ABOUT THE AUTHOR

Mark Ray once shared a dressingroc
Border in a NSW Colts team in the
After that their career paths took rat.
directions. Ray did play three senior g.
NSW in 1981-82 before representing T
from 1982-83 to 1985-86. He began his
journalism as a photographer for the *Exa.* ...r in
Launceston in 1983 before moving to Melbourne
to join the *Herald*. Since 1987 Ray has covered
every Test match played in Australia and tours to
England, New Zealand and South Africa. His most
recent book was *Cricket: The Game Behind The
Game*, a collection of his photographs. Since
November 1989, Ray has been the chief cricket
writer for the *Sunday Age*. He lives south of
Sydney with his wife and four children.

Border and Beyond is an enlightening account of 10 years Australian cricket would never have enjoyed had it not been for Allan Border. Mark Ray's excellent research and understanding of the game help put into perspective a period in cricket's history which has never been subjected to such pressures before. Allan Border with all the distractions of the modern game has stood the test of time, and more.

Martin Crowe

Border and Beyond is a compelling read and a powerful insight into a unique period of Australian cricket. The book takes us through the 'behind the scenes' politics and gives the reader a feel and understanding of what really goes on. It also looks at the two major figures of the time, Allan Border and Bob Simpson, and gives us a valuable peep at the intricate and complex personalities of these men.
Congratulations Mark Ray. At last a cricket book written without fear of retribution.

Mike Whitney

An illuminating, powerful analysis of the most durable cricketer in the game's history.

Jim Maxwell

The book is an engrossing read about how a demoralised and depleted Australian team raised itself to be the number one team in the world. The role of Allan Border in getting Australian cricket to believe in itself again has been chiefly instrumental in its top position in the world of cricket today. I would strongly recommend this book to a student of cricket history to get an insight into the way Australian cricket shaped up under the much underrated Allan Border.

Sunil Gavaskar

Mark Ray's reflections on Allan Border's career and his influence on the game are like the former Australian captain himself, honest, straight to the point, with no airs and graces.

Ian Chappell

Mark Ray is one of the world's most perceptive cricket writers, and this is a cool, well-informed book that will interest anyone who wants to know what really happens in the game.

Matthew Engel
Editor *Wisden Cricketers' Almanack*

Cricket lovers will be grateful to Mark Ray for his revealing and careful examination of an important period in the game's history. His book is studded with absorbing issues, not the least of which concern Bob Simpson's attempts to politicise the media and Simpson's unseemly public rows with cricket writers.

Jack Pollard OAM
Leading Australian cricket writer

Completely absorbing account of a dramatic period in Australia's cricket history: frank to the point of blush-making, rousing in its insight into the struggles and triumphs of the Border years.

David Frith
Editor *Wisden Cricket Monthly*

Mark Ray's meticulous research and marvellous insight into the game combine to reveal the inside story of one of the most fascinating eras in Australian cricket history. He seeks many diverse opinions and pulls no punches. This is the real Border – keratoses and all.

Geoff Lawson

A fearless, precise, enlightening and entertaining account of a fascinating epoch in Australian cricket.

Mike Coward

... the Border years are a vital part of Australian cricket history, and Mark Ray's experience at the business end of the game as a player gives him an important edge in the writing of the story, which makes this an essential tome.

David Gower

BORDER
& BEYOND

MARK RAY

an
ABC
BOOK

ACKNOWLEDGMENTS

The one person I do not have to thank for an extended interview for this book is Allan Border. With his manager organising for another Border book to be published in the summer of 1995-96, Border did not feel free to offer his thoughts to this project. As this was only the second or third time Border had refused me a comment or interview in the past nine years, I could hardly complain. Others who did offer their views included Ian Chappell, Greg Chappell, Bob Simpson, Laurie Sawle, David Richards, Ian McDonald, Malcolm Gray, John Benaud, Geoff Lawson, Michael Whitney, David Gower and Mike Coward. Many others, including Border's teammates and opponents and my colleages in the media, provided comments, judgments and ideas – sometimes specifically for this book, sometimes in informal conversations during Border's decade as Australian captain. I thank Mike Coward for his advice, criticism and encouragement at crucial times and Stuart Neal (ABC Books) and Ken Merrigan (sports editor of the *Sunday Age*) for their patience.

Published by ABC Books for the
AUSTRALIAN BROADCASTING CORPORATION
GPO Box 9994 Sydney NSW 2001

Copyright © Mark Ray 1995

First published November 1995

National Library of Australia
Cataloguing-in-Publication entry
Ray, Mark.
   Border and beyond.
   Bibliography.
   Includes index.
   ISBN 0 7333 0480 X.
   1. Cricket – Australia. I. Australian Broadcasting
   Corporation. II. Title.
796.3580994

Designed by Kaye Binns-McDonald
Set in 11/13pt Goudy by
Midland Typesetters, Maryborough, Victoria
Printed and bound in Australia by
Australian Print Group, Maryborough, Victoria

1995-5

5 4 3 2 1

CONTENTS

SO

CLOSE...

ALL Test cricketers carry vivid memories of their first Test match. The memories, usually a mixture of the pleasant and the painful, last forever. In Justin Langer's case, a single image from his Test debut, against the West Indies in Adelaide in January 1993, is burnt into his memory. It was the devastated look on the weathered face of his captain, Allan Border, an instant after Border had seen his best chance of leading Australia to a Test series win over the West Indies snuffed out by the raised right index finger of umpire Darrell Hair.

Hair had just given Craig McDermott out caught behind off Courtney Walsh to end a brave 40-run last wicket partnership with Tim May, which had taken Australia to within two runs of victory and an unbeatable 2-0 lead in the series. Instead, the West Indies won by one run, the narrowest margin in the history of Test cricket, levelled the series and, most significantly, regained the psychological advantage.

For the 37-year-old Border, who had taken the Australian team from the depths of despair in the mid-1980s to within two runs of the pinnacle of world cricket eight years later, it was the end of a dream. A week later, his last Test match against the West Indies would end in three days in a major defeat on a green, lively pitch in Perth. And to make the defeat more personal, Border would make his first pair in a long and distinguished career.

Showing the wear and tear from 10 years as captain, a position he never really wanted, Border would play his final Test match in Durban, South Africa, 13 months later. He had taken Australia to a World Cup win and to series victories over every country but the West Indies. He'd needed a lot of help along the way, and perhaps one of the reasons Australia could not beat the West Indies in his time was because of the conservative personalities of Border and his closest adviser, coach Bob Simpson. But through it all, Border remained the very public heart and soul of Australian cricket. The cricket public suffered along with Border in the dark early days, celebrated with him in the good times and, on that day in January 1993, reacted with a similar mixture of disbelief and angry frustration to the realisation that Border's Australians had still not beaten the West Indies.

For the 22-year-old Langer – like Border, a short, tough and determined left-hander – the end of the Adelaide Test provided an insight into how difficult and emotionally draining cricket at the highest level could be. It was cricket's version of innocence confronting experience. For Langer, the memory of that look on his skipper's face would serve as his inspiration.

'I remember seeing AB when we lost,' Langer said. 'Seeing his face made it a big ambition straight away to be in a winning series against the best in the world.'

Australia had gone to Adelaide leading the series 1-0. A win there would have given Border's side the series and the honour of achieving what for so long had seemed cricket's impossible challenge: becoming the first team to beat the West Indies in a series since New Zealand did it in 1980. Arguably, that achievement would also have earned Border's Australians the unofficial and conditional title of world champions of Test cricket. For Border, the win would have closed a circle, long and tortuous, that began in 1984 when he became captain of a dispirited Australian team and set about rebuilding it with little leadership experience but plenty of determination – the quality that had always inspired his batting.

The Adelaide Test had been a great match even before the dramatic last day's play. Australia bowled out the West Indies late on the first day for a modest 252 but had fallen 39 runs short in

2

its first innings, succumbing to the pace of Curtly Ambrose. Then the West Indies collapsed in their second innings for 146, showing their fragility against good spin bowling during a brilliant seven-over spell from Tim May that netted him figures of 5/9.

In the evening, after stumps, you can play some great shots as you look out across an empty cricket ground. There are few sights that offer as many possibilities. As a group of Australian players walked from the Adelaide Oval after stumps on the third day, Allan Border glanced across to the stately old scoreboard. '186 to win, eh,' he said.

In previous series, Australia had developed a habit of collapsing under the pressures of a fourth-innings run-chase. Border knew that 186 was tantalisingly close but also far enough away to give the West Indian pace attack time to cause some trouble.

Langer's role in the game had been pivotal. His West Australian teammate Damien Martyn had pulled out of the match after injuring an eye during fielding practice and Langer was flown in from Perth on the night before the game to replace him. Having been asked by Border whether he was prepared to bat at number three, Langer said he would love the chance. That opportunity came late on the first day after Mark Taylor was out to Ian Bishop's third ball, the ninth of the innings.

Langer arrived at the crease for his first taste of Test bowling with the score 1/1. Ambrose and Bishop were racing in, attacking the nervous Australians in the final minutes before stumps. Bishop had been considered the fastest bowler in the world before a serious case of fast bowler's back had forced him out of the game for more than a year. This was his first series after recovering from the injury and he had struggled for most of the summer. That evening, Bishop's rhythm had returned and, with it, his express pace.

Langer took strike with the new Bradman Stand at his back; David Boon, one of the heroes of his youth, was watching anxiously at the other end, and three balls remained in Bishop's over. All three were fast and short. Langer avoided them skilfully. Boon handled Ambrose's second over well enough, leaving Langer to face Bishop again. At that stage, Langer had faced three deliveries in Test cricket and was yet to put bat on ball. Bishop's first ball was short of a length and very fast. Langer tried to swerve his head out of the way, was too late and was hit on the back of the helmet. The impact split the helmet and left a slight depression in Langer's skull. With a helping hand from Desmond Haynes, Langer stayed

Dogged defence: Justin Langer stops another West Indian thunderbolt during his dramatic Test debut in Adelaide in January 1993.

on his feet and, after a delay in which he convinced Boon he was all right, faced up to the next ball. It was another short one and Langer, showing great courage and presence of mind, ducked under it well, his eyes fixed on the ball throughout another challenging split second. Langer let the next ball pass with little trouble but pulled away in distress as Bishop was sprinting towards him for the fourth ball of the over. Boon was joined at Langer's side by team physiotherapist, Errol Alcott, and, soon after, by the ground doctor, Adelaide surgeon and former South Australian player, Don Beard.

Although he had taken a blow to the helmet 12 days earlier while fielding at short leg in a Sheffield Shield game, Langer was allowed to stay on the field. Two balls later, with the light fading, he finally felt the comforting sensation of wood on leather as he successfully played his first shot in Test cricket, a defensive dead bat but a triumph in the circumstances. The few hundred spectators

4

still at the ground applauded warmly. Two overs later, bad light stopped play. Langer had been out there for 26 long and tense minutes, faced 15 balls and had still not scored a run. But he had managed to show the cricket world that he at least had the courage to be a Test batsman.

It was Boon who was forced off the field the next morning, after he was struck a painful blow on the point of the elbow by a veering Ambrose lifter. In 70 Tests, Boon had never left the field injured while batting, even staying in the centre to have stitches inserted in his chin in Jamaica during Australia's tour to the Caribbean in 1991. So intense was the barrage from the West Indians that Langer finally fell to his feet after a ball from Kenneth Benjamin pounded into his stomach. After treatment, Langer carried on until he was caught behind off the same bowler for twenty. He had bruises on both forearms, both thighs and his ribcage, and his left forefinger was bloodied. Welcome to Test cricket, son.

'When I got the ball in the stomach, it was like being hit by a bloody gunshot. Oh mate, it knocked the wind out of me,' Langer told the press that evening. 'You watch it on TV and you hear about the West Indies and you think they can't be that bad. It was my hardest cricket of all time, really hard. But that's what Test cricket is about, isn't it? It's the best cricket you'll ever play. I thoroughly enjoyed it. It was superb.'

Rain interrupted play with Australia reaching a promising though traumatic 3/100 by stumps on day two. Ambrose ran through Australia's batting on the third morning, but by stumps that night, West Indies were all out for 146, leaving Australia that 186 to win and Border with plenty to think about overnight. Seventeen wickets had fallen for 259 runs on that third day, evidence of the ferocity of the play, with the Australians desperate for an historic win and the West Indies cracking under the pressure.

Langer, exhibiting all the signs of masochism required of top-order batsmen facing the West Indies, was back at the batting crease early on the fourth morning, this time with the score on 1/5. Taylor soon followed Boon back to the showers, and when Australia lost another four wickets for 10 runs in the hour after lunch, thanks to another piercing spell from Ambrose, Australia was 7/74, still 112 difficult runs from home. Border's hopes rested with Langer, his young mirror image, and the tailenders Shane Warne, May and McDermott.

At one stage during his 72-minute stand with Warne, Langer

called for a new pair of batting gloves from twelfth man Tony Dodemaide. While on the field, Dodemaide asked Langer and Warne if everything else was all right before heading back to the players' viewing room high up at the back of the Members' Stand. Before Dodemaide had gone 10 metres, Langer called him back.

'Tell Maysie and Billy not to think for a minute we're going to lose this,' he said. Dodemaide was impressed. The young bloke's got a bit of shit in him, he thought as he jogged back to the dressing-room.

Langer and Warne had added 28 to take the total past the 100 mark when Bishop trapped Warne leg before for nine. May, celebrating, if that is the word, his thirty-first birthday, joined Langer to add another 42 runs, runs that only marginally raised hopes in the viewing room. When Langer, mentally exhausted after four hours' resistance, edged an attempted pull shot to wicket-keeper Junior Murray to be out for a defiant 54, the only half-century of the match, Australia still had to make 42 to win with only number 11 McDermott to support May. For the next hour and a half, as workers from the nearby city centre rushed to the ground and people in thousands of homes, offices and workplaces throughout the country gathered nervously around television sets, May and McDermott edged closer to that winning target.

Ambrose was spent by this stage, his energies exhausted after carrying the West Indies attack for most of the summer. Courtney Walsh, the underrated into-the-wind workhorse with the gentlest of off-field manners, launched the final assault.

As May put his body behind each delivery and tried to work the ball away with impressive technique, McDermott nicked and nudged, trying to hit Australia home. One way or another, the score mounted, as did the excitement. In the Australians' viewing room, Langer had settled next to Dodemaide in the front row. Border was directly behind them in the back corner. No one had dared to speak to the skipper for ages. He sat in silence and reverted to an old habit: throwing a ball from his left hand into the palm of the right in a vain attempt to relieve the tension. The sound of that 'worry ball' thudding into his captain's hands is the only sound Dodemaide can recall from those last minutes.

With three runs to win, McDermott launched into an off-drive but, instead of hitting Walsh past Richie Richardson, who had stationed himself at mid-off to talk with his bowlers, McDermott slightly mishit the shot and the ball fell short and wide of the West Indies captain. After Richardson spilled the difficult diving chance, he stayed on his backside juggling the ball.

'Stay cool, boys. Stay cool,' was the message from the skipper.

Soon after, with only two needed to win, McDermott paddled a ball off his legs towards square leg. In the instant it left the bat, it looked like the winning runs. McDermott's teammates, like people all over the country, moved to the edge of their seats until a hand came down and knocked the ball to the ground. Desmond Haynes, the great opening batsman, had had a wretched summer, his feet and reflexes looking like those of a man well past his prime. In that last half an hour, he had been fielding at short leg, and every time a shot went near him, he seemed to be a metre out of position. But this time Haynes was in the right spot and he reacted quickly enough to stop McDermott's shot.

Two balls later, McDermott tried to avoid a short ball from Walsh which clipped his helmet and, in Hair's opinion, his bat on the way past. West Indies had won. In the viewing room, Border jumped to his feet, turned his back on the field and hurled that 'worry ball' into the wooden floor with so much force that it rebounded high enough to hit the ceiling.

We were all stunned [Langer said]. There'd been this amazing tension building and then when we were so close and it was all over. Nobody said a word. I heard AB's ball thump into the floor and I turned to look at him. It had been so close and then it had been stolen away from him, especially after the guys had played so well in the series up to then. It was something I'll always remember – just that look of disappointment on his face. I can't remember him saying anything . . . just that look, a look as if something precious had been stolen from him.

The Australians waited in their seats until May and McDermott dragged themselves from the field, up the steps of the Members' Stand, along the corridor in front of the viewing room and back into the dressing-room where their teammates joined them. Border went over to McDermott to check if the umpire's decision had been reasonable. Satisfied, he consoled the two tailenders and then sat on his own. McDermott, in particular, was devastated. The mood was solemn. No one dared to speak to Border although most eyes were watching him.

Two years later, when Langer was named in the 15-man party to tour the West Indies under new captain Mark Taylor, he recalled those moments in the dressing-room in Adelaide on Australia Day 1993.

7

I was the young kid in the team and I was taking it all in, the atmosphere, taking in what had happened that day. I'd been watching AB for a long time and I'd admired him so much for all that he'd achieved. I felt that sense that I was a young guy from the next generation watching the old leader near the end of his career. And from then on, the memory of that look on AB's face ignited an ambition in me to one day beat the West Indies. They'd obviously been a thorn in Australia's side for a long time. It'd be great to beat them.

As Langer flew to the Caribbean with Taylor's team for another tilt at that world crown, Border was at home in Brisbane preparing to achieve his other unfulfilled ambition, to play in Queensland's first Sheffield Shield-winning team. At the end of the Shield season, he was to fly to the West Indies to try his hand, reluctantly of course, as a commentator for pay television. As he watched play from the calm of the commentary box, he no doubt recalled the highs and lows of his battles with the great West Indies teams that dominated his era. His two greatest innings – 98 not out and 100 not out at Port-of-Spain in Trinidad in 1984, 630 chanceless minutes of resistance against the might of Malcolm Marshall and Joel Garner; the 3-0 savaging by a rampaging West Indies team in the first three Tests in Australia in 1988-89; the consoling win in Sydney in that series in which he took a career best 11/96 including 7/46 in the first innings; the bitter series in the Caribbean in 1991 when Australia went down 1-2; the lost chances of the 1992-93 series, another 1-2 loss; and, back in November 1984, the second Test match in Brisbane, when his mate Kim Hughes tearfully resigned the Australian captaincy, leaving a hole that Border was to fill for the next 10 years.

RELUCTANT

LEADER

F OUR days after Kim Hughes's resignation as Australian captain in late November 1984, Allan Border was in quiet, out-of-the-way Launceston playing for Queensland against Tasmania. Hughes had finally given in to the pressures of critics, less than supportive teammates and the merciless West Indies, who had just inflicted their fifth successive defeat of Hughes's Australians in the second Test in Brisbane. As Hughes's deputy, Border was the hot tip to replace him as Test skipper. Border's Queensland teammates thought so anyway. One of them went to a local toy shop and bought a plastic sheriff's badge which was duly pinned on the Queensland captain's chest.

'What's the story with the badge, AB?' one of the Tasmanians asked as the home side joined the visitors for a beer after play.

'Ah, they reckon I'm gonna get the job as Test skipper,' Border said with a shrug of the shoulders.

The next Australian captain was holding a beer in one hand and nursing a broken little finger on the other. Roger Brown, a tough, fast-medium bowler from local club Mowbray, got a ball to

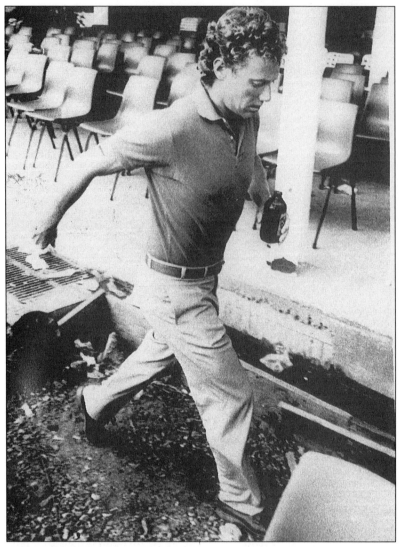

The captain quits: Kim Hughes leaves the press conference at the Gabba in Brisbane after announcing his resignation from the Australian captaincy.

lift sharply and inflict an injury that Garner and company had not managed in seven consecutive Tests. At least Border never let on whether the West Indians had broken any of his bones. Perhaps he saw little need to conceal an injury from the Tasmanian attack. He did retire hurt on 29, a minor victory for the home side, but came back soon after and went on to an undefeated 144 runs.

I was one of the Tasmanian players that day who watched in

admiration as Border, broken finger and all, cut, swept and drove with the confidence of a world-class player enjoying the relative comforts of domestic first-class cricket. We tried hard to get him out, to stem the flow of runs, but the bugger was far too good. In retrospect, those days are one of the joys of Shield cricket for the many players who make up the numbers. Unlike the thousands of fans who pay their money and watch from the distance of the stands, you have the chance to study the world's best up close, to realise just how good they are.

Typically, in the dressing-room later, Border was just another Sheffield Shield player enjoying the traditional beer and conversation with teammates and opponents. He just happened to be a day or two away from the highest honour Australian cricket can bestow. But throughout his career, Border often managed to be both a great cricketer and an ordinary bloke. It was his greatest attraction to the fans in the stands.

During that game, Greg Chappell, less than a year into his retirement from first-class cricket and already a selector, confirmed the speculation to Border. The Australian Cricket Board (ACB) and the selectors had little choice. A few alternatives had been mentioned in the media, but the only other possible candidate was David Hookes and there was too much doubt about his ability to maintain his place in the team on weight of runs. In the end, Australian cricket followed two of its oldest traditions – picking the vice-captain as the one already officially designated as the most suitable successor and preferring a top-quality player as captain to a proven leader who might have to be carried as a player.

Border was not quite unprepared for such an onerous job. When he was Test captain, Chappell had been impressed by Border's reading of play, judging him sharper than Hughes. Chappell began some two years before the 1984-85 summer to suggest to Border that he at least consider that he might end up Australian captain one day. Border's initial reaction had been to say he wanted none of that trouble and strife. Chappell kept at it until, by the time he had become a selector for '84-85 and the Australian team was falling apart under Hughes, Border gave ground.

'Once the season got under way,' Chappell said, 'he said he was still not that keen but that he might as well get in there and have a go.'

ACB chairman Fred Bennett and chief executive David Richards had been on the phone in the days following Hughes's resignation, seeking from colleagues at the board and the selectors their views on who should be the next captain. As Border was on his way home to Brisbane from Tasmania, Bennett and Richards met him at the Tullamarine Travel Lodge near Melbourne Airport on 3 December to convince him to take the job. Upset at the pain his mate Hughes had suffered and reluctant to take on such a tough challenge in difficult times, Border told them he had never sought the role of captain and was reluctant to change his mind now.

One of Border's most celebrated character traits is his determination and it was in full swing that day in Melbourne. After four or five hours of intense but amicable discussion, Bennett and Richards convinced Border he was the man to lead Australian cricket out of the wilderness and that he would have all the support from the ACB he needed to achieve that goal. That Border was so wary of the job but then battled at it for so long speaks volumes for his determination and tenacity.

So, at 29 years of age with 63 Tests already to his name, Border was chosen as Australia's thirty-eighth Test captain. And on 4 December in Ansett departure lounge 4 at Melbourne's Tullamarine Airport, he held the first of hundreds of press conferences as the national team's leader.

As the years of his tenure passed, the symbolism of that scene would become more and more apparent to the journalists present, some of whom were to attend most of those Border press conferences. Throughout his long career, teammates lost count of the times Border batted for Australia with a broken finger. Some said that when he went out to bat with such an injury, they were certain he would score runs. An airport transit area was the perfect setting for a player who had been the first Australian to classify himself as a fully professional cricketer, a player who would survive the rigours of touring life in every cricket-playing country in the world during the next 10 years. No cricketer in the history of the game spent more time on the road than Allan Border – at airports, on planes, in buses and taxis.

Alongside the humbled, self-effacing new captain were the men behind the scenes – ACB chief executive David Richards and team manager Bob Merriman. If they looked more nervous than Border, it was because they knew that their man had very little captaincy experience, just nine games in charge of Queensland, and had never seen himself as a potential leader. As well, he had developed a reputation as a moody character with no great liking for the cricket media. For Border and the people who had appointed

*Captain elect: Allan Border before a Sheffield Shield match in Launceston
in December 1984. During the game Border learned officially
that he was about to succeed Kim Hughes as Australian captain.*

him, the road ahead covered unknown territory. To travel it
successfully, Border would need and would receive the support of
a back-up crew that would help him through the hard times to
the successes of the late 80s and early 90s.

Sensibly, Border played the media as he always played a good
bowling attack in a crisis – solid defence, no rash shots and no
pretensions to being anything other than under the hammer.

*Basically I'm here just to answer any questions you may have.
I would just like to point out that I have been a little disappointed at
the circumstances surrounding my appointment. But I would like to
go on record as saying it is a great honour and I can just assure
everyone that I will give it 100 per cent and do my best. You learn
all the time and obviously I've got a long way to go yet . . . I'm quite*

sure this job is going to be pretty demanding and, in the current circumstances, pretty tough.

In his report the next day in the *Sydney Morning Herald*, Mike Coward noted that there ' ... was an endearing simplicity and honesty about everything he said'. That confessional openness would characterise Border's dealings with the cricket media, if not always the wider media, for the next 10 years. In fact, he was often too honest for his own good and there would be times when a Border press conference would quickly turn into an investigation into the man's spiritual well-being. Border never planned these soul-searching sessions. He just answered probing questions honestly and, although this honesty might not have served team interests on every occasion, it exposed Border's raw emotional states to the public gaze, building a powerful bond between Australia's cricket followers and their captain.

Still, at that first press conference, neither Border nor the journalists listening to him could have had any idea just how prophetic the new captain's words would prove to be.

'A long way to go yet ...' ended up being 93 consecutive Tests as captain, one of his many world records. Not one match missed through injury or illness or accident or fatigue. Of those playing world cricket at present, only the West Indian Brian Lara or the Indian Sachin Tendulkar have the remotest hope of breaking that record, assuming that both will one day be appointed their country's captain.

'Pretty demanding and, in the current circumstances, pretty tough' could not have been more accurate. For the next three years, Border would hardly lead Australia to any significant success until the 1987 World Cup. He was about to head into the darkest period of his captaincy career, probably the darkest in the history of Australian cricket. And the 'current circumstances' that dispatched Hughes and landed Border in front of the media that day in Melbourne were as difficult as any that had ever faced the game in Australia.

GRIM

BEGINNINGS

A USTRALIAN cricket was in a mess in 1984. The ACB and its selectors had allowed some senior players to pick and choose overseas tours and this had created instability. At times, Greg Chappell led the team; at other times, he rested from a tour and Kim Hughes took control. A team that included three truly great players in three departments of the game – batsman Chappell, bowler Dennis Lillee and wicket-keeper Rod Marsh – could cope with instability through sheer class. A team without those giants could not. When the 'Big Three' retired in one hit, after the fifth Test against Pakistan in Sydney at the end of the 1983-84 season, a huge hole opened in Australian cricket.

To emphasise the depth of that hole, each of the 'Big Three' set records in their last match. Chappell became the first Australian to score 7000 Test runs, doing so by making 184 and so ending his Test career as he began it, with a century. Lillee became the first bowler, from any nation, to take 350 Test wickets, and Marsh, the first keeper to reach 350 dismissals. It might have been a fluke that all three set records in their last Test appearance in the same

The Big Three: Dennis Lillee, Rod Marsh and Greg Chappell retired at the end of the 1983-84 season, leaving a huge hole in Australian cricket.

match, but it was also a neat and telling way to remind Australian cricket that it was losing three giants.

When a team is struggling to rebuild after the loss of three such fine players, and when many people within and without the team have reservations about the captain, the last people that team needs as opponents are the West Indies. After that successful series against Pakistan, Hughes, perhaps cursed from way back, faced 10 consecutive Test matches against Clive Lloyd's commando unit – five Tests in the Caribbean early in 1984 and five more in Australia six months later.

Before the Australians left for the Caribbean, Hughes and Geoff Lawson led a revolt over clauses in the players' tour contracts. As match programs became more crowded, placing heavier and heavier burdens on players, disputes between the ACB and its players over contracts and payments would surface every few years during Border's time as captain. Hughes, in this instance, gained widespread respect for the way he fought for the players' rights. However, influential critics were still calling for Hughes to be replaced as captain.

In April, Sydney's *Sun-Herald* achieved a rare coup by placing two of Australian cricket's most implacable foes side by side on a page headlined: 'Aussie cricket – where now?'. Underneath the heading, Ian Chappell and Bob Simpson – the former the ultimate anti-establishment figure from World Series days and beyond, and the latter the hero of the anti-Kerry Packer establishment – agreed on two things. First, that Kim Hughes should be replaced as captain and, second, that the best man for the job was Allan Border.

Like Simpson and his brother Ian, Greg Chappell had never had much confidence in Hughes's captaincy and believed Border would eventually replace him. This might have been behind a telling comment Chappell made after reaching the 7000-run mark.

'I'm quite sure someone will get past it in the not-too-distant future. Even in the current side, Kim Hughes and Allan Border are well on the way. They have both got to 4000 very quickly, which puts them well over halfway. I guess it depends on who is the more resilient.'

It took no giant leap of the imagination to believe that Chappell definitely knew who was the more resilient. He and the rest of the cricket world would soon find out.

Chappell made that comment in early January. Four months later, Australia had lost the series in the Caribbean 3-0. While Hughes had managed only 215 runs from his 10 innings with a highest score of 33 and an average of 21.5, Border had established himself as by far the best of Australia's batsmen, one of the very best in the world. Strengthened by a tough pre-tour fitness campaign, he had coped brilliantly with the pace of Michael Holding, Malcolm Marshall and, in particular, Joel Garner. The latter took on Border in a personal duel of the highest quality, a duel that ended with Garner making a point, as the teams left the field at the end of the series, of publicly shaking hands with the man he had failed to dismiss in five intense Test matches. Border made 521 runs at 74.42. The next best was Wayne Phillips with 258 at 25.8.

Not only had Border established himself as a great batsman in the Caribbean in 1984, but in the second Test at Port-of-Spain, Trinidad, he played two of cricket's greatest innings, back-to-the-wall efforts that raised him to hero status. His 98 not out and 100 not out not only saved the Test for Australia, but were made in the toughest of situations as his teammates collapsed against the pace and power of the West Indians. In all, Border batted for 10 and a half hours and never gave a chance.

'As always, he laid his body on the line and that inspires people,' teammate Geoff Lawson recalled. 'You just had to be there. It was unbelievable. The two greatest Test innings I've ever seen. You are in awe of those kind of performances because you know how difficult it is.'

A bright-eyed Dean Jones, a week short of his twenty-third birthday, made his Test debut in this game. In the first innings, Jones joined his future captain to overcome a nasty damp pitch and hostile bowling to post a century stand. Jones remained a Border fan from that day.

The West Indians were also deeply impressed by Border's skill and courage. Holding wrote later of how Border rose above the disunity and lack of spirit in the Australian team, and the wicket-keeper, the popular and gentlemanly Jeffrey Dujon, would say that the greatest disappointment of his career was that Border did not make two centuries in that match. High praise indeed. The West Indies, however, had less regard for Hughes and were determined to continue their assault on the vulnerable captain when the contest resumed in Australia a few months later.

As summer approached, the world of Australian cricket was bracing itself for another onslaught from the best cricket team in the world. Despite expressions of hope from a new three-man selection panel – new chairman Laurie Sawle, Greg Chappell and Rick McCosker – and a successful two-week visit to India in September for a one-day tournament, the atmosphere before the 1984-85 series was rife with impassioned and concerned debate. Major preoccupations included the rights and wrongs of the West Indians' short-pitched bowling tactics, methods that might be employed to either counter those tactics or nullify them, the increasing number of no-balls and the deadening effect that was having on cricket as a spectacle, the poor quality and lack of direction of the Australian team and its captain's various weaknesses. Most newspapers sought the opinions of experts, and the public was invited to write in with its views on bouncers, Kim Hughes and the uncertain future.

Former New South Wales captain Ginty Lush recommended the pitch be lengthened by half a metre to give batsmen more time to cope. Another former New South Wales captain, ABC Radio's respected commentator Alan McGilvray, supported Lush's idea. Greg Chappell called on the umpires to restrict the West Indies' use of short-pitched deliveries, arguing that the West Indian attack was more daunting than England's in the 1932-33 Bodyline

Classic Border: The skipper plays his signature cover drive.
With the square cut, the pull and the cover drive,
Border could destroy any bowling attack in the game.

series because the former boasted four very fast bowlers, while England had only one, Harold Larwood.

Australia's batsmen were worried too. Dean Jones admitted that that winter, while the West Indians were completing a 5-0 Test 'blackwash' of England in England, he had spent two nights a week in an indoor centre ducking and weaving deliveries sent down by a bowling machine turned up to full speed. The only problem was that the machine was still not as quick as the West Indians.

Cricketers the world over had been slow to embrace modern gurus like body-movement specialists, dietitians and sports psychologists but, after a first taste of these latest magicians during a camp at the Australian Institute of Sport in Canberra before the brief trip to India, some of the Australians changed their minds.

With the arrival of the West Indian team imminent, a few leading batsmen swallowed their pride and visited the Sydney consulting rooms of hypnotherapist Arthur Jackson. No harm in trying.

In the *Sydney Morning Herald*, Jackson, who had worked with many leading international cricketers, described the psychological pressures, the loss of self-esteem and the mental anguish suffered by a batsman forced to face ball after ball rearing into fingers, ribcage or shoulders at great speed.

'A batsman who has to take avoidance action against such a ball undoubtedly develops a negative emotional reaction to similar balls in the future,' he said. 'It's the same as burning your hand on a hotplate; you're very wary of hotplates for some time afterwards.'

With help from the ACB, which programmed the first two Tests on the fastest, bounciest pitches – Perth and Brisbane – the West Indies turned up the heat on Hughes and his team and comfortably won both games.

In Perth, the public's worst fears were realised when Michael Holding smashed through the Australians' first innings, taking 6/21 off 9.2 overs of blistering speed on a juicy pitch. That game was over early on the fourth morning.

The victory margin was narrower in Brisbane but the game lasted only a few hours longer. Tasmania's 23-year-old right-hander, David Boon, made his debut in this game, scoring 11 and 51. When Boon walked out to face Joel Garner in the first innings, the score was 4/81. Border was at the other end. At the Adelaide Oval, Boon's Tasmanian teammates left off watching their batsmen out in the middle to gather around a television in the back dressing-room. They had to watch their colleague begin his Test career in the toughest possible situation. Boon survived the few deliveries left in that over before seeking reassurance from the only friendly face in sight.

'You all right?' Border enquired.

'I can't move my legs,' the nervous Boon replied.

'Hang in there,' Border said. 'You'll be right.'

When Boon began to linger too long at the crease in the second innings, Malcolm Marshall asked the ultimate question.

'Boonie, I know it's your first Test match, but are you going to do the right thing and get out or do I have to come around the wicket and kill you?'

In that first innings, Hughes was caught at long leg off the shot he had promised before the series that he would eschew – the hook. One trait that had annoyed Hughes's critics had been

Fearsome: West Indies' giant fast bowler, Joel Garner, was one of a four-man pace attack which pounded the Australians during the 1984-85 series.

his tendency to shoot from the lip without thinking beforehand. To announce such a tactic so early in the series was unnecessary. To then show that he did not have the mental discipline to adhere to it was fatal to Hughes's chances of retaining the captaincy.

Before the third Test in Adelaide, Border presided over a team dinner at which, by ACB arrangement, a renowned after-dinner speaker was to offer encouragement.

I don't think I've ever felt so nervous or inadequate in my life [Border would reflect]. Thankfully it went okay and Sir Donald [Bradman], in particular, was marvellous. He talked about Bodyline and the comparisons with the West Indies pace attack. He was very good. In fact he seemed a lot more switched on about cricket today than some of our illustrious cricketers from the more recent past. Some ex-players seem to have forgotten how difficult the game can be. It's disappointing to realise that these past players, whom you would expect to know, don't seem to realise what we have been up against.

What Border and his team were up against in the third Test in Adelaide was another defeat, this time by 191 runs, despite Geoff Lawson's superb match figures of 11/181, including a career-best 8/112 in the first innings. However, in Melbourne over Christmas, the Australians fought back and at least staved off a fourth defeat, largely due to a fighting second innings century from opener Andrew Hilditch. Border offered support with 41 in a successful rearguard action.

The new captain also offered support to Lawson, who had been fined by Merriman for 'conduct unbecoming' although, to Border's great annoyance, the umpires had filed no official report. Border organised for the $500 fine to be paid from the team kitty rather than Lawson's pocket. This was the first public example of Border's intense loyalty to teammates and the first of many clashes with officialdom.

Hughes, his spirit broken, made a pair in this match and never played another Test. As one fine player left the game in tragic circumstances, another arrived. At 19 years of age, Craig McDermott had won his first Test cap for this match after turning the Tasmanian dressing-room into a casualty ward during that match in Launceston a few weeks earlier. Although he took six wickets in Melbourne, it was to be that many years at least before McDermott was fully established as Australia's leading fast bowler.

By now, Border – who, as captain, had lost one Test and

drawn one – was looking to Sydney's slower, turning pitch for a respite from the West Indies' pace barrage. He got more than that. Australia won by an innings in four days, thanks to spinners Bob Holland and Murray Bennett, who took 15 of the 20 West Indian wickets to fall. The loss was the first suffered by the West Indies in 27 Tests and their first innings defeat since 1968-69. In that sense, the game was a disappointing end to the career of the leading architect of the West Indies' world dominance, captain Clive Lloyd, who ambled slowly from the Sydney Cricket Ground to the warmest of standing ovations after top scoring in the second innings with a fighting 72. Lloyd's 74 Tests as captain was a world record. Ten years later, his opposite number in the final three Tests of this series, Allan Border, would break that record by 19 Tests.

The Hughes resignation was not the only controversy that summer. Lawson and Desmond Haynes had clashed in Brisbane, Lawson and Gordon Greenidge in Melbourne and Border, Steve Rixon and Viv Richards in Sydney. The heat generated by playing against such ruthless opponents as the modern West Indies was always substantial, and there would be similar incidents in future series. Still, at his press conference after the fifth Test, Border drew comfort from the improved results in Melbourne and Sydney.

'I feel the turning point was the draw in Melbourne,' he said. 'We had some new faces and a new attitude. We thought of getting to Sydney and stopping the rot – stopping the West Indies' run of success. [Of the Sydney win] I won't forget it. It was something very special to me. Everyone should take heart from this victory.'

Australia's summer was far from finished after the Sydney win in early January. With the West Indies and Sri Lanka, Border's team contested the Benson and Hedges World Series Cup: 10 games each plus three finals between Australia and West Indies. The latter won the trophy but not before Border had regained top form with 580 runs at 64.4 and a century against both opponents. His 127 off 139 balls in Sydney against the West Indies in the first final was a stunning attacking performance.

Then, as if to stretch to breaking point the durability of the toughest players, the Victorian Cricket Association celebrated the founding of their state by inviting all seven Test-playing nations to contest the Benson and Hedges World Championship of Cricket through the second half of February and into March. Australia and West Indies lost interest and energy and India beat Pakistan in the final. The first match, between England and Australia at the Melbourne Cricket Ground on 17 February in front of 82,494 fans, saw the light towers turned on for the first time – lights that would shine on Border many times during the next 10 years.

Too much cricket? No wonder that had been yet another hot topic during that overheated summer. The Australians now had three weeks off before playing their first match in the Rothmans Trophy tournament in Sharjah in the United Arab Emirates. After that, they were to head to England for an Ashes series. Despite the hopes raised by the Melbourne and Sydney Tests, Border realised his new job was far more demanding than he had imagined. During that summer of upheaval, Australia dropped 46 catches in all international matches. There was much work to be done.

What Border did not realise was that he was about to enter a two-year period of frustration, disappointment and depression brought on by the prolonged difficulties of rebuilding a shattered Australian team, his own misgivings about his leadership abilities and the attractions of a few million Krugerrand.

ABROAD

AND ALONE

WHILE in Sharjah in the United Arab Emirates for a brief tour in late March 1985, Allan Border gave another press conference and, as usual, it was part-confession, part-public prayer for a better future. He conceded he was 'not a natural leader' and would have to 'work a little more at being a diplomat and filling the other roles'. What he was enjoying, though, was the close involvement with his players.

I enjoy the captaincy only from the point of view of being in charge of those guys who really want to make things happen. Certainly I enjoy it because of the involvement with the team, and the team has responded well. The players here who are going to England are now very keen to get there.

There is nothing like hindsight to add poignancy and significance to words delivered informally to a handful of familiar journalists in an airport lounge, the lobby of a hotel or at the dressing-room door. As Border would soon learn, some of those players he thought were going with him to England for the 1985 Ashes series had already succumbed to the lure of South Africa's

Krugerrand and would instead be playing for an Australian rebel team in the banned republic. In fact, unbeknown to Border, more than half the team that played the first Test against the West Indies in Perth had signed for the rebel tour by 9 November, the day the Test match began. In all, seven players from the Ashes touring party were named as defectors to South Africa – Wayne Phillips, Graeme Wood, Terry Alderman, Rod McCurdy, Murray Bennett, Dirk Wellham and Steve Rixon. The first to change his mind was Bennett. Phillips, Wood and Wellham were persuaded by Kerry Packer to follow Bennett back into the official fold. The problem was that Packer spoke only one language, money, and Border and his loyal teammates found it hard to accept into their midst players who had originally decided to leave Australian cricket and then been bought back into it by a billionaire media magnate.

Border discussed the situation with Greg Chappell and ACB chairman Fred Bennett, but was still unhappy. Finally the team met in Melbourne just before the tour and voted not to go ahead unless the three players were replaced. Border left the meeting, went down to the ACB offices in Jolimont and informed the board of the stand the players were prepared to take. Informed of 'certain things', mainly legal constraints preventing those players from being removed from the squad, Border was forced to relent and tell his players they could not jeopardise the Ashes tour. With the board's encouragement, the three one-time defectors had to state their full commitment to the Ashes tour in front of something of a kangaroo court presided over by their suspicious teammates. It was an ugly scene, but one that Wellham, one of the three, and Geoff Lawson, one of the tour faithful, later thought had not caused too much damage to team morale. But what of the effects on a captain unsure of himself, desperate for some success and for whom loyalty to the team was paramount?

In his autobiography, Border described the situation as a 'real crisis', and expressed his hurt at the actions of former teammates who had not only deserted his Australian team but never revealed to him the clandestine negotiations that had been going on for some time. He recalled a session in a hotel bar in Sharjah, only weeks before the Ashes tour, in which he talked emotionally of his confidence about the immediate future of his Australian team. Border wrote:

> I look back to a particular night during the 1985 series in Sharjah and I realise that several people I'd liked and respected made a bloody fool out of me. We were in a bar having a few drinks. I

*was happy because I reckoned we'd assembled quite a cricket team.
We'd had more than our share of setbacks, but we were getting it all
together and our future knew no bounds. I poured out my heart –
and it hurts even now to realise that a lot of guys who heard me rave
on that night about the future knew damned well that they weren't
going to be part of it. But they didn't say a word – then or
later . . . The truth about South Africa didn't hurt. The lack of
honesty did.*

So did the loss of so many top players. To have seven players
already chosen for a tour pull out at the last minute has to have
serious repercussions on team strength, if nothing else. Take one
player: Terry Alderman. In his first Test series, in England in 1981,
Alderman took 42 wickets. In 1989 in England, he took 41. It is
fair to assume he would have taken about 40 in 1985, and so would
have been the most outstanding bowler on either side and, quite
possibly, the difference between the teams.

No doubt Border carried that knowledge amongst a heavy
load of excess emotional baggage when he flew out to London for
his first full series as Australian captain. As he noted before the
1994-95 Ashes series, his first as a spectator: 'Maybe it goes back
to Bodyline, but there's an unspoken responsibility on Australian
captains to do extra well against England.' Not only was he playing
against the 'old enemy', but against some good mates as well,
people like Graham Gooch, David Gower, Mike Gatting and Ian
Botham. Personal as well as national pride was at stake.

Border began the 1985 Ashes tour with four hundreds in the
opening four first-class games. Even Bradman had not managed
that. It seemed the Australian captain had reverted to the basics.
He might not yet have developed into a fine captain; he might
not have been able to trust completely in the loyaltly or quality
of all his teammates; but he could bat. Border was never a captain
for one-on-one conversations with teammates. They were expected
to follow his lead, and in 1985 in England, he set the perfect
example – out in the middle at least. Off the field, he rarely sought
the advice of senior teammates and had little of substance to say
at team meetings. As David Gower recalled in his autobiography:
'He batted very well in '85, but was generally out of control as
captain.'

Laurie Sawle, chairman of selectors since the start of the
1984-85 season, holidayed in England that northern summer and
followed part of that tour on an 'unofficial look-see basis'. He was
concerned about his captain.

*Good mates: Opposing captains Allan Border and David Gower
chat at the end of the first Test of the 1985 Ashes series.*

It was AB's first real go at captaincy, his first tour, and apart from the Lord's Test, we fell apart pretty badly. He was a reluctant captain. He was groping to find his way. In '85 he was fairly raw and battered and uncertain whether he could do the job. Allan in the centre is tremendously courageous but to have this thrust upon him made him doubt whether he could do it. The only feeling the selectors had about it was we hoped he could come to grips with it and learn to handle it. We felt for him, as did the country. There was an inner turmoil eating at him. But Australian cricket was just about in ruins then. I believed we needed a long-term captain. You've got to have that to rebuild a team. He'd shown us that he had the capacity to do the job and the best way to get that out of him was to give him all the support we could.

As Sawle admitted 10 years later, that support did not really begin to fall into place until the 1985-86 season back in Australia. Events since the Hughes resignation had moved too quickly for the selectors to fully plan and choose the personnel to form Border's off-field support team. The loss of a squad of senior players to South Africa, including the disillusioned former captain, slowed the painstaking process of sorting out which players had the desire and determination to struggle on with Border.

The experienced Bob Merriman was in England as manager, and former Test pace bowler Geoff Dymock as assistant, but Border felt pretty much alone. The hurt he suffered from the defections to South Africa made him even more wary of opening himself too much to his teammates. That, together with his doubts about his abilities as a leader and his natural tendency to hold his deepest feelings to himself, made him a solitary figure. Just how much that distance from teammates contributed to their collapse in the final two deciding Test matches is still hard to judge, but it cannot have helped.

Many close observers of Border's time as Australian captain wondered whether the hurt suffered in these difficult early years affected him to the end. At the start of the 1984-85 summer, the summer he would have the Test captaincy thrust upon him, he spoke to a magazine about 'the fear of failure' as a driving force in his career. Some commentators believed these early years increased that fear and caused Border to struggle to develop into an imaginative, adventurous captain such as Richie Benaud and Ian Chappell. Certainly, Gower felt the loss of the Ashes in '85 had a lasting effect on Border, saying it was '... probably the most

Lone hand: Border struggled as captain during the 1985 Ashes series, but his batting was a class above the efforts of his teammates.

important lesson of his career – an experience he never forgot or ignored in planning all future contests'.

Australia lost the first Test at Headingley, won at Lord's thanks to Border's 196, Greg Ritchie's 94 and leg spinner Bob Holland's second innings 5/68. Two draws followed before the Australians folded, losing both the final Tests by an innings and, most importantly, the Ashes regained in Australia in 1982-83. Border topped the tourists' first-class and Test batting averages, making 597 runs in the Tests at 60.33. Next best was Ritchie with 422 at 42.2. Wood, Phillips and Kepler Wessels were inconsistent, Wood's 172 in the third Test his only score over 50 from five matches. Boon looked out of his depth against England's spinners, his feet stuck embarrassingly to the crease through nerves and uncertainty. Few people in England that season thought they would see David Boon again, let alone be forced to grow so familiar with the nuggety figure who would pound their bowlers in the 1989 and 1993 series.

However, the most enduring images from that series are those of the two captains, the two left-handers – Gower gliding shots through the covers with grace and ease, and Border thumping deliveries to the boundary rope with pugnacious short-arm jabs. The difference was that Gower batted secure in the knowledge that if he failed someone else would get the runs off this Australian team. Border stood alone, a batting collapse never far away. His great performances in the Caribbean in '84 had not been telecast to Australia and so remained more myth than memory, but the '85 Ashes series was watched every night by thousands of Australians. This was when the public's image of Border as the epitome of the embattled leader, the backs-to-the-wall champion, took hold. That image would finally change but not for some time, not until the passing years dimmed Border's stroke play a little, until players such as Boon developed into world-class batsmen capable of sharing the burden.

Greg Chappell has always believed that Border's greatest strength was his contrariness, his capacity to buck against adversity. In England in 1985, Border expressed that contrariness as a batsman only. At that stage, he knew no other way.

Ian Chappell saw another way for Border to express his contrariness. Chappell, as convivial a companion in the dressing-room after a day's play as he was an uncompromising opponent on the field, thought Border's obvious closeness with the likes of

Gower, Botham, Gooch and Gatting was sending the wrong message to Border's teammates and the Australian public – that losing was not hurting that much. Chappell put this view in various articles, but Border was not impressed. Before the 1989 Ashes tour, Phil Jarratt of the *Bulletin* asked Border how he looked back on Chappell's critcisms of his friendly behaviour in '85.

> *Oh, shit! Look, Ian hates the bloody Poms [Border said]. It's hard to comprehend how much he hates them. I'm afraid I find it hard not to build up some kind of relationship with blokes you play against so often. But after the last Ashes tour I did give a lot of thought to the possibility that some of our younger players misinter-preted that mateyness and that it had an effect on their game. Maybe this time I'll make it my responsibility to be a bit tougher. But I tell you what – I'll make a point of having a beer with Both and the boys afterwards.*

This would not be the last time Border would disagree with Ian Chappell on a cricket issue, but later come around in his own good time. So often the discussions would end in an argument that the pair agreed to disagree on cricket and to confine their conversations to less important topics such as baseball, golf or the meaning of life. But in '89 in England, Border went even further than Chappell was suggesting and rarely mixed with the Englishmen off the field. On it, he never spoke a friendly word. Australia won 4-0 in '89, regaining the Ashes lost in '85.

Craig McDermott, in his first overseas series, bowled very well in England in 1985 to take 30 wickets, and Geoff Lawson, despite poor health, took 22. But their wickets made up 52 of the 69 to fall to Australian bowlers and came at too high a price. As the 1986 edition of *Wisden Cricketers' Almanack* noted, England scored at 60.67 runs per 100 balls, the fastest rate in Ashes history. Border's mates in the England side had gorged themselves on wayward bowling. Gatting made 527 at 87.83 and Gower a gluttonous 732 at 81.33 with three centuries, one a double.

The two captains led from the front, but Gower's team played by far the better cricket. Even England's selectors could do no wrong with choices like opening batsman Tim Robinson and swing bowler Richard Ellison enjoying significant, if short-lived, success. England was settled and confident; Australia inexperienced and lacking in direction and leadership.

For Border, more traumas lay ahead. Back in Australia for the 1985-86 season, he and his team would continue to struggle, losing its first Test series on home soil to New Zealand. Border would contemplate, then threaten resignation. But behind the scenes, the cavalry was coming. Gower's glory days ended in less than a year. He was sacked as England captain after losing the first Test of the 1986 series against India, although the damage had been done a few months earlier in the Caribbean. As they had done and would continue to do, the West Indies laid waste to another team and another captain. Now led by Viv Richards, the West Indies inflicted on England another 5-0 'blackwash'. At least Australia did not have to face the West Indies until 1988-89, by which time, the rebuilding process would be well under way.

DAZED

AND CONFUSED

'OUR New Hero' declared the posters for Adelaide's now-defunct daily paper, the *News*, on Tuesday, 14 January 1986. Above the headline was a picture of Australian all-rounder Greg Matthews. The lively 'new wave' cricketer had grabbed the headlines midway through the summer of 1985-86 with some excellent batting performances in the three Test matches against New Zealand. Although Australia lost the series 1-2, Matthews's efforts had people talking of a turning point for the Australian team.

Matthews's popularity was inspired by the way he played as much as the runs he scored. To a somewhat apologetic team, Matthews brought a manic enthusiasm, spiced with eccentricity, which threatened to become infectious. After a grim couple of years, Australia seemed to have found a cricketer with flair, passion and commitment – a colourful cricketer for grey times.

Matthews's profile was established in the first Test in Brisbane, when he joined his captain with Australia's second innings about to collapse at 5/67. Richard Hadlee had taken a stunning 9/52 in

the first innings to rout Australia for 179 on a green pitch. New Zealand declared at 7/553, leaving Australia 374 to score just to force the visitors to bat again. With a monstrous innings defeat looming in the first Test of the summer, the two left-handers added 197 for the sixth wicket. When Matthews lifted off spinner Vaughan Brown down the ground for six, he posted his third first-class hundred and his first in a Test match.

During the 1985 Ashes tour, Matthews had asked a senior teammate what it was like to score a hundred for Australia in a Test. 'Better than sex,' said the teammate. He might have been right, too, judging by Matthews's exultant reaction to his first Test century. It would take years for Border to come to terms with Matthews the bohemian cricketer, but that day in Brisbane, many cricket watchers had to admit that perhaps a non-conformist with a 'weird' hairstyle, a stud in his ear and a vocabulary straight out

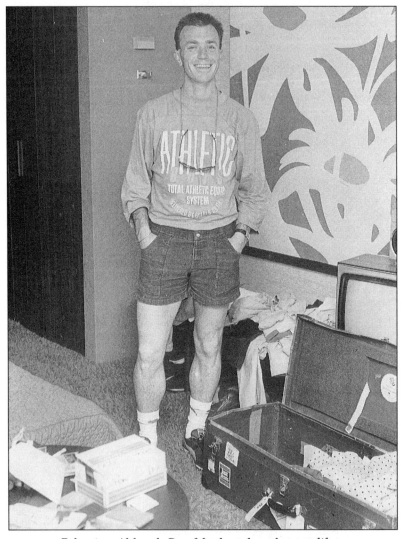

Bohemian: Although Greg Matthews brought some life to a struggling Test team, his captain Allan Border never quite came to terms with the unconventional all-rounder.

of a New Orleans jazz club might actually be able to play the grand old game after all.

Matthews was out for 115 and, when Hadlee bowled Bob Holland for a duck for New Zealand to win the Test by an innings and 41 runs, Border was left undefeated on 152 after seven and a half hours of stoic resistance. It was a terrible start to a summer of Tests against the modest opposition of New Zealand and India, a summer in which Australia was expected to show some progress. That Border and Matthews's ultimately futile partnership gave hope to people and raised Matthews to cult figure status said as much about the cricket public's desperate need for some encouragement as about Matthews's passion and courage. A few more like him alongside Border and things would start to improve.

Australia beat New Zealand in Sydney, a venue now established as the one Border-friendly ground in the country, but lost in Perth to give the visitors their first series win over Australia. Richard Hadlee's brilliant 33 wickets at 12.15 apiece was the difference. Border led the Australian batting, again in customary rearguard actions, with 269 runs at 55.8, with Matthews next with 247 at 41.16. Although it would be ungracious towards New Zealand cricket and dismissive of Hadlee's genius to say such a loss proved how low Australian cricket had fallen, it was a decidedly embarrassing result.

After the Perth Test, Border said he would be prepared to stand down as captain should the selectors suggest it.

You start to wonder if you are the right bloke for the job [he said]. If there is an obvious choice that I believe could do a better job, I'd be happy to stand down. But I don't really think it's my captaincy. Rather it is the way we have been playing. My own enjoyment of the game is suffering. If you keep losing, the selectors have got to keep trying to change.

A few days later, Border's first year as Australian captain was marked, if not exactly celebrated, in the press. In that time, Australia had won three Tests out of 12 and lost a number of fine players to South Africa. Mike Coward in the *Sydney Morning Herald* noted how the captaincy had aged Border, but wrote that: 'Allan Robert Border is Australian cricket circa 1985.' He then summed up: 'He, and he alone, has given the Australian cricket lover something to cling to; something to hope for. He believes in Australian cricket when many people, eminent players included, have chosen to turn their backs on it.'

In the *Australian*, Terry Brindle wrote: 'Border is not about to give the job away, even if he finds it frustrating and sometimes unrewarding. That would smack of despair and there is nothing in Border's character or behaviour to suggest he is a quitter.'

True enough, although his offer a few days earlier to stand aside showed again that Border was prone to reveal his misgivings in public in a way that cannot have filled his battling team with confidence. On that offer to stand down, Richie Benaud commented that Border had been 'led into one of his many conversations on the possibility of retiring from the captaincy'.

Brindle wrote that what was really troubling Border was 'the suspicion that failure does not hurt, the nagging belief that players have become inured to defeat and will do just enough to satisfy standards of their own'. He continued: 'Border has no reason to believe that Australia's lack of success is a reflection on his personality. Leadership by example is powerful enough, assuming the led have the perception and ability to follow.'

Again, true enough, although leadership by example alone is one dimensional. Had Border been a more willing and more natural captain, one capable of examining his players' personalities and finding out how to get the best out of them, the slow torture of these years might have ended sooner. The same could be said of Border's on-field tactics at that stage. He was slow to read play, reluctant to set unorthodox fields for his bowlers and unable to give them much advice beyond the clichéd 'keep working'. Brindle was right to suggest that not all Border's players boasted his commitment, but there were others with that commitment who were expecting personal advice and direction but not receiving them.

Greg Chappell believes Border was slow to learn the arts of tactical captaincy because of his general reluctance to take on the job after seeing what it did to Kim Hughes and because he had little confidence in his bowlers in those days.

He was keenly aware that he didn't have a potent attack [Chappell said]. And for a little while he felt sorry for himself. That contributed to the fact that he didn't take to the job with a great deal of relish from the start. He also felt betrayed by the guys who went to South Africa. All in all I don't think he was in a frame of mind that allowed him to take on the job in the most positive way. It was different with me and Mark Taylor. I got the job when we had a pretty good all-round team. Allan came to it in a very different situation. Mind you, it was a also a great opportunity for him. And later he took great pride in the fact that he'd been able to pull a good side together.

In the three weeks from mid-December into January 1986, Australia played three drawn Tests against India. Although Australia's batsmen fared better now that Richard Hadlee had gone home, the bowlers missed the injured Geoff Lawson, the one

The Hadlee Hoodoo: The brilliance of New Zealand's Richard Hadlee during Border's early years as Test captain made life very difficult for Australia's emerging batsmen.

39

experienced bowler who had not gone to South Africa. The Australian fieldsmen also let Border down, another stream of dropped catches reflecting a continued lack of self-confidence. Australia took only 26 Indian wickets in the series, and the visitors posted first innings scores of 520, 445 and 4/600 as well as several protests at what they perceived as poor and biased umpiring. Had it not been for some strangely conservative captaincy from Sunil Gavaskar, Australia would probably have lost this series too.

However, the home summer of 1985-86 was not a complete write-off. In the first Test against India in Adelaide, Australia chose three new players – batsman Geoff Marsh and two new pace bowlers, Merv Hughes and Bruce Reid – and David Boon made his first Test century. In the second game in Melbourne, a 20-year-old all-rounder from Bankstown in Sydney's western suburbs, Stephen Waugh, made his debut, batting at number six, surprisingly ahead of the in-form Matthews, who made a first innings undefeated hundred. In the second innings, Border was last man out for an heroic 163 and, with stout support from tailenders Ray Bright, Bruce Reid and Dave Gilbert, just managed to take the game out of reach of the conservative Indians.

In the third Test in Sydney, keeper Wayne Phillips moved down the order, allowing Marsh to open with Boon. In their first stand together, the old friends from Australia's 1977 under-19 team added 217, Boon making another century and Marsh 92. Australia also regained some pride by winning the World Series Cup, Waugh revealing abilities in these games that he had not been able to display in the Test matches. This was the first example of Border's teams salvaging pride by playing well in one-day cricket, despite repeated failures in the longer, more demanding form of the Test match.

Border had been teased in the recent past by the occasional promising performance from a player, only to see that man soon fall by the wayside. Had he been able to see five years into the future, his spirits would have lifted. In Boon, Marsh, Waugh and Hughes, the selectors had found players with sufficient ability, pride and commitment to travel the road ahead with the skipper and, eventually, to form the toughened core of the team that would find success in the late 1980s. Matthews and Reid would play their parts, too, although form, injury and selection vagaries would limit their appearances. Behind the scenes, things were improving too. Not before time, the ACB was marshalling the back-up staff its reluctant captain needed so badly.

With Border on the flight to New Zealand in late February was another new face, that of former Australian captain Bob Simpson. Simpson was going on the month-long tour as assistant manager, but in practical terms, he was on a reconnaissance mission to decide whether he would accept an appointment as the Australian cricket team's first full-time coach.

As far back as 1981, the ACB had been considering appointing someone to run practice sessions and work with individual players on their skills and mental approach. Initially, the ACB held back because there was widespread cynicism in the Australian cricket community about the value of a travelling coach. Cricket in Australia had always prospered by relying on natural talent rather than the academic coaching and over-analysis that was the preferred method in England. Allied to this was the view that the Australian team had always been and should continue to be run by one man, the Australian captain. Fiddling with this set-up was seen as something of a betrayal of Australian cricket's finest traditions.

Simpson's comment on his appointment that he hoped to make himself redundant acknowledged this view. He meant that if he did his job well enough, the team would soon become self-sufficient and be able to revert to the old system where the captain was the only person in charge. As the years passed, Simpson argued that the increased amount of cricket in the 1980s demanded that international teams have coaches. And in that period all other Test-playing countries did appoint coaches. Simpson was probably correct in this, but the question remained as to how wide a coach's powers should be.

Captains might have needed assistance in running their teams, but did the coach have to be a selector? It was a question of degree, of job description. When the South Africans toured Australia in 1993-94, their officials and media were amazed at how much influence Simpson wielded. Their coach, Mike Procter, ran practice, advised players and held occasional press conferences. That was all. Even among those critics who agreed that the Australian team needed a coach, the suspicion remained that Simpson desired and gained too much power. Yet, for most of his decade as captain, this set-up suited Border.

These misgivings would continue to lie behind the persistent criticisms of Bob Simpson's controversial and high-profile reign. Simpson's personality, in particular, has always attracted criticism, courted it in fact. But it would be wrong for observers to see that criticism as inspired solely by personal feelings. There has always been a strong element of serious cricket thinking behind the criticism, the overview being that Simpson's conservative approach as Test captain and later as coach ran counter to the traditional attacking philosophy of the Australian game.

One commentator who studied many of Australia's captains was ABC Radio's Alan McGilvray. In his book *McGilvray: Captains of the Game*, he said of Simpson's first stint as Australian captain from 1964 to 1968, during which 14 of 29 Tests ended in draws: '. . . the Simpson years, where victory at any cost – more particularly avoiding defeat at any cost – produced grinding cricket of a kind that made attrition an art form.'

McGilvray also noted Simpson's prickly personality: 'Simpson was highly protective of his position and his record, and would take on anybody he considered to be undermining them.' He then linked that personality to Simpson's captaincy: 'Nothing had come easily for him and it was perhaps inevitable that the doggedness of his cricket eventually would be reflected in the doggedness of his captaincy.'

Shades of Allan Border there, too, and that is why Ian Chappell always argued that the combination of two such dogged characters as Simpson and Border was not a happy one.

This view of Simpson as someone outside the better traditions of the Australian game is confirmed by the scarcity of Simpson fans among former Australian and Sheffield Shield players. Among ex-players in the media, Keith Stackpole would be Simpson's strongest supporter, with Bill Lawry and Tony Greig always positive. From 1988 onwards, the Australian press corps could be split roughly into three groups: a few who praised just about everything Simpson did, quite a few who criticised him regularly and a few others who chose to remain neutral.

The English press tended still to see Simpson as the white knight who rescued his country's cricket team when the Packer barbarians stormed the castle. As well, they pointed to the coach's role in restoring a poor team's reputation, comparing his success with the bungling of the England team set-up from '86-87 well into the 1990s. But as will become more and more apparent, comparing Australia's cricket standards with England's was liable to be very misleading.

Still, in 1985, Border was struggling with the captaincy and his team was battling to stay competitive. The need for off-field support was urgent and the ACB began to act. Bob Merriman had been appointed full-time manager in late 1984 and, with the strong support of ACB chairman Fred Bennett and the Cricket Committee, which included Border and the state captains, the board began to look around for a former Test player to become Australian team coach.

Bennett and David Richards sounded out Ian Chappell, who said he would not be interested, partly because he did not believe an Australian team needed a coach and partly because he was committed to his media career with Channel Nine. Chappell was not impressed when Bennett told him Simpson was a contender. His view was that if the team had to have a coach, the conservative and often prickly Simpson was the last sort of person to partner a pessimistic and obviously reluctant leader such as Border. Chappell never wavered from that early judgement.

Two other candidates for the coach's job were interviewed by the ACB, but neither had Simpson's record as a player nor his experience as coach of a successful Sheffield Shield team. The ACB was still grateful to Simpson for the way he returned to Test cricket at age 41 to captain the team left after the defections to Packer's World Series Cricket. Board members were also aware of his tendency to be provocative and divisive. They were prepared to handle those problems if and when they arose in return for his undoubted skills as a meticulous, disciplined coach who stood a good chance of pulling a decent team together.

Before he signed on, Simpson asked to be sent to New Zealand to see what he was letting himself in for. What he found disturbed and excited him. 'I was somewhat horrified to find such a lack of cohesion in the team itself, in the personnel, their desires and ambitions,' he recalled. 'I realised there was a lot to be done. But it was a good time to start, a challenging time.'

Simpson reported to the selectors that some players were taking a cynical approach to their cricket, playing primarily for themselves and damaging what was left of team morale by disparaging any success their teammates might manage.

You could see there were blokes with a genuine desire but also that there were others who just wanted to be in the side and not contribute much more. They were happy to do just enough to stay in the team but were never prepared to go beyond the pain barrier. They'd say to a teammate who'd done well: 'Congratulations, mate, it must have been easy out there.' There was a bit of that around. You had to wonder how genuine some of them were. We had to remind them about taking pride in the Australian Test cap. I think some of them had forgotten just how fortunate they were to be the selected few with the talent to play for their country.

Simpson's brief largely involved running practice sessions, never something to inspire Border though he trained hard himself, and relieving the captain of some of his media commitments. Simpson set about instilling the work ethic into the team, increasing the intensity at practice sessions and beginning to work on specific skills with specific players.

Through practice I tried to show them that through a good workout they could become better fieldsmen, better runners between the wickets. I tackled the easy things first. Once they saw themselves improving I hoped they'd understand the value of working hard at practice. At first I was amazed that I had to tone down the intensity from what I'd been doing with the New South Wales team I'd been coaching for the previous two years. But we were lucky to have Swampy [Marsh], Boonie and Steve Waugh, and Allan of course – players who had the tenacity to go through with it. I always thought those three could make it. They had the right attitude, the work ethic and enough skills. They thrived on it. I still remember spending hours under a tree at Hamilton hitting short catches to Swamp and Boonie. That was when Boonie started to learn to field at short leg. It was the first time they had had anyone to take them one on one and work on specific areas.

The confidence of the players had been at a low ebb for some time and had been reflected in their poor catching under pressure. Drop a catch in front of a big crowd and you not only let the opposition off the hook, but you invite public ridicule which then damages your self-confidence. It was a vicious circle that had surrounded this team for a couple of years.

'They'd catch well at practice but then drop them in games,' Simpson said. 'It was a slow turnaround. It took some time till the players understood that they had the capacity to do it. They were still very nervous and you had to get them to be confident under match pressure by working on their concentration.'

Even his harshest critics would admit that Simpson runs an excellent practice session, especially the fielding. He has been a master at hitting catches and ground balls just far enough away from each player to stretch his mobility, enhance his skill and test his commitment. It is an essential skill for a cricket coach and Simpson's practice sessions with Border's team gradually took on the noisy, enthusiastic tone that would characterise them for the next decade. The only drawback with Simpson's fielding drills was that occasionally they got too intense and a player suffered a minor injury.

Simmo is always big on watching the ball [Boon said some years later]. From the start he always told us that everything in the game is about watching the ball. That's why his fielding drills – the close, sharp stuff – also help your batting. And he was always on about having soft hands when catching or batting, being able to drop your hands when defending against fast bowlers so any edge or mishit wouldn't travel far.

While Simpson began working at close quarters with Border and his players, the selection panel under Laurie Sawle's chairmanship was well into its rebuilding program, sorting through the Sheffield Shield competition for the most talented players who also had the temperament and dedication to make it as Test cricketers. Greg Chappell explains:

Basically we sat down and said: 'All right, AB's struggling, so we have to build a structure around him. The guy is reluctant and a bit volatile but he is the only one of his generation who is going to be able to do the job. If we lose him we're in trouble so we have to give him time to come good.' Then we thought we had to get players around him who were going to give him total support, 100 per cent effort. It was no good having blokes with flair who are going to be up one day and down for the next ten. We had to get blokes who had a love of the green cap – the likes of Geoff Marsh, David Boon, Steve Waugh. We knew we had a limited number of players capable of playing the game at that level. So we had to identify them, get them in the team, let them know they're in for the long run and allow them time to learn the game. We had to give Allan the sort of guys who would be inspired by his leadership, who were going to see that he was prepared to run through brick walls and who'd be prepared to follow him through.

By the end of the third Test in Auckland in mid-March, it seemed that Allan Border had come up against a brick wall that resisted even his determined battering. Australia had drawn the first two Tests. Boon, Greg Ritchie and Matthews scored runs in the first, with Matthews making his third century of that extended summer. Border saved the second Test by making 140 and 114 not out, the latter innings coming in a total of 7/219. Border's effort enabled him to join Greg Chappell, George Headley and Clyde

Walcott as the only players to score two hundreds in a Test match twice. He also passed Neil Harvey to move into third place behind Greg Chappell and Don Bradman on the list of Australia's highest run-scorers in Test cricket.

However, life turned sour again in Auckland for the third Test when Australia, having enjoyed a lead of 56 on the first innings, collapsed for 103 in the second to allow New Zealand to win the series with an eight-wicket victory. Only Boon came through unscathed, showing great application to carry his bat through the innings for 58 runs. Overall, it was a classic case of a side lacking belief in itself crumbling under pressure. It also confirmed the popular view that when Border failed, the team fell apart. The latter point was hardly surprising: at this stage, Border had played more Tests than the combined total played by the rest of his team.

After the Test, Australia again collapsed chasing a modest target of 186 in the first one-day game at Dunedin. Border was near breaking point. After a loose practice session in Christchurch before the next one-day game, Border, in response to some probing questions on his feelings about the captaincy, blurted out that he would resign unless the team lifted in the remaining three games.

'They're going to have to show me whether they really want to play for Australia and whether they really want to play under me. I'll find out over the next three games and my decision will be made after that.'

As he conceded in his autobiography, Border had not planned the outburst. Again, it had just come out as his thoughts responded to a persistent line of questioning and turned into words ideal for bold headlines. The players, without Border, met that night and pledged their support. Senior ACB people, startled by the unexpected threat and worried they might lose their only option as captain, rang Merriman and encouraged him to calm Border.

'It was a very tense 24 hours,' Sawle recalled. 'We knew he was a bit fragile at that time and was still struggling to come to grips with the whole thing. We were in a transition period and there was no one who could've replaced him.'

Simpson was equally shocked. 'It came out of the blue. I knew he'd had his disappointments, but maybe he'd been subjected to them longer than I'd appreciated. He just blew his top. It was a leading question and his honesty led him on.'

Almost immediately, Border regretted his emotional outburst, but the team's support, conveyed after the meeting by vice-captain

Ray Bright and Merriman, had little immediate effect. The next day, he lost his temper with his team, sitting 20 metres from the rest during a drinks break in the second one-day international and prompting Ian Chappell, among others, to advise him to take a break from the game. Nevertheless, the players lifted to win the final two games of the series and Border was saved the dilemma of deciding whether to stick to his words.

Again, he had expressed his feelings openly to the press without thinking through the ramifications. In his autobiography, Border later wrote: 'I'd grown thoroughly tired, since that Christchurch press conference, of answering questions about captaincy. Nobody seemed interested any more on what we might or might not do on the field at any particular time. No, everybody wanted to know about the captaincy, would I quit, would I continue, had I mellowed.'

Border was getting caught in another vicious circle. The press had grown preoccupied with his painful tussle with the captaincy and had turned it into the major story, the very public and personalised drama of Australian cricket. This was understandable. The cricket itself was pretty poor, and Border stood out from the rest of his players so much that what future they might have rested squarely on his shoulders. But the situation also made it hard for Border to forget his troubles and concentrate on the cricket. The pressure never seemed to ease.

Certainly, Ian Chappell was amazed by what Border had said in Christchurch.

> *I wrote that it was ridiculous for an Australian captain to think of quitting. If most other captains had said that, the ACB would have said: 'Okay, piss off.' The only reason they didn't then was they felt there was no one else to captain the side. You never talk about quitting. I understand he was trying to shock the players into playing better, but it shows his lack of knowledge of men. It was like an army commander telling his men they were going to retreat. You might be thinking it but you never let the men know that.*

Once more, Ian Chappell's views on Border resulted from a radically different way of thinking.

> *The underlying reason Allan and I were always going to argue about cricket was that he's a pessimist and I'm an optimist. So in making criticisms like this I should take a step back and imagine how a pessimist would think. And I suppose a pessimist would think of resigning. As a pessimist Allan always saw a disaster around the next*

corner. Allan will blame that on the fact that in those early days there always was a disaster around the corner and he can do that with some justification. But also it had to do with his outlook.

Perhaps another reason for Border's low spirits was the sheer volume of cricket he'd been forced to play. Since Hughes's resignation in late November 1984 to the end of March 1986, 16 hectic months, Border led Australia in 18 Tests for three wins, eight draws and seven losses. As well, Australia had played 37 one-day internationals for 18 wins. And since the 'Big Three' of Greg Chappell, Dennis Lillee and Rod Marsh retired at the end of the 1983-84 season, Australia had won only three of 25 Tests and lost five Test series with the sixth drawn.

Yet, in '85-86, Border's form with the bat was so irresistible that he earned enough points from umpires to be named the Benson and Hedges Sheffield Shield Player of the Year despite appearing in only four games. For the record, he made 568 runs from his seven Shield innings at an average of 94.67. Whether disappointed, frustrated or nearing a nervous collapse, Border overcame all when he held a bat in his hand. It said a great deal about his determination and powers of concentration that he could play so well while consumed by self-doubt about his worth as a leader. And to prove his massive superiority over his butter-fingered teammates, Border also won Channel Nine's Classic Catches award for his diving one-hander in the slips to dismiss John Reid off Dave Gilbert in the first Test in Brisbane.

So if Border was about to crack up, it must have been because of terminal Test match disappointment rather than exhaustion. The amount of cricket he had played had forced him to confront loss and failure as a captain far too often for his own good. It was a situation that ought to have had Border spending the winter in retreat at a Buddhist community in Tibet. But he had one more shock left for his followers. Instead of rest and recuperation Border – defiantly wearing his badge as Australian cricket's first full-time professional – chose to increase his workload by joining Essex and the six-day-a-week treadmill of English county cricket.

THE WORST

6

SUMMER

A LLAN Border likened his busman's holiday playing for Essex in county cricket in 1986 to 'turning the cold water tap full on your head when you've got a hangover'. Given the amount of cricket he had played in the previous 18 months, a more appropriate metaphor might have been 'drinking a beer the morning after a big night guzzling whisky'. Although diluted, it was essentially the same poison and another bout of nausea was a distinct possibility.

Not so with someone of Border's iron constitution. When he left Essex before the end of its season to lead the Australians on a three-Test tour of India in September and October, Border was refreshed. For a few months at least, he had been just another player with none of the onerous responsibilities of captaincy. Being the senior overseas pro was hardly an imposition on such a resolute, working cricketer.

Border had enjoyed watching Essex's Keith Fletcher go about his captaincy with the sort of low-key approach Border preferred. The Australian pro had been impressed with Fletcher's ability to inspire his players with quiet one-on-one chats rather than loud and long speeches to a full dressing-room. Whether Border actually learned anything of genuine substance from Fletcher remained in doubt according to some observers, who thought Border still spent too much time inside his own head and not enough swapping ideas with his teammates, particularly his bowlers.

While in England, Border had watched an improved Indian team under new captain Kapil Dev beat England 2-0. The Australians had found the Indians a provocative and touchy lot during the previous antipodean summer, and Border knew the tour to India had the potential to be a trying experience for an emerging team unsure of itself at home let alone in such unfamiliar territory. At least on this tour he would have the support of Bob Simpson, who had been formally appointed cricket manager during the winter.

Relations between the teams during this series were tense. In his report for the 1988 edition of *Wisden Cricketers' Almanack*, R. Mohan noted that '... there were far too many incidents of gamesmanship, with the Indians reacting to the pattern of behaviour set by the visitors'.

The question of who started what remained an issue with the Australians on the subcontinent and in the Caribbean throughout Border and Simpson's time together, as did their poor playing record. The Border-Simpson record in England was superb, but to an Australian cricketer, England is friendly, familiar and unthreatening. As soon as the Australians under Border and Simpson ventured further than England, behaviour problems and poor match results ensued. Outside England, Australia's overseas record in the Border-Simpson years was four wins from 24 Tests, with 12 draws, seven losses and one tie. Australia won one of those seven Test series.

Still, on this their first overseas tour as a partnership, Border and Simpson's team took a major step forward in its painful journey towards respectability by tying the first Test at Madras and drawing the second and third.

After the traumas of the previous two years, the fact that the Australians held firm under intense pressure in appalling weather conditions to force the second tie in Test match history showed Border and Simpson that they had the raw material for a decent team. In Australia's first innings of 7/574 declared, Boon made his third Test century (all against India), Dean Jones his first and Border his nineteenth. Jones turned his century into an epic 210, the latter stages of which he barely remembered so poor was his physical condition. Soon after he was dismissed, he collapsed and was taken to hospital and put on a saline drip.

When Jones moved into the 170s, he was vomiting regularly and his body was racked with trembling. He told Border he was too ill and exhausted to continue. Instead of merely telling Jones to 'keep going', as was his custom in those days, Border actually tried a little psychology. 'All right, if that's the way you feel. Let's get a real Australian out here. A Queenslander.' (Greg Ritchie was due in next.)

It was not particularly subtle but it was a start. And it worked. Jones, like Boon, Waugh and Matthews, knew well enough that the one thing that inspired Border and that he demanded of his players was pride in the baggy green cap, pride in playing for Australia. When he questioned Jones's pride, Border helped lift the young Victorian to heights rarely if ever reached by a batsman. If Border also helped put him in hospital for a while that night, so be it. This was a Test match after all.

Greg Matthews played brilliantly in Madras, although as the game has receded into history, his efforts have been overshadowed by Jones's epic. As well as making 44 and 27 not out with the bat, Matthews took his first five-wicket haul in a Test innings in India's first and followed it with another in the second. He bowled unchanged from the ninth over on the final day until he had Maninder Singh trapped leg before with the fifth ball of his thirty-eighth over. There had been one ball left in the match and one run needed for an Indian win, but Matthews and Border kept their nerve.

Given the terrible conditions and the fact that Border had declared both Australia's innings to push for a win, this was a great performance from an inexperienced team. Simpson said later that he doubted there had ever been a tougher Test match. Finally, Border was showing more confidence as a captain. He had declared on the morning of the fifth day to leave India 348 to win off a minimum 87 overs, and had abandoned the more conservative line of bowling medium pacers to take up time so as to put pressure on India. Instead, he attacked with the spinners, Matthews and Ray Bright, in an all-out effort to win. Border had also received the sort of stout-hearted support from teammates that he had been longing for since becoming captain. Jones had shown a capacity to soar to the heights; Boon and Matthews, a willingness to put their heads down and work away for hours like their captain did so often.

What might have happened to Border's fragile morale had any of his decisions backfired in Madras, and Australia lost a match in which they had made all the running, hardly bears thinking about. Going so close to a great victory only to have it taken away in the final over in such trying conditions could have induced Border to snap for the last time. Mike Coward thinks so.

Coward covered that tour and relived it in *Cricket Beyond the Bazaar*, his 1990 book on Australian cricket's history on the subcontinent.

> *Looking back after nine years, the Tied Test was a near thing for Australian cricket [Coward said]. AB had been consumed by self-doubt for some time. You could see him growing older in the job. The original self-doubt he'd brought to the job of captain had grown a great deal. At times I thought he looked as close to a nervous break-down as an elite athlete could go. His state of mind was the main talking point in Australian cricket and if he'd lost that Test match it would have been an unjust result and very damaging at such a delicate time. I doubt if he could have coped.*

Yet, some unusually attacking tactics from Border himself, some long-awaited, sustained, good play from key team members and, not to be forgotten, some luck in the form of the obliging umpire V. Vikram Raju saw Australia avert another crisis and gain some much-needed confidence. The second Test was badly affected by rain and the third in Bombay dominated to a draw by three local heroes – Sunil Gavaskar (103), Dilip Vengsarkar (164 not out) and Ravi Shastri (121 not out). Despite not winning a Test match and losing the one-day series 2-3, Border had good reason to approach the coming Ashes series with some optimism.

Six months later, as the Australian team bus left for the airport and the flight home from Sharjah, manager Ian McDonald announced that Bob Simpson had been appointed a selector for the next three years. As he relates in his autobiography, *The Gloves Are Off*, Tim Zoehrer was not exactly overjoyed at the news.

'I'm finished. What about you?' Zoehrer said to Greg Ritchie.

'I'm gone too,' the Queenslander replied.

For some weeks, Zoehrer had been under the impression Simpson did not want him in the team. In chats with the keeper, Simpson had been referring regularly to the better practice habits of New South Wales keeper Greg Dyer. It was the sort of tactic Simpson would use for years to come. He likes to keep some players on edge by mentioning their closest rivals and by dropping hints, subtle and otherwise, that he is not happy with them. It seemed to be Simpson's version of the divide and rule theory of political operation.

During the 1989-90 season, a senior player told me that not a week went by when Simpson was not on speaking terms with at least one player. This was different from Border's approach. The captain could lose his temper with a player but he very rarely held a grudge after his temper cooled. Once he had made his point, Border got on with the job. With Simpson, a transgression against his authority was never forgotten and both parties knew it. This made for a charged atmosphere in the dressing-room.

One notorious episode which has never been fully explained was the fining of Greg Matthews for an alleged incident at a function in Sharjah in April 1987. The fine of $1000 was hefty, but Matthews was assured that that was to be the end of the matter and the selectors would decide his future on purely cricket criteria. Yet there were many times in the next few years when Matthews was the best cricketer in the Sheffield Shield but did not win senior selection.

The ACB has never revealed details about what Matthews allegedly did, allowing the matter to become the subject of unfair and unsubstantiated rumour. One view is that Matthews was a troublemaker and deserved the penalty. The other view is that the team hierarchy did not know how to handle his eccentricity, thought it was harming team spirit and so overreacted to a minor incident to make a point.

Dirk Wellham, in his book *Solid Knocks and Second Thoughts*, said that the incident arose from a combination of Matthews's frustration at being overlooked for the Sydney Test against England and Simpson's critical view of a few of Matthews's 'misdemeanours'.

Matthews still hopes to return to Test cricket and so prefers to let the matter rest.

Whatever the niceties of that episode, it confirmed the suspicion that Simpson was the one setting and enforcing the rules governing off-field behaviour. Throughout his years as coach, Simpson made sure his players constantly monitored where they stood with him. It was a significant aspect of the team dynamic and it drove the players to distraction and, finally, to action. This was one of the main issues that led to Simpson's standing down as a selector after the tour to South Africa in 1994. With Border's retirement expected at any moment, the ACB called its four most senior players to a meeting in Melbourne to discuss a range of issues. When asked whether they thought it best that Simpson continue as a selector, the four – Mark Taylor, Ian Healy, David Boon and Steve Waugh – answered in the negative. A few months later, Simpson stood down as a selector.

However, that development was eight years in the future. In the spring of 1986, the players knew their coach had become a very powerful figure in Australian cricket. A few of them also knew their days in the team were numbered. Not that this was necessarily unjust nor entirely up to Simpson: there were three other selectors on the panel, the team was still struggling badly and there were a few players whose inconsistency was not winning them many friends.

Before arriving in Australia, England had lost its previous three series, losing eight of 11 Tests, winning none. The two former great powers of the game were in poor shape, but although the '86-87 series would no longer be a top-of-the-table clash between cricket superpowers, there were still 110 years of tradition and pride at stake.

England – now under Mike Gatting, who had replaced the sacked Gower – had done its best to increase the confidence the Australians brought home with them from India. England blundered around the states in the lead-up games, dropping catches and inspiring Martin Johnson of London's new daily, the *Independent*, to declare that 'England have just one problem: they can't bat, they can't bowl and they can't field'.

Although Border never trusted the game in general nor form in particular, he walked out to toss with Gatting in a positive frame of mind. On the morning of the match, the selectors surprised by making Geoff Lawson twelfth man. Lawson was the only experienced bowler in the team but had played only two Sheffield Shield games after a 10-month spell recovering from a crippling back injury. Instead, Border had at his disposal a pace attack of Bruce Reid, Merv Hughes and Chris Matthews, who boasted nine Tests between them. Their inexperience proved costly, probably decisive for the entire series.

Australia's pace bowlers wasted the new ball and a pitch green enough for Border to decide to bowl first after he won the toss. But England's batsmen enjoyed a free rein and ended the rain-shortened first day comfortable at 2/198. The next morning, Australia took two quick wickets for no addition before Chris Matthews dropped David Gower at third slip, still with the score on 198 runs. That was Australia's last chance. Gower and Ian Botham, neither having scored at this stage, began a stand of 118 that turned the game.

After Gower and then Jack Richards were dismissed, Border set seven and at times eight fieldsmen on the boundary to deny Botham the strike. It was a defensive tactic that backfired. Border, no doubt recalling Botham's destruction of Australia at Headingley in 1981, and realising his bowlers this time around might not be good enough to deny the great all-rounder with tight, consistent bowling, opted to protect them in the hope that Botham would be frustrated out. This was a classic example of Border the conservative captain. The self-doubts had still not been fully dispelled, the memories of Australia's worst loss in living memory, the dreaded Headingley '81, had not been fully exorcised. Border knew that his bowling resources were dangerously thin. He was taking no risks.

Botham, sensing the Australians' vulnerability, was not about to throw his hand away. He had shown discipline throughout his innings and was happy to milk the Australians of any easy runs on offer. Occasionally, he launched an assault, once moving to and past his 100 by blasting 22 off a Hughes over, but in general, he played like a man determined to give England a strong start to the series.

Like Border, Botham relished an Ashes contest and he always lifted when an Australian was 22 yards away. His innings on the second day of the series changed the course of the summer. The two teams had been struggling in the various series leading to this encounter, but there was one major difference, as proved by Botham's innings in the first Test and Gower's form throughout. England had in its number at least two truly world-class players and a few others with significant experience; Australia had one world-class player on the field in Border, another, Lawson, languishing in the dressing-room and little experience among the others.

England won by seven wickets in Brisbane, bringing on a Border 'dummy spit' and further speculation about another threat to resign. At the end of the match, Border refused to attend the cheque presentation at the now familiar television ritual. Boon was asked to deputise while the skipper expressed his anger and frustration at and to the press before packing up and leaving the ground. Border described this loss, after winning the toss and bowling on a helpful pitch, as the worst in his time as captain.

*England's hero: Ian Botham's performances in the Brisbane
and Melbourne Tests of the 1986-87 series crushed any hopes
of a prompt revival in the fortunes of Australian cricket.*

England had the better of a draw in Perth, drew again on a flat pitch in Adelaide, then retained the Ashes in Melbourne by thrashing Australia by an innings and 14 runs in three days.

Simpson looks back on this series as the lowest point in his years with Border.

We'd gone really well in India and we went into the first Test in Brisbane expecting to win. We bowled badly. It was a big win for England and away they went. That series was the greatest disappointment. Getting beaten in three days in Melbourne was a shocker. All the things we'd been working on went out the door and we had to start from scratch again. Craig McDermott had lost form and been dropped. We had to drop Boonie. Blokes you thought you could build a team around. But I'm a great believer in history and I thought it'd change somewhere along the line as long as we worked and planned along the way.

Boon had been battling poor form throughout the series but rallied in Adelaide in the third Test to score a hundred in the first innings. He made a duck in the second, failed in the Melbourne Test and was dropped for Sydney. Technically, he had forgotten where his off stump was and consequently had become indecisive, hesitating for that crucial split second. Boon's four hundreds in the previous 12 Tests and his excellent opening partnerships with Marsh had been a highlight of the recent improvements, recognised by the selectors when they appointed Boon vice-captain. Dropping him was a bitter blow to Border, Simpson and the other selectors.

For Boon, it was devastating. From the time he was a 10-year-old batting prodigy in Launceston, he had been talked of as a future Test player. Despite Tasmania's relative isolation and its poor practice facilities, Boon had never taken his eyes off that ultimate prize. When he finally began his Test career, it was against the might of the West Indies pace attack. But he survived that and battled on to the stage where he was making Test centuries and playing a significant role in an improving team. Then, all of a sudden, his eyes and mind had become confused and could not tell his feet where to move. He lost his spot in the Test side. A childhood dream and an adult career were threatened and a huge amount of emotional investment apparently cast aside. Being dropped is difficult for any cricketer to handle; for a Test player, it can be savage.

My most vivid memory of that summer was seeing Boon staring bleakly at the ground while fielding at fine leg for his club

Launceston at the city's Northern Tasmanian Cricket Association ground during a round of club matches. A few days before, he had been a Test cricketer, playing in an Ashes series, the highlight for any Australian cricketer. Now he was a solitary figure in a provincial game, avoiding the action by fielding on the boundary in front of rows of empty seats. It was a sad sight in a disappointing summer.

One player who felt deeply for Boon was Dean Jones. Jones had already suffered setbacks and disappointments. He made his Test debut way back in 1984 in the West Indies, yet failed to make the 1985 Ashes tour, a major disappointment given that a full squad of Shield players was unavailable because of their rebel tour to South Africa. The stocks were thin, yet Jones still could not win a berth to England. Jones wrote to Boon, offering him sympathy and encouragement, telling him the setback would make him a tougher player in the end. Boon appreciated the gesture and still has the letter.

England had no such personal dramas. The tourists also won the World Series Cup and another one-day tournament, the World Series Challenge, held to coincide with the staging of the America's Cup yacht race off Fremantle. By the early 1990s, all cricket countries were crowding the program to bursting point and stretching the players to breaking point with one-day tournaments, citing every conceivable reason except the most obvious – money.

The only light for Australia in this dark season was, as usual, the Sydney Test match. Against Australia's spinners – this time leg spinner Peter Sleep and surprise debutant off spinner Peter Taylor – England failed on the final day, losing 5/31 in the final 70 tense minutes. When Sleep slid a low delivery through John Emburey's defence with one over remaining in the match, Australia had achieved its third consolation win in Sydney in the past three seasons and its first Test win in more than a year.

After the game, Border refused to draw much comfort from a rather meaningless win in the final game of a wretched series. Bruce Reid and Dean Jones were two of the last to leave the Australian dressing-room on the final night. Jones had made an undefeated 184 in the first innings, thanks to what appeared to be a poor umpiring decision in his favour before he had reached double figures. Reid took 2/74 in the first innings and 1/32 in the second, that one being tailender Gladstone Small. When the skipper saw the two still celebrating in the dressing-room hours after play, he confronted them.

'What are you two smiling about? You didn't take the hard

wickets and we didn't win the series.'

Two selections for the Sydney Test were significant. Dirk Wellham, with whom Simpson had worked closely at the Western Suburbs club in Sydney and then in the New South Wales squad over the previous two years, had come in for Boon. And Greg Matthews had been made twelfth man to allow Taylor to make his debut.

Although Wellham had been in good form in the Sheffield Shield, his was a surprise selection. The suspicion in cricket circles was that Wellham's experience of playing and captaining on the slow, turning Sydney Cricket Ground pitch had been drafted in to help Border. There were certainly times during the match when Wellham seemed to be directing traffic out in the middle more than the captain.

Border was definitely not happy with Wellham's selection, especially given that he had replaced one of the skipper's closest mates, David Boon. As well, Wellham had been one of those players who signed for the rebel tour to South Africa and then pulled out and went to England with Border's 1985 team.

Depressed: David Boon contemplates life after being dropped by the selectors during the 1986-87 Ashes series. Five years later, many thought Boon the best batsman in the world.

Matthews batted well in the first four Tests, averaging 53.75 mainly from the number seven spot, but Border lost confidence in his bowling. The selectors wanted Matthews to be the all-rounder, which meant his bowling had to be Test class. One problem was that Border could not relate to Matthews the cricket bohemian and was decidedly unsympathetic when setting fields for him in Test matches. A captain such as Ian Chappell would have found time to talk with Matthews to try to find out what made him tick in an effort to get the best out of him as a player. Border was not that sort of captain and had just about dismissed Matthews as a 'head case'.

Matthews's performances with the bat in the Tests leading to this series had been excellent. He made a century in each of the series against New Zealand and India at home and New Zealand away – this, after averaging 45 with the bat and topping the bowling figures in the series in India. Those efforts should have earned him an extended trial as a batting all-rounder at number six. This would have allowed the team to carry another spinner when necessary, rather than rely so heavily on Matthews. It would also have given Matthews more time to learn about bowling in Tests and Border more time to learn about handling players with personalities and tastes a little different from the usual conservative, steak-and-chips cricketer.

Again, the selectors had the right to search for the balance they thought would best suit the team, but the fact that the captain and Matthews did not get on did not help swing the decision the player's way. For his part, Matthews could look at the career of Steve Waugh, who was carried in his early years in the Test side more on potential than performance, and wonder why he was not granted similar support. So much for 'Our New Hero'.

In his reporting on the '86-87 Ashes series in the 1988 edition of *Wisden*, English journalist John Thicknesse, after acknowledging Border's dogged batting which produced two centuries, noted: '... but as captain he lacked spark and the ability to inspire a young team much in need of it. Hard task as he had, he did not look the man to lead the Test team from its troubled run.'

Thicknesse would have held his view even more strongly had he been told that during those tense moments towards the end of the Sydney Test, Border had been so unsure of which bowlers to use to finish off England's stubborn tail that, at the fall of one wicket, he gathered his senior teammates into a huddle and called for a vote.

THE TURNING
POINT

D ESPITE the excited crowds, the coloured uniforms and
the glare of the spotlights, one-day cricket is a defensive,
often predictable game. Allan Border and Bob Simpson
had this in mind when they prepared their game plan for the 1987
World Cup in India and Pakistan.

During his career Simpson had been a quick and aggressive
runner between wickets and, as coach, he encouraged his players
to use running between the wickets as a tactical weapon rather
than a routine which merely followed the playing of a shot. The
reasoning was that the team that took the most singles in a one-
day match would almost always win it. It was the safest way to
build a platform to an innings. Minimise the risks, hit the occasional
bad ball for four and gradually accumulate the runs, while keeping
wickets in hand for the slog in the final 10 overs.

When Australia first started playing one-day internationals
in the 1970s, they took the opposite approach, trying to hit
boundaries from the start. Often, that ended in batting collapses
and low scores. But that approach was to be expected of teams led

by Ian Chappell. They were early days in the evolution of one-day cricket in Australia, and Chappell did not have the advantage Simpson and Border enjoyed of being able to play plenty of one-day games every summer and so learn from the present as well as the mistakes of the past. But also, Chappell's imaginative attitude to cricket and his innate daring were not suited to a defensive game such as one-day cricket although, given time, he would no doubt have adjusted his approach.

The way Chappell's teams played one-day cricket reflected his philosophy. The approach Border and Simpson developed definitely reflected their more conservative, safety-first attitudes. It became a cold, calculated, mathematical exercise and for a long time, it worked very well.

One of the major advantages Border and Simpson exploited for the World Cup was the fine opening combination that had developed between Geoff Marsh and David Boon. The latter, reinstated for the World Cup, was the more powerful hitter with a wider range of shots in his repertoire and was designated as the more attacking of the two. Marsh was essentially a deflector but could hit a boundary with a crisp cover drive when the bowlers pitched full. His role was to lay the foundation of the innings, trying to bat through the 50 overs if possible, aiming to reach a hundred himself while allowing the stroke players to go for their shots, secure in the knowledge that Marsh was at the other end rotating the strike and stabilising the situation when a wicket fell.

Boon and Marsh were followed by Dean Jones, a fast and frenetic runner between wickets and one of the most inventive stroke-makers in the world. It was the perfect line-up for the game plan and the perfect game plan for the batsmen involved. So perfect, that it served Australia well for years until New Zealand and Pakistan countered it in the 1992 World Cup by employing a more daring brand of top-order batting and varying their bowling in unexpected ways. New Zealand broke the long-established rhythm of the Australian batting by opening with a gentle off spinner, and Pakistan used its fast swing bowlers to take wickets rather than merely save runs.

Australia's bowling was a blend of Craig McDermott's pace, the accuracy and awkward bounce of tall left-armer Bruce Reid, the niggling accuracy and slow-ball variations of medium pacers Steve Waugh and Simon O'Donnell and the spin of Peter Taylor or Tim May and, occasionally, Border himself.

Waugh, in particular, had developed into a tough, cool-headed all-rounder. He had also invented a slower ball that came out of the back of his hand like a wrist spinner's wrong 'un. This meant that his fingers pointed towards the sky as they did for a normal delivery but the back of his hand faced the batsman. As well, the seam of the ball remained upright as in his more conventional deliveries. It was a difficult ball to bowl and none of his teammates was able to master it despite hours of experimentation in the nets; it also took several years before opposing batsmen began to pick it.

McDermott had regained the confidence and form that deserted him in India the year before when he had been convinced by Simpson to cut his run-up and pace on the bare, unresponsive pitches. Simpson had been a useful leg spinner in his time and knew something of that art, but he never understood pace bowling. The changes he made to McDermott destroyed the bowler's rhythm, his form and, for a while, his morale. But all had come back by the time of the World Cup and McDermott ended up equalling the tournament's record wicket tally with 18 at the fine average of 10.94.

Although the Australians arrived in India as 16 to 1 outsiders, Border was guardedly optimistic. He was happy with the tactical plans and he knew his team had been playing more one-day cricket than any other team, thanks to a full domestic program which drew so much criticism from visiting teams and commentators. Also, a few players whom he and the selectors felt had been disruptive were not in the squad – Greg Matthews, Tim Zoehrer, Wayne Phillips and Greg Ritchie. Border and Taylor were the only two over 30, and Border would say early in the tour that it was the happiest and most closely knit team he'd captained. In fact, Border, his players and the travelling journalists all sensed a change in spirits occurring in the early days of this tour. The turning point in that tumultuous month and in Border's decade as captain came not after the victory over England in the final at Calcutta's Eden Gardens, but a month earlier in familiar Madras. It was there that the Australians held their nerve to beat India, the reigning champions and the home side, by one run in front of 50,000 roaring supporters.

The way the Australians constructed that win was significant, following the game plan closely and setting a pattern for the next few years. Batting first in intense heat, Boon and Marsh added 110 at the start with Marsh going on to reach the same score off 141 balls. Australia ended with 6/270, then, with fine fielding, disciplined bowling and impressive grace under pressure, dismissed India for 269 with one ball remaining. The Indian top order began in a flurry, McDermott going for 31 in his first four overs. But the Australians came back to take hold of the match late in the day. McDermott destroyed the middle order with a burst of four wickets, Steve Waugh stayed cool in the final overs and Border and Jones excelled in the field.

That night, the lobby of the Taj Coromandel Hotel filled with Australian supporters, while upstairs in manager Alan Crompton's suite, Border's side stayed together, celebrating with beer and spirits supplied by the Australian High Commission and agreeing that 'a special feeling' was in the air. Players who were there still consider that night as highly significant. As does Mike Coward.

'It was a bigger party that night than the one after the final in Calcutta. It was a cathartic moment when the team came together and first really believed in its own value. They only lost one game after that in the tournament, the one game when they did not bat first.'

Another journalist who covered the tournament, Bruce Wilson, the vastly experienced European correspondent for the now-defunct Melbourne afternoon daily the *Herald*, was enthused from the start, quickly coming to believe that this team was 'the core of Australian cricket to come'. Wilson watched Border closely throughout and became an ardent admirer.

> It is impossible to exaggerate the importance of Border to this team [Wilson wrote]. He is a father figure and, more than that, a mate to his younger players. He is guarding them and when it becomes necessary making them snap to attention. But he is also, week by week, welding them into that most elusive of teams, a touring side with one mind, one heart and one will. Border said that while he disliked the concept of one-day cricket, he thought that he could use this tournament to mould the future of Australian cricket.

Australia beat the strong Pakistan team in Lahore in one semi-final, while England knocked India out of the event in Bombay. When the game's oldest enemies met in Calcutta on 8 November 1987, the majority of the crowd of 80,000 enthusiastically supported their fellow 'colonials'. Australia won 5/253 to 8/246.

The English cricket journalist and author Scyld Berry wrote in his book *Cricket Odyssey* of the emotional after-match scenes that were played out in a soft, surreal twilight.

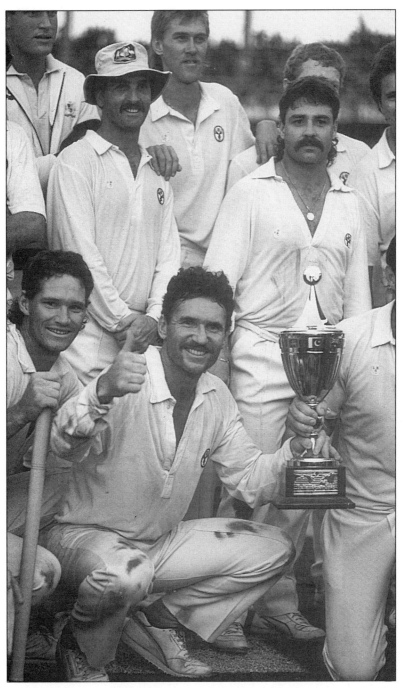

A win for the underdogs: Allan Border and his young team celebrate their victory over England in the 1987 World Cup Final in Calcutta.

The more I reflected on Australia's winning, the more pleased I felt. Border received the Reliance World Cup, held it high, and did nothing vulgar like kiss it or stick the lid on his head. The Australians did a victory lap and were most generously applauded, but only I suspect because they were asked to do so: most seemed too abashed and pink behind the ears to have thought of such an act of self-aggrandisement. And my heart was warmed when Border was lifted respectfully on to the shoulders of two of his players. One year before, we had seen him in Brisbane, after Australia lost the first Test to England through no fault of his, and he was a wound-up, weary and dejected man. No more deserving current Test skipper could have taken hold of the fourth World Cup.

Like all the journalists there, Mike Coward was moved to watch Border in his first moment of genuine triumph. 'When Dean Jones and Craig McDermott lifted Border onto their shoulders, you could almost see all the suffering draining from his body. He started to look young again. Australia was no longer the laughing stock of world cricket. It was the end of the great depression and Border grew as a captain from that moment.'

After the game, Border, in a warm gesture, spoke of the 'love' of the Indian people for his young team and how their support in the final had pushed the Australians forward. What had not pleased him was news that in Sydney and Melbourne, Channel Nine, Australia's exclusive cricket telecaster, had left the final after Australia's innings to run a Hollywood movie. Border's long-awaited moment of triumph and relief was not seen by the two largest audiences in the country.

It would be a long time before cricket on the Indian subcontinent would be taken as seriously as cricket in England or Australia. Channel Nine did not show the Test series from Pakistan in the spring of 1994, Mark Taylor's first as captain. And only the advent of pay television with its opposition telecasters prompted Nine to acquire the rights to the 1996 World Cup in India, Pakistan and Sri Lanka.

In the middle of a bizarre Japanese garden at the opulent Oberoi Grand Hotel, players from the other teams joined in the winners'. celebrations. No one seemed to begrudge Border's hard-working underdogs their unexpected victory. For most of the night, Border sat cross-legged on the floor sipping beer from a can while his younger teammates sang and danced with joy. Next to him for a long while sat England's Graham Gooch, his old mate from

Essex. Gooch, like many of the senior players in the world, liked and respected Border and was genuinely pleased to see the Australian skipper enjoy success at last.

The next morning, Border headed to the pool for a spell of rest and recuperation, clutching a batch of congratulatory messages and faxes from Australia. The hotel switchboard was so overloaded that day that the Australian journalists gave up trying to get through to their offices back home.

As well as McDermott's fine bowling, Marsh made two centuries, Boon was second to Gooch in runs made, the two openers averaged 61 per partnership and Waugh became known as the 'Iceman' for his calm under the pressure of bowling in the last hectic overs. Most pleasing of all was that Australia succeeded without a major contribution from the skipper's bat.

Simpson, like Border, looks back on the success of that World Cup campaign as the undoubted turning point of the Border era.

Yes, it was the major turning point. It was when the blokes realised they were good enough to take on anyone in the world. We put in a very good program before the Cup. We had two weeks in Madras in very, very tough conditions. And the win against India in the first match was the thing we needed to kick us off. That was the big one because we realised we could beat anyone in the world. We got through tight situations. The enthusiasm was terrific. We also learned that unity, team spirit and camaraderie would take you through a hell of a lot.

Not long after the Australians returned home, they began a summer of three Tests against New Zealand, a Bicentennial Test against Mike Gatting's England team and Australia's second Test match against newcomers Sri Lanka. That was to be followed by the toughest tour in the game, a three-Test series in Pakistan, after which Australia hosted the West Indies for five more gruelling Test matches. In that time, Laurie Sawle's long-term plans to improve the depth and structure of Australian cricket at youth and club levels would be set in motion, and he and his fellow selectors would begin working towards regaining the ultimate prize, the Ashes, on the 1989 tour to England.

THE REBUILDING

BEGINS

E VERY summer, two days before the opening Test of the
season, the ACB and its major sponsor throw a cocktail
party for the players from both teams, officials, sponsors and
media. The nights are always lively, informal affairs where a few
drinks loosen up relationships normally a little strained by the
pressures of the summer. The Australian players always enjoy these
nights, using them to release any tension that has developed in
the lead-up to the start of another Test series.

In early December 1987, the first Test was in Brisbane against
New Zealand, the team that had beaten Border's Australians in
their two previous series. Richard Hadlee was back and there was
speculation in the media about how the improving Australians
would cope this time with the 'Hadlee Hoodoo'. After the ACB
cocktail party, most of the Australians and the travelling press
adjourned to the familiar surrounds of their home base, the Parkroyal
Hotel. A colleague and I spotted Australia's opening batsmen
settled into one corner of the hotel's small, dimly lit bar. This was
the first series I had covered so I was more familiar with David

Boon from our days in the Tasmanian team than I was with most of the journalists. My mate and I joined Boon and Marsh. The openers were in good form, flush with their success at the World Cup and looking forward with enthusiasm rather than foreboding to the next challenge, the great Hadlee on the Gabba's traditional bouncy, seaming pitch. That 'special feeling' first noticed in Madras two months before was still in the air.

Boon and Marsh had been mates since touring England together in the Australian under-19 team in 1977. The friendship which had formed then helped the pair develop the opening partnership that had added great stability to Australia's batting in the preceding few months. Boon and Marsh are fairly quiet blokes although both can fire up in the right situation. This night, Boon was in one of his chirpy, mischievous moods, delivering one-liners at the expense of anyone who approached him and threatening to hurl abuse at the nearest administrator. He was playing his shots. Marsh was playing with his usual caution, content to push singles and rotate the strike. Occasionally, Marsh adopted the role of Boon's minder. When the Tasmanian said he was heading across

The leader and his lieutenants: David Boon and Geoff Marsh were two of Allan Border's staunchest allies during the rebuilding process that occupied the second half of the 1980s.

the bar to finally tell some ACB official what he really thought of him, his partner interrupted.

'Boonie, Boonie,' Marsh whispered. 'Settle down.'

'Nah, stuff him,' Boon said as he swaggered away from us, weaved his way through the crowded bar and out across the lobby to the gents' toilet.

'Shit, he's a great bloke, isn't he?' Marsh laughed, the deep affection for his close friend obvious in his admiring eyes. Border and Simpson's efforts to build team unity off the field seemed to be working well.

On the field two days later, the improvements continued. After Australia's pace attack of Craig McDermott, Merv Hughes and Bruce Reid dismissed New Zealand for 186, Boon and Marsh added 65 for the first wicket against Hadlee, Danny Morrison and Ewen Chatfield. Marsh fell for 25, but Boon carried on to finish with 143, his fifth and highest Test century and a triumph of technique and temperament against Hadlee, one of the greatest bowlers in the game's history. Boon's innings which set up Australia's victory confirmed that the Australians' success in the World Cup would be built upon.

Border's team drew the next Test in Adelaide on a pitch that favoured batsmen far too much. New Zealand made 9/485 declared in its first innings but Australia replied strongly with 496, thanks to an innings of 205 from Border. When the Australian captain pushed a single to square leg to move to 71, he passed Sir Donald Bradman's career aggregate to move into second place behind Greg Chappell on the list of Australia's Test run-scorers. Border was bemused by the applause of the crowd until New Zealand's Martin Crowe enlightened him.

'You've got the Don,' Crowe revealed.

Border ended the third day on 105 and added another 100 the next day to post his first double century in Test cricket. In the process, he passed Greg Chappell's 7110 runs to become Australia's greatest-ever Test run-scorer. His 205 left him in seventh place on the list of the game's greatest run-makers.

Border was typically humble about the achievements, particularly passing Bradman. 'To pass Sir Donald's total is a great achievement, but you have to get it in its true perspective. It's taken me nearly twice as long as the little fellow. It's just mind-boggling as to how good he must have been.'

The most remarkable aspect of Border's innings was that it was achieved in 10 hours of intense heat, admittedly spread over two days. Temperatures in Adelaide for this match hovered around 40 degrees Centigrade, and Border's determination to deny New Zealand's push to level the series required all his formidable powers of concentration and stamina. Steve Randell umpired that game and recalls noticing Border continually glancing up at the scoreboard and mumbling to himself.

'After a while, I heard what he was saying. He was talking to himself all the way through: "Come on, concentrate, concentrate. Work hard." It was very tough out there in the heat. It was an amazing innings.'

Australia went on to draw the third Test in Melbourne and so win the series 1-0. It was Border's first win in six full series as captain, and only came after some very tense moments in Melbourne when Australia's last pair, Craig McDermott and Mike Whitney, defied Hadlee and New Zealand for 4.5 overs to save the game and the series lead. It was the sort of situation which would have seen the Australians crumble under the pressure a few years before. This time they held firm. It was another step forward.

Off the field, the selectors and the ACB were putting together a range of initiatives which would not only consolidate Border and Simpson's work with the senior team, but establish an infrastructure at lower levels that would become the envy of every other cricket-playing country. The architect of much of this long-term rebuilding was the quiet, self-effacing former high school headmaster, chairman of selectors Laurie Sawle.

Sawle had been a moderately successful left-handed opening batsman for Western Australia in the state's early years in the Sheffield Shield. He also led the university club in Perth to several premierships and club championships as he moved from first-grade captain, to selector, secretary and finally president. That experience gave him an appreciation of the grass-roots level of the game. In his career as teacher, principal and finally at the Western Australian Education Department's head office staffing high schools, Sawle combined his interest in youth with what must have been a natural talent for choosing the right people for the right jobs. He employed all of those interests and skills in his work as a national selector.

'The Colonel', as Sawle has been known since his teachers' college days, was the man who stabilised Australia's selections in the mid-80s. At one stage, there were about 40 former Test players going around in the Sheffield Shield competition. Sawle and his co-selectors Greg Chappell and Rick McCosker knew there were not that many players of international quality in the country. The previous selection committee had tended to work in an ad hoc manner. When a player produced a couple of outstanding performances in the Shield, he would win a Test cap. Only the very best players prosper in Test cricket from their first game. Most soon find the going tough and are dropped. The good ones fight back, regain their Test place and often go on to enjoy successful careers. The weaker characters never return and too many of those tried in the early 1980s were found wanting. Sawle realised that this sort of scatter-gun selection policy was harming Kim Hughes's team, and after he became chairman in 1984, he worked at settling things down.

Former Test batsman and New South Wales captain John Benaud is a fine judge of cricketers with a simple, aggressive attitude to the game. Benaud served as a selector from 1988 to 1993 under Sawle's chairmanship and describes him as 'the most unrecognised person in Australian cricket'. Benaud even talks in terms of 'the Sawle era', so highly does he regard the Colonel's influence.

Three things have characterised Laurie's work as a selector [Benaud said]. He has always believed that stability was important, that the selectors should plan for the long term. Secondly he has been a very good chairman because he doesn't press his opinions on the rest of the panel. He allows the other selectors to fully express their views and discussions are always open and constructive. In my years on the panel, there was never a raised voice or a formal vote. We talked things through. The third thing he has been strong on has been youth cricket.

Sawle brought one major advantage to his work as a national selector: his other role as a Western Australian delegate to the ACB. This meant the selectors had a voice on the board. Long-term strategies could be worked through thoroughly and both bodies had a fair idea where the other was heading. Because of this, the whole rebuilding process that began soon after Border took over the leaking ship in 1984 developed into a well-coordinated operation. While Border's personal support group of Simpson, team manager Ian McDonald and physiotherapist Errol Alcott formed around the new captain, Sawle led the ACB in restructuring Australian cricket at the lower levels so the future could be assured.

In his role as chairman of the Australian Youth Cricket Council, Sawle redeveloped youth cricket from its previous base

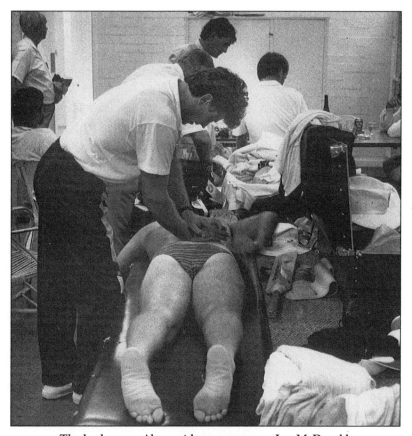

*The back room: Along with team manager Ian McDonald,
physiotherapist Errol Alcott provided valuable support throughout
the Border era. Here Alcott works on Terry Alderman.*

in state schools to the system of under-age national carnivals and Australian representative teams that now produces almost all of Australia's Test cricketers. The ACB had recognised this need by the late 1970s, but it was not until Sawle took over that the whole operation was set in motion. As well, by the early 1980s, there was more corporate sponsorship available. Barclay's Bank came in to support the under-19 program and the production line was off and running. Sawle also organised for a Test selector to chair the selection committee for the national under-19 team. Benaud filled that role for much of his time as a senior selector.

The reason I thought it would be a good idea to have a national selector involved at under-19 level was that we would know what talent we had coming through [Sawle said]. As well as John Benaud and now Steve Bernard, I followed the under-19s closely for six or seven years from the mid-1980s. That's where I first saw the Waugh twins, Ian Healy and Mark Taylor play. I used to attend every under-19 carnival. Knowing what talent we had coming through meant we could fast-track them, accelerate their progress towards the Test team.

Sawle was also instrumental in organising some Young Australia tours to Zimbabwe, and in the introduction of the four-day Australian XI match against the visiting international team that now acts as both a showpiece of the younger talent pushing towards the Test team and as a de facto sixth Test of the summer.

At club level in the major cities, Sawle pushed the idea of changing the rules from games where the first innings were limited to 100 overs, after which a compulsory declaration was made, to the old system where a team could bat as long as it liked and where winning meant taking all 10 wickets. The 100-over games were played in all the major cities in the 1980s, and eventually produced a defensive style of play essentially the same as one-day games only twice as long – and twice as boring. Bowlers were used to restrict scoring. Fieldsmen were run-savers not attacking weapons. Taking wickets was largely unimportant and scope for imaginative captaincy was virtually non-existent. Spin bowlers were seen as a liability. This view, combined with the reigning fashion for fast bowling, forced the finger spinner into a negative role and the wrist spinner into obsolescence. This approach was far removed from first-class and Test cricket and was not producing the wicket-taking bowlers Australia needed.

Sawle always believed that the most valuable bowlers were those who moved the ball away from the bat: in particular, swing bowlers and leg spinners. Terry Alderman's decision to play in South Africa denied Border the country's best swing bowler from 1985 to 1988. A few other swing bowlers were tried but none came anywhere near Alderman's class. Since Richie Benaud in the 1950s and early 1960s, Australia had not chosen a regular leg spinner. Several had enjoyed reasonable success but none was a regular match-winner.

The pre-eminence of pace in the 1970s – with Dennis Lillee and Jeff Thomson in Australia followed by the emergence of West Indians Andy Roberts, Michael Holding, Joel Garner and Malcolm Marshall, as well as India's Kapil Dev, Pakistan's Imran Khan, New Zealand's Richard Hadlee and England's Bob Willis and Ian Botham – meant that every kid in the local park wanted to run 30 metres and hurl the ball down as fast as he could. This trend

Working relationship: That was how Allan Border always
described his partnership with coach and selector
Bob Simpson, a pivotal figure during this period.

reduced the game's variety and therefore its spectacle. Over rates slowed to an alarming degree and short-pitched fast bowling, perfected by the West Indians, narrowed the range of shots available to batsmen. The game's entertainment value was diminished.

Leg-spin bowling had been a traditional strength of Australian cricket throughout the century, and Sawle believed a good leg spinner should be part of every Australian team, especially one which aspired to end West Indian dominance.

The other major development came in 1987 when the ACB established the Commonwealth Bank Australian Institute of Sport

Cricket Academy. This institute was set up to further fast-track the best young cricketers in the country by providing them with a live-in centre for a period of intense tutoring from the best coaches in the land. The idea was to prepare these elite cricketers so they could adjust more quickly to Sheffield Shield cricket. The very best of them would then graduate to Test cricket sooner and with a better chance of success.

After Australia had performed poorly at the 1976 and 1980 Olympic Games, the federal government had set up the Australian Institute of Sport (AIS) in 1981 as a means of reinvigorating a sporting community which had fallen behind world developments. The then general manager of the ACB, Graham Halbish, thought of the idea of linking a cricket academy to the AIS to speed up the process of filling the gaps left in Sheffield Shield ranks by the defections to South Africa. Halbish deliberately chose the term 'academy' because he wanted it to give the young cricketers a broader education than just expert coaching in batting, bowling and fielding.

Initially, Halbish's idea of an academy was received with suspicion by the Australian cricket community which had always prided itself on its ability to educate its young players through practical means such as strong junior and club competitions. Australians had always been wary of the English approach, considering it overly theoretical and obsessed with technique. After all, the game's greatest batsman, Don Bradman, had taught himself to bat in the backyard of his home in rural Bowral. This was an Australian tradition and was not to be fiddled with without good reason. Halbish thought the poor state of Australian cricket in the mid-1980s reason enough and he convinced his colleagues at the ACB that drastic problems demanded drastic solutions.

The academy was set up in Adelaide, a city which boasted good weather and the best practice facilities in the world. Strangely, some of Australia's greatest cricketers from the successful era of the 1970s were not encouraged to contribute. Ian Chappell and Bob Simpson had never seen eye to eye, and when appointed national team coach, the latter went to great lengths to state his view that the peer influence which had passed on Australian cricket's knowledge and traditions from one generation to the next had fallen away during and immediately after Chappell's era.

Yet there was a period in the mid- to late 1980s when the ACB declined to use the experience of Chappell, Dennis Lillee and Rod Marsh at the academy. In fact, in that period, Lillee

*Directing the traffic: Bob Simpson during an Australian practice
session. A great slips catcher in his day, Simpson used fielding
drills to improve the Australians' battered self-confidence.*

successfully pursued a coaching career in India, Sri Lanka and New
Zealand but did little coaching in Australia because the ACB was
not prepared to pay him a decent fee. At times, Simpson used his
considerable clout with the ACB to stifle any academy involvement
by the leading players of the Chappell era – an era that was one
of the most successful in the history of Australian cricket, certainly
far more successful than the period when Simpson captained
Australia in the 1960s.

All this began to change when Rod Marsh took over the
academy in 1991. Marsh had recently been summarily dismissed
from the Channel Nine commentary team by Kerry Packer for
criticising the god of one-day cricket on radio. The ACB's Graham
Halbish contacted Marsh soon after and offered him a new job.

Marsh runs a tight ship, but he works as much on attitude as the technical side of the game. His view is that the players who come to the academy, usually straight from the previous summer's under-19 carnival, are already good cricketers with a sound grounding in the basics. Marsh sees his job as encouraging their natural self-confidence and the traditional attacking approach that has characterised Australian cricket for most of its history. The young players train very hard but are expected to find outside employment during normal working hours. Marsh, who learned his cricket in the no-frills ways of the late 1960s, has made some concessions to modern sport by expanding the non-cricket courses first begun by his predecessor Jack Potter in such areas as psychology, media relations, public speaking, computer programming and business studies. Most significantly, Marsh has brought back into the fold the great players of his era.

When the new group of cricketers arrives in Adelaide in April, Dennis Lillee and John Inverarity spend a week with them. Lillee even takes the lads to a pub to tell them stories about the game. This is the sort of cricket education that has kept Australian cricket alive for more than a century. As Ian Chappell, one of Marsh's expert batting coaches, says: 'I learned a lot about cricket in the hours after play when I sat around the dressing-room after a Shield game sharing a beer and listening to people like Richie Benaud. That is crucial for a young cricketer's education.'

Marsh has also introduced a broader range of specialist coaching clinics, where a group of the most promising spin bowlers, wicket-keepers or pace bowlers will come to Adelaide for a week and be tutored by former Test players. As well, a recent graduate of the academy who has gone on to success at Shield and hopefully Test level is brought back as a role model.

Marsh has introduced a greater emphasis on matches for the academy players. Their team tours the country each summer playing state Second XI teams and international touring teams. Most of all, he encourages his students' natural flair, believing that modern cricket must be entertaining.

From its earliest days, the academy attracted interest from other countries. By 1994-95, most of those nations were beginning to establish academies of their own. Even conservative England had begun thinking about it, no doubt because in early December 1994, Marsh's academy team thrashed Mike Atherton's touring Englishmen not once but twice in two limited-overs games at North Sydney Oval. The contrast between the plodding English professionals and the spirited young Australians was amazing. The English establishment was so impressed and embarrassed that the British government's Minister for Sport, Iain Sproat, later came to Australia to inspect various AIS operations, particularly Marsh's academy.

The idea that a group of 19- and 20-year-olds with very limited first-class experience could beat the cream of English cricket twice in such an uninhibited and entertaining way impressed the English cricket media. One of those, Hampshire captain and *Sunday Telegraph* columnist Mark Nicholas, paid Marsh a visit.

The crux of the whole thing is the playing and, most specifically, to teach the boys to be entertainers [Marsh told Nicholas]. A few years down the road, I can see players who are not fun to watch not being chosen. There won't be room for the bloke who grinds out a hundred no matter how good he is. In four-day cricket, we score at four an over not by slogging but by aggressive cricket. The opposition score at just over three an over and only because we set attacking fields. We do not defend and we insist that there are slips or close catchers in position all the time. It is not always the right way to win a game but the philosophy is the important thing.

Marsh, the former anti-establishment World Series rebel, even had good words to say about the ACB. This was not exactly surprising, as it employs him, but the compliments seem warranted.

You gotta give it to 'em. They look ahead and try new things, plan for the future – yellow balls, night Shield games, the A team concept, the academy and more. They know the problem is that cricket is fighting for pole position in a country riddled by the surge of interest in basketball and baseball, never mind the leisure activities that are on tap these days.

Although the academy attracts the praise, cricket people from Marsh down know that it *should* succeed, because the players who go there are already well on their way to first-class and Test careers. They are hand-picked by a thorough talent-spotting system fine-tuned in large part by Laurie Sawle. In the Australian team which toured the West Indies in 1995, there were eight graduates of the academy – Michael Slater, Justin Langer, Ricky Ponting, Greg Blewett, Damien Fleming, Glenn McGrath, Brendon Julian and Shane Warne. Perhaps all would have made it to the top anyway, but in most cases, the academy brought them through more quickly. However, the most gifted of them, Shane Warne, might have been lost altogether.

While he was still a young leg spinner/batsman at the St Kilda Club in Melbourne, word began spreading around Victorian cricket circles that Warne appeared to have a special talent. St Kilda's shrewd captain/coach Shaun Graf was impressed and passed on the word. Test selector and former leg spinner Jim Higgs alerted senior people, and soon Warne, despite minimal achievements, toured the West Indies in 1990 with an Australia Youth team, then found himself in Adelaide being tutored by another former Test leg spinner, Terry Jenner. In those days, Warne was a chubby character whose dedication did not match his potential. But the system of talent-spotting and fast-tracking that was now in place in youth cricket and in the states kept the young leggie in the system.

Although Warne parted company with the academy earlier than anticipated, the Victorians quickly brought him into their Shield team with encouragement from Higgs and Sawle. As the latter says: 'The word was around about Shane – that he was a very talented young leg spinner. What we had to do was put every opportunity in front of him.' They did, and Australia now has its greatest leg spinner since O'Reilly – perhaps the greatest ever.

Some six years after England thrashed Australia in the 1986-87 series, Australian cricket had rebuilt itself impressively while England had plunged into a steady and prolonged decline. As Australia under new captain Mark Taylor thrashed England for the fourth consecutive Ashes series in 1994-95, England's young captain, Mike Atherton, writing in London's *Daily Telegraph*, exhorted his administrators to learn from Australia's rebuilding.

The problems within the England side are analogous to those faced by Australia in the mid-1980s [Atherton wrote]. The Australian side then were losing regularly with a disparate set of individuals. Australia then decided upon a policy of stability under the wise chairmanship of Laurie Sawle. They identified young players with the technique, talent and temperament to succeed in Test cricket ... They endured some tough times, but the World Cup victory in 1987 began to forge the Ashes-winning side that we have seen since 1989. England must follow suit.

When the English are surrendering the Ashes regularly and admitting they must learn from the ways of the old enemy, Australian cricket must be in good shape. However, although the treatments being administered to Australian cricket were beginning to take effect by 1987-88, Allan Border's team had to endure another two difficult Test series before being discharged in good health at the end of the next Ashes series in England in 1989.

POLITICS

IN PAKISTAN

I AN Botham miscalculated a little when he joked in 1984 that 'Pakistan is the kind of place to send your mother-in-law for a month, all expenses paid'. The jibe cost him a £1000 fine and, no doubt, some time explaining to his own mother-in-law the clichéd reference to those much-abused relatives. Yet Botham spoke for most international cricketers who saw a tour of Pakistan as a visit to cricket hell. At least after you had been battered by West Indian fast bowlers in the Caribbean, you could enjoy a few numbing rums on a cruise boat at night. Not so in alcohol-free, Islamic Pakistan, where a night out would more likely consist of a walk along the hotel corridor to a teammate's room.

Three years after that joke, Botham's friend and captain Mike Gatting became embroiled in an ugly incident in the second Test at Faisalabad in December 1987 when he clashed heatedly with umpire Shakoor Rana. A day's play was lost as the umpire waited for an unconditional apology from the angry and aggrieved England skipper. It was one of the lowest points in international cricket history and, less than a year later as they prepared for their tour to Pakistan, Allan Border's Australians were determined to cope better than Gatting's Englishmen.

As they assembled in Brisbane before leaving, ACB chairman Malcolm Gray had impressed on the players the need to maintain patience when they felt that they were receiving the worst of playing conditions or umpiring decisions. Since the 1979 tour to India, Australian cricketers in the Indian subcontinent had tried, largely unsuccessfully, to live up to a motto leg spinner Jim Higgs had seen on the wall of a tenement building in Madras. 'To lose patience is to lose the battle', the sign warned. The patience of the 1988 Australians had all but vanished by the first day of the first Test in Karachi.

The Australians were upset when umpire Mahboob Shah ruled in favour of Javed Miandad in two leg-before decisions. Javed went on to make a double century and put the first Test out of Australia's reach. Although the players were furious, it was coach Bob Simpson and manager Col Egar who lost their cool completely. These two were supposed to be the ones to maintain control over a team of young, inexperienced cricketers, yet it was they who embarrassed Australian cricket by ranting and raving about the umpire in such a public manner that a representative of tobacco company Will's, Pakistan cricket's sponsor, lodged a formal complaint.

Simpson and Egar issued a statement saying they would continue the tour 'under protest', and at one stage, Border conceded to the press that the Australians might under some circumstances abandon the tour. Simpson and Egar were later forced to change their tune after ACB officials told them it was not their role on tour to try to right all the perceived wrongs of Pakistan cricket. Simpson blames a leading question from the press to Border and the captain's somewhat naive answer for that now-infamous suggestion that the Australians might have considered abandoning the tour. Simpson says that course of action was never considered.

However, apportioning blame after the event did no good. The damage had been done in exactly the way Gray had warned against. Surely it would have been better to have adopted a similar approach to England's after the Gatting-Rana dust-up. The Test and County Cricket Board (TCCB) forced Gatting to apologise to Rana, a move that upset the England players and smacked of a typically English concern for appearances. But the undertaking to tour was honoured and the issues sorted out later in a calmer mood by the game's administrators, not angry players and management too close to the action to judge things from the widest perspective. Instead, the TCCB, not satisfied that conditions in Pakistan would improve sufficiently, decided to say thanks, but no thanks to any offer of a tour until 1996.

Some observers saw in Simpson's overreaction to events in Pakistan in 1988 a pattern that had characterised most of his career. Simpson has always been prone to conspiracy theories, to blaming anything and everything except mistakes made by him or his team. Throughout his career he seemed to have the knack of polarising people and deeply upsetting opponents, overseas hosts and even teammates.

Simpson's book *Captain's Story*, published in the mid-1960s, upset a lot of people. The most notable was former teammate Ian Meckiff who, in November 1966, sued Simpson over comments about Meckiff's motives behind his suspect bowling action. Meckiff, who claimed that Simpson had held him up to 'public scandal, hatred, ridicule and contempt', won an unconditional apology. Another comment by Simpson that West Indian officials needed to clean out chuckers from their game 'with the thoroughness of health officers weeding out vermin' caused great offence in the Caribbean, and was still a source of friction when Simpson returned as Test captain during the Packer split in 1978 and again as team coach in 1991. A comment about Indian umpires moved the secretary of the Indian Board of Control to say that it was only 'a figment of his imagination born out of prejudice, with a definite purpose of ridiculing the umpire'.

On the field, Simpson could become so infuriated when things went against him that he lost concentration on the game. Ian Chappell recalled a Test in South Africa in 1966-67 in which a Simpson tantrum had a great bearing on the outcome of the match. Australia led by 126 in the first innings in the first Test in Johannesburg, and had South Africa 6/349 in the second when an obvious edge from South African captain Peter van der Merwe was caught by keeper Brian Taber in front of Simpson at first slip. When the umpire did not give it out, Simpson lost his temper.

> *Simmo was going on about 'cheats' and things like that and was so upset that when van der Merwe edged the next ball to him at first slip he dropped it. Instead of saying to himself: 'Bugger it. Let's get on with the game', he carried on again about the umpiring. Then van der Merwe nicked the next ball straight to second slip where Keith Stackpole, after all the carryings-on next to him, dropped it as well.*

*Van der Merwe went on to get 76 and Dennis Lindsay 182, and in
the end, we had to chase 500 to win. We lost the game then won
the second Test in Cape Town. We could have had a 2-0 lead.*

*All teams get bad decisions. It's a matter of how you handle
them. That is my greatest criticism of Simpson: that in his time, with
Border giving him a free rein, the Australians developed an approach
of dishonesty. Not that they were cheats, but because they weren't
prepared to look in the mirror and correctly apportion the blame. And
I had the same criticism of Australia under Kim Hughes. It was the
food in India, the pitches in Pakistan or whatever. Anything except
the fact that we weren't playing all that well. And the thing is that
once you admit you're not playing well enough, you can start thinking
about rectifying it.*

Chappell cited some examples of how Richie Richardson kept
himself and his team under control in the tense 1992-93 series in
Australia.

'In the first Test, Curtly Ambrose thought he had Mark
Taylor caught down the leg side early in the match, but it was
ruled not out. Ambrose was obviously upset but Richie went over
to him and calmed him down. With Viv Richards as captain there
would have been a real carry-on.'

On the last day of that match, as Australia tried to bowl to
victory, Border and his players lost their cool as several decisions
went against them. Not for the first time, Border had heated words
with umpire Steve Randell. Later, Merv Hughes and Border were
reported for dissent. Australia failed to force a win from a strong
position, and many observers believed that inability to cope with
adverse decisions cost Australia the game, probably the series.

Chappell also recalled Richardson doing handstands at mid-
on after another poor leg-before decision went against his bowlers
in the close and decisive fourth Test of that series in Adelaide.
'To me that showed the difference between the two sides. If the
West Indies had taken the same approach as Australia, they would
not have won in Adelaide.'

In his 1994 autobiography, Ian Botham discussed the resurgence
of sledging under Border and how his attitude changed from the
affable losing captain of his early years to the uncompromising
competitor of the later years. Botham wrote: 'Sean Fitzpatrick, the
great All Black rugby captain, once said that to be a good winner
you have to be a good loser. But AB didn't see it that way. He
was not a good loser; he had no time for it at all. In fact, I'm sure

it was his absolute hatred of coming second that was at the root of him allowing his players to go over the top on the field.'

Whether the Australians in the later years sledged too much is open to debate, although the fact that every other cricket nation complained about it suggests there was substance to the allegations. In private, the Australians argued that most teams indulged in sledging but did it in a less obvious way than they did. Certainly, there is truth in Botham's judgement that Border was not a particularly good loser. His players, team management and the travelling press came to know that well enough over the years. They all realised that after a poor performance or a bad loss, it was wise to be very careful when approaching the skipper. He was likely to snap at the slightest provocation. However, unlike Simpson, Border did not hold grudges.

The combination of Border's hatred of losing and Simpson's paranoia and volatility proved to be at times an explosive mix, at other times a fatal distraction.

While Simpson and Egar raged about Karachi's poor pitch or Shah's suspect umpiring, some journalists covering that unfortunate 1988 tour noted that Australia had dropped six catches in Pakistan's innings, including two off Javed when on 126 and 186. The Australian team was aware that in his 43 Tests on home soil, Javed had been given out leg before wicket only three times. To them, this was strong evidence of Pakistani skulduggery. Presumably, they did not know or chose to ignore the fact that Bill Lawry, Australia's fine opening batsman of the 1960s, was never given out leg before by an Australian umpire in the 30 Tests he played on his home turf.

The journalists travelling with the Australian team in Pakistan agreed that it had suffered from some poor umpiring. Where the press corps split was in assessing the reaction of Egar and Simpson. Those who criticised Simpson and Egar's behaviour were seen as traitors. According to Mike Coward in *Cricket Beyond the Bazaar*, Simpson, typically oversensitive to media criticism, accused Coward (the *Sydney Morning Herald*), Trevor Grant (the *Age*) and Phil Wilkins (the *Sun-Herald*) of 'disloyalty to the cause of Australian cricket'. Rod Nicholson (the *Herald*, Melbourne) and Terry Brindle (the *Australian*) supported Simpson and Egar. This split in the press corps remained for several years until Nicholson and Brindle moved from cricket duties within a few months of each other in 1992.

Protected species? The Australians' complaints about umpiring decisions
in Javed Miandad's favour during the controversial 1988 tour to
Pakistan upset the locals and split the Australian press corps.

The inconsistency typified by attitudes to the Javed-Lawry statistics began to plague Australian cricket from the tour to Pakistan in '88 into the 1990s. The political split in the press corps was a factor in this. Visiting teams would complain about Australian umpiring, sledging, fiercely parochial crowds at one-day internationals and the hectic travel and playing schedules. It was as if some influential figures in Australian cricket – PBL Marketing, which promoted the game, a few nationalistic media people and, behind the scenes, coach Simpson amongst others – overreacted to the successes which followed the early failures. A dangerous jingoism began to pervade Australian cricket.

Certainly Simpson, the former Test captain who rode to the establishment's rescue after Kerry Packer's World Series revolution split the cricket world, knew he had his critics in the press and the Channel Nine commentary box, which was made up largely of former captains from Packer's World Series teams. Prompted by this knowledge, Simpson was often overzealous in promoting the worth of the team he was coaching.

In a column in the *Sydney Morning Herald* in January 1992, after it was revealed that umpire Steve Randell was going to sue India's former great batsman Sunil Gavaskar for comments he made in the media about Australia's poor umpiring, Peter Roebuck wrote:

> *Debates about umpiring here are merely a side-issue in this more important matter. Quite simply, Australian cricket stands accused of wanting genuine hospitality, and of tolerating an hysteria which has led to [crowd] violence in limited-over games and to a sense of grievance among visitors.*
>
> *. . . the real cause of this suspecting boastfulness and the accompanying propaganda which is unleashed from within the Australian camp, is an enmity and tension in high circles going back to the upheavals of 1977 . . . Even now those animosities have not been stilled and it is they which cause the paranoia and suspicion sometimes evident in this national game. Writing about it is no easy task, for a scribe is constantly, if privately, condemned if he fails to toe the party line . . . Most objective observers simply want to enjoy the cricket of Australia and its guests, have no time for boastfulness nor the manipulations of one or two dismal characters.*

Simpson and Roebuck had been at odds for some time as the latter was one of a few critics who regularly drew attention to what they saw as the less satisfactory aspects of Simpson's work. In December 1989, Roebuck noted that Simpson's contract as Australian team coach was up for renewal in the near future, and then proceeded to examine the pros and cons of the position of a cricket team coach, or manager, the English term which Roebuck preferred. Although the article tended to the view that coaches were necessary in the modern game, the *Sydney Morning Herald* ran this sentence: 'Simpson is not universally beloved and is, accordingly, blamed by some for deceits, and dismissed as redundant in victory, which serves only to cloud argument about the relevance of managers.'

In March 1990, the *Herald* ran an apology, saying that 'the word "deceits" was inserted through a copy-taker's error. Mr

Roebuck's word was "defeat".' This was not enough for Simpson who began legal proceedings which ended with him winning a substantial out-of-court settlement.

In a column in the *Sunday Age* in December 1991, I wrote of 'a worrying self-righteousness' that had begun to creep into Australian cricket. An example I cited was an incident at the end of the first Test against India in 1991-92 when an unnamed ACB official accused India's Manoj Prabhakar of 'chucking'. This was a gutless act, surely one well below the supposed dignity of a nation that considered itself above the underhanded tactics it thought it saw in third world countries. That some of the Australian press gave this anonymous accusation credence by reporting it confirmed that the split in the press corps caused by the controversies in Karachi in 1988 was still affecting coverage of the game in Australia.

In his early years in the coaching job, Simpson often made the point that he wanted to clean up the image and behaviour of the Australian team. Not for him the jeans and longish hair and aggressive on-field behaviour of the Ian Chappell era. His teams were to be clean cut, dressed in proper team uniforms and would adhere to the highest standards of behaviour.

Perhaps early on this was the case, but then when you are losing all the time, you do tend to be fairly quiet on the field. As the Australians became more competitive, so their on-field demeanour changed. Simpson's constant jibes at the alleged sins of the Chappell era and his sanctimonious support of his team began to wear thin.

In fact, in the early 1990s, Australian players were among the first to be reported and fined by the International Cricket Council's (ICC) new system of match referees, but until the summer of 1994-95, Australia's administrators, and Simpson in particular, defended their players with vehemence. Journalists who pointed out inconsistencies were again considered disloyal.

The split in the press corps was reflected in the coverage provided to the public. Simpson enjoyed strong support from Nicholson and Brindle, both of whom praised the efforts of the Australian team to an extent which others considered exaggerated. It was as if Australian teams had always been poor performers, that the terrible state of affairs in the mid-80s was the natural order of things. The emergence of this improved team in the second half of the decade was promoted as something of a miracle. Sure, the mid-80s were a terrible period, but no one who knew anything about Australian cricket believed it would last.

One example of the way the politics surrounding Simpson and the team affected the media coverage occurred during the series against India in 1991-92, when Geoff Marsh's form fell away badly. Journalists who called for the West Australian to be dropped from the Test side were described by Brindle as suffering 'east coast jaundice'. Marsh had been a close ally of Border and Simpson in the rebuilding of the team, and Nicholson and Brindle seemed to view his critics as traitors to the cause. This was absurd. All the journalists liked and respected Marsh and found criticising his batting unpleasant. They also understood that Marsh deserved loyalty for coming through the hard times with Border and Simpson. It was a question of degree, not principle. In the end, a simple cricket judgement had to be made: Marsh had lost form so badly that he did not deserve to remain in the team. Marsh knew this and had been expecting the chop for some time.

Later that season, the selectors did drop Marsh. He never regained his spot in the Test side, although Simpson convinced the other selectors to hold the door ajar by keeping an opening spot relatively free for Marsh's return. Michael Slater's obvious talent and his rapid rise during the 1992-93 season closed that door for good.

The late 1980s and early 1990s were the period when Simpson's power base grew markedly. After the celebrated 1989 Ashes win in England, Nicholson and Brindle pushed the line that Australia was an outstanding team and that much of the credit for that should go to Simpson. These assessments verged on the jingoistic and were not borne out by match results, particularly those on overseas tours. All of this strengthened Simpson's influence as a selector and his standing with his employers, the ACB. This, in turn, increased his hold over the national team. With Border reluctant to play politics and the ACB reluctant to rein in Simpson, the coach/selector became a powerful figure, particularly inside the Australian dressing-room.

Simpson's view that the Australian press ought to be partisan supporters rather than objective observers and critics was illustrated by events on the Australians' acrimonious tour to the West Indies in 1991.

At the end of the fourth Test in Bridgetown, Barbados, in which West Indies took an unbeatable 2-0 lead, West Indies captain Viv Richards still had one shot to fire. As he left the dressing-room to attend the post-match press conference, Richards warned his teammates that he was about to speak his mind about the Australian coach. Richards, a champion of black rights and a political captain, had been annoyed by Simpson's comments that the West Indian batting was fragile, and by his whingeing to West Indies officials during the series about the home team's slow over rates and generally cynical attitude. At the press conference, Richards, armed with a large cigar, launched a blistering verbal attack.

> You can quote me on this: he's a moaner and a bad loser, and a very sour sort of guy. I've seen him over a number of years and seen the way he operates. I may say I'm not the greatest admirer of Bobby Simpson. I dismiss anything that Simmo says. I'm not a guy that listens too much to Bobby Simpson because I don't think we do have the greatest respect for Bobby Simpson. Every now and again he will say 'thank you' and 'well played' or whatever's the case, but you treat people the same as you are treated. I'm going to tell you that again. Bobby Simpson ain't our cup of tea at all. If he says this [congratulates you] sometimes you don't know. You don't know what's in a man's heart. A man can tell you the world but you never know what's in his heart.

Simpson's supporters in the press saw this as an unforgivable and unfair attack. Others, while questioning Richards's taste, tempered their outrage and made the point that Australia's over rates, for instance, were only marginally better than those of the home side. In private, some of the Australian players did not see much wrong in Richards's assessment of Simpson's character but they had to toe the party line in public.

As the Australian team was preparing to head home from the Caribbean, I wrote a feature on Simpson for the *Sunday Age* which was headlined: 'Is Simpson the fire beneath the smoke?'. In it, I argued that it was likely Simpson had brought on Richards's attack, citing examples of Simpson's propensity for upsetting the hosts of countries he visited with Australian teams. I argued that Richards might have been guilty of poor taste in the way he vented his feelings so gratuitously at a post-match press conference, but that he was correct. In many respects, Simpson had shown himself over his long career to be prone to moaning and to be a bad loser. The article also said that many of Richards's criticisms of Simpson were shared in private and occasionally in public by many respected people in Australian cricket.

Not surprisingly, Simpson objected to the article and told me so the following season. Other members of the cricket community, though surprised at the vehemence of the article, did not disagree. One senior player told me he thought I had 'got it right'.

Eighteen months after the story's publication, during a period when Simpson had engaged in unseemly public arguments with two of his critics in the press, Roebuck and the *Australian*'s Malcolm Conn, the *Age*'s chief cricket writer, Patrick Smithers, called for calm on the Simpson issue. In doing so, he provided evidence for my assertion that Simpson would have provoked Richards to some extent. Smithers also illustrated Simpson's willingness to politicise the media, to try to use the press for his own ends.

Smithers related how, during the flight to the Caribbean for that 1991 tour, Simpson had made it clear to the travelling press corps 'that anything they said or wrote that upset Viv Richards was okay by him'. It was a naked attempt to enlist the support of the Australian press on the side of the Australian team and its coach.

Simpson's accusation that some members of the press corps in Pakistan in 1988 had shown disloyalty to Australian cricket typified his attitude to the cricket press. So concerned is he with the press that he has all reports faxed to him at the team hotel whether he is in Australia or on tour overseas. He wants journalists to be uncritical supporters of Australian cricket, more like public relations people than reasonably neutral observers. Many ACB officials of that era thought the same way, a fact which concerned the more broad-minded of the local game's administrators.

The most unfortunate aspect of Simpson's attitude is that often the latest press reports become a major topic of conversation in a dressing-room that should be concentrating on the cricket. During the season following the publication of my piece on Simpson, several players told me that Simpson had been criticising me in the dressing-room, warning players to be careful in their dealings with me.

Fortunately, as players remain in the team and deal more regularly with the press, they are able to make up their own minds about whom to trust or not. In recent years, many players have expressed the view in private that life in the Australian dressing-room would be far more pleasant if Simpson ceased his active engagement in the day-to-day workings of the fourth estate.

Certainly, Simpson's attitude to the press and the Channel Nine commentators created a highly political backdrop to the middle and late years of the Border era. The controversies in Pakistan in 1988 marked the end of any innocence in the world of Border's Australian cricket team.

There was some action *on* the field in Pakistan in 1988. Australia recovered well from Karachi to draw the second and third Tests. Bruce Reid and off spinner Tim May took 14 wickets apiece and seamer Tony Dodemaide supported Reid well with the new ball. Unfortunately for Australia, Dodemaide would struggle to maintain that form, May would be in and out of the Test side for many years and Reid, hampered by a long, thin body and a fragile back, would miss more Tests than he would play in the remainder of his career.

Reid's case was something of a tragedy for Border. The tall left-armer was a world-class bowler but was never able to muster the fitness to play consistently at Test level. Most people thought Reid terribly unlucky to have been born with such a fragile body. Others wondered whether he had done enough physical training in his early years to strengthen that body. But there was no doubt that had Border been able to call on a pace attack of Reid, Hughes and McDermott for a few series in the early 1990s, Australia's results, especially against the West Indies, might have improved dramatically.

That first Test at Karachi was very much a baptism of fire for a red-headed 24-year-old Brisbane wicket-keeper who had been the surprise choice for the tour after playing only six first-class matches as Queensland's number two. By the end of the 1995 series in the West Indies, Ian Healy had played 73 Tests for Australia and had developed into one of the team's best players – a fine keeper, attacking number seven batsman and tough vice-captain to Mark Taylor.

Allan Border topped the Test batting in Pakistan, averaging 57.5 and scoring Australia's only century of the series, a long and typically dogged 113 not out in the second Test at Faisalabad. It was to be Border's last Test century for four years and 61 innings until his 106 in the third Test against Sri Lanka in Moratuwa in 1992. During that 'dry' spell, he still averaged 50 plus, but that was not enough to satisfy more and more critics, who began saying that Border had lost his touch and should make way for one of a number of younger batsmen.

THE

10
BOGEYMEN

W HEN the West Indians took the field at the Gabba in
Brisbane for practice two days before the first Test in
November 1988, they were a different team from the
merry pranksters who had been strolling around the states during
a month of casual lead-up games. The in jokes that had kept them
giggling during weeks of travel and practice had died away. The
players' thoughts had turned inward, ignoring outside distractions.
When I asked the great fast bowler Malcolm Marshall for a couple
of minutes of his time to help with a story I was working on, the
usually affable Bajan declined.

'Not now, man. Test match.' Suddenly, life had become
serious.

The reporters who watched that day were chilled by what
they saw. The ruthless, remorseless West Indian cricket team, the
best in the word, was preparing to launch its first attack of the
new summer. They had just thrashed England in England 4-0 and
now it was Australia's turn – again.

No other team of the modern era has been able to coast through lead-up games at two-thirds effort, then lift to a peak for the first Test of a series. The West Indian teams of the 1980s knew they were good enough to pick and choose when to play at their best. When you are used to winning and your opponents used to losing, you can afford such luxuries. It was yet another way the West Indies found to intimidate their opponents. The message was: 'When we need to concentrate and get some match practice, we will. Otherwise, we'll just relax and wait for the next big game.'

Apart from a few of the younger players, Viv Richards's West Indians were a jovial lot in the early weeks of that summer. Some of those younger men were touring Australia for the first time and, still unsure of themselves, did not mix much with the locals – fans, opponents or media.

The newcomer who attracted most attention, and shunned it all, was giant fast bowler Curtly Ambrose. Ambrose was 200 centimetres (6 feet 7 inches) tall, and played his cricket with the bored attitude of someone who would rather have been playing basketball, his first choice as a teenager in the village of Sweetes on the island of Antigua. This strange, slow, British game of cricket did not fill him with enthusiasm. But then Ambrose rarely showed much of anything to anyone. At times, he did not even seem to enjoy the company of his teammates all that much. But one thing was obvious: he could bowl. By the end of the summer, West Indian predictions about the future of this newcomer would be confirmed. The West Indies had unearthed another great fast bowler. Ambrose took 26 wickets in the five Test matches at an average of 21.46 and won the Man of the Series award. He was quick, though not express, and his height allowed him to lift deliveries off a length into the ribcage with painful regularity. These qualities, allied with an accuracy similar to Joel Garner's, made him a formidable opponent.

With Ambrose, Marshall's experience, Courtney Walsh's into-the-wind consistency and the erratic but express pace of Patrick Patterson, the West Indies had yet another formidable pace attack. And they exploited it to the full.

Before the series, Allan Border's Australians were dealt a savage blow by their administrators who, in a bid to maximise crowds in Sydney and Melbourne over the Christmas and New Year holiday period, scheduled the first two Tests for the relative backwaters of Brisbane and Perth. The West Indies would begin their campaign to retain the Frank Worrell Trophy on the two

Winners can laugh: Viv Richards never lost a Test series as West Indies captain and proved to be a difficult and provocative opponent for Border's Australians.

fastest, bounciest pitches in the country. The visitors could not have drawn up a better program themselves. By the time they reached Melbourne for the third Test, the score was 2-0 in their favour and the heat between the teams was near to boiling point.

West Indies won in Brisbane by nine wickets, giving Richards good reason to remember his hundredth Test match. A week before, he had scored his hundredth first-class century, against New South Wales in Sydney, and in Brisbane he took his hundredth Test catch. However, what Richards probably remembers more than anything from the Brisbane match were the first three balls he received.

The Australians knew Richards would swagger out to the crease in his usual arrogant, hip-swinging style. In fact, they expected him to strut even more than usual given that he would be the centre of attention. The Australians had decided that whichever paceman was bowling would greet the West Indies captain with a couple of bouncers. It happened to be medium pacer Steve Waugh, which increased the surprise. Waugh was a determined character and a difficult early period in international cricket had toughened him even further. He had always had a good bouncer, too, and in this case, he increased the warmth of the greeting by giving Richards not two but three bouncers in succession. It was a daring, imaginative and provocative gesture from the 23-year-old all-rounder. Richards was nonplussed and quietly impressed. Here was one Australian at least who would stand up and fight. Richards was further impressed when Waugh made a counter-attacking 90 in Australia's rearguard second innings.

The second Test in Perth degenerated into hand-to-head guerilla warfare, with Hughes and the recalled Geoff Lawson bowling a lot of short-pitched deliveries during the West Indies first innings. Lawson suffered terrible luck on the first day, seeing four catches put down off his bowling. Worse was to follow when he was felled by a lifter from Ambrose that veered in from outside off stump off one of the many cracks that were opening up all over the pitch. Lawson, broken jaw wired by surgeons, returned to the ground the next day and was photographed alongside Ambrose. The latter cooperated for the photograph but never said a word. Lawson was out of cricket for seven weeks and, when he returned to play for New South Wales against South Australia, had to appeal through teeth still clenched tight by the wiring in his jaw.

Ambrose's felling of Lawson highlighted the problem of persistent short-pitched bowling, which had by then developed into one of the game's major controversies. As this violent season progressed, the issues of slow over rates and short-pitched bowling would come to occupy many minds.

Border, seeing the anger rise in the home team's dressing-room, declared Australia's innings as Lawson was stretchered off the WACA. Hughes kept the fires burning by dismissing Gordon Greenidge with the first ball of the innings. Although he did not realise it, Hughes had just taken the seventh Test hat-trick by an Australian and the first for more than 30 years. Amazingly, the hat-trick stretched over two innings and three overs. Hughes finished with 8/78, a magnificent performance which established him as a regular member of Australia's bowling attack for the next five years.

Richards set Australia a ridiculous 404 to win with less than a day to bat on a pitch made dangerous by dozens of surface cracks. From the elevated vantage point of the press box, I could see the light from the afternoon sun reflecting off the pitch in a mottled pattern, suggesting a loose, uneven surface. Later, after the post-match press conference, I made a point of walking out to the pitch, standing on the popping crease and imagining Ambrose steaming in at me. As I looked down the wicket I saw dozens of curved, loose pieces of dry, hard soil, all about the size of dinner plates. It was a frightening sight for any batsman to have to face every minute as he waited for another missile to be fired his way. The Australians had shown tremendous courage by even turning up on that last day. No Test cricketer should have been asked to bat on such a pitch, let alone against the West Indies. Australia made 234 and West Indies won by 169 runs. Two-nil.

After three relatively calm weeks of one-day matches, during which swing bowler Terry Alderman became the first of Kim Hughes's rebels to be reinstated to the Australian team, the two Test sides assembled in Melbourne for the Christmas Test. It was to be Border's hundredth. There would be few celebrations.

Border was furious to find a moist, green pitch which promised more help for the West Indian quicks. In many ways, this pitch was worse than the one in Perth. The bounce in Melbourne was just uneven enough to cause batsmen to miscalculate by centimetres. The result was that they would fend away one lifting ball with the top of their bat only to have the next ball, off the same length, pound into their fingers, crushing the bones hard against the handle of the bat. Border said later he had never seen so many batsmen hit in a Test match. It was an ugly spectacle, especially on the last day when Australia, again with a nominal target of 400 for a win, had to survive 97 hostile overs to keep the series alive.

Near the end of play the previous evening, Patterson had had words with Border, complaining about the short balls he was receiving from Steve Waugh. Border was not exactly moved to offer an apology. Incensed, Patterson tried to enter the Australians' dressing-room after stumps to continue the discussions, but was forced to stew over it until he got the new ball in his hand the next morning. That summer I was working on the Melbourne afternoon paper the *Herald*, and my sports editor, Geoff Slattery, asked me to ring Patterson early on the final morning. Patrick and I had been teammates in the 1984-85 Tasmanian team and he was happy to take the call. When I told him the Australians were very upset, he just grunted.

'Why?'

All-out attack: Patrick Patterson only knew one way to bowl – flat out. During the Melbourne Test in 1988-89, he produced a ferocious spell of bowling which left the Australians battered and bruised.

'Because of all the short stuff, Patrick.'

'Good.'

Patrick sounded as if he was determined to have the final say by bowling very fast on that fifth day. Sprinting in from the southern end, he produced the fastest bowling of the series, firing ball after ball at the Australians. It was brutal cricket. With the final edition of the *Herald* done, Slattery came down to the Melbourne Cricket Ground to witness first hand the end of a ferocious Test match. We left the enclosed press box to sit down near the fine-leg boundary, where you are quite close to the action. While the crowd booed its distaste for the West Indies style of play, we saw the most frightening hour of cricket imaginable.

With Australia's top order back in the pavilion applying ice to their bruises, Patterson launched another attack on the bottom half of the batting order. So fast did he bowl that wicket-keeper Jeff Dujon, standing closer to us than to the stumps, took every ball above his head. Dujon held his ground by planting his feet as firmly as he could on the turf an instant before taking the force of each ball with his arms and shoulders. Time and time again, his torso snapped back as another missile hit his gloves. From where we sat, we could hear either the crack of deliveries hitting the keeper's gloves or the sickening thud as they were intercepted by the batsmen's bodies.

Batting, as *Wisden* editor John Woodcock later wrote, 'became largely a matter of evasion'. And on that nasty pitch against such nasty bowling, evasion was often impossible. Patterson ended the suffering with a burst of 4/4 in 13 balls. The series was finished as a contest. Three-nil.

Umpire Tony Crafter had chided Ambrose and Patterson for overuse of the short ball in the first innings, but they seemed to ignore the warning. Umpires had not been encouraged by the game's administrators to strictly apply the law regarding intimidatory bowling and it was easy to understand why Crafter chose not to inflame the situation by doing so. A solution to this problem had to come from the International Cricket Council.

After an ignominious duck in the first innings of his hundredth Test, Border battled for 167 minutes in the second for an equal top score of 20 in a total of 114 runs. He took any number of deliveries on the body, but some of his teammates fared worse. Dean Jones, back in the team after a lengthy absence, was taken to hospital for X-rays for a suspected broken rib. Graeme Wood suffered a broken finger. Ian Healy had been hit twice in the protective box and, suffering nausea as well as severe bruising, was seen by a doctor in the dressing-room. Most of the other batsmen had bruises all over them. Jones said his fingers felt like they had been playing a piano non-stop for 10 hours. As well, Waugh had been cut on the chin after being hit by Ambrose in the first innings, and West Indies opener Gordon Greenidge had retired hurt after suffering a cut eye from a ball from Terry Alderman.

After the game, Border refused to criticise the West Indian tactics, but was severe in his criticism of the pitch.

That's not a Test wicket out there. I've played against a lot of short-pitched bowling, but I don't think I've ever seen blokes get hit so much in all my time. That tells me there is variation in pace and bounce. They utilised the conditions perfectly. There was no point in throwing the ball up to the bat. The West Indies are a tough side to play on any surface, but I can't see why we give them the advantage. They've got four fast bowlers and we give them a green wicket. If we had four fast bowlers of that ability we'd use them the same way. But there is absolutely no pleasure in it. You walk in just wondering where your next single is going to come from and nobody really likes to get hit by a cricket ball at 90 miles per hour. If every country had an attack like the West Indies, Test cricket would die pretty quickly.

That last comment summed up the dilemma facing the game's administrators. If those tactics were adopted worldwide, they would all but destroy the game. Yet, if the legislators acted to curtail short-pitched bowling, the West Indians would cry foul, arguing that they did not invent this sort of cricket and that there had never been any talk about restricting short bowling when Australia and England had boasted powerful pace attacks. The West Indies tactics had, after all, been developed after their team had been battered by Lillee and Thomson in Australia in 1975-76. The West Indies' view was that any move against short bowling would be born out of jealousy and designed merely to end West Indian dominance of world cricket rather than for any higher goal. But as the MCG crowd made plain that day, such cricket was boring. Over rates were scandalously and cynically slow, and the range of shots available to batsmen strictly limited.

ACB chairman Malcolm Gray publicly expressed his disappointment at the way the series was being played. 'It has been an unrelenting battle with slow over rates and relentless short-pitched bowling,' he said. 'That is not really conducive to attracting crowds.'

After Border's press conference, it was Richards's turn to face the microphones. Could he recall a match in which so many batsmen had been hit? Simmering as only Richards can, the reply was swift and to the point. 'Yes. I was here in 1975. The crowd was chanting then. They were chanting "kill, kill, kill" as your bowlers ran in. We hear people say we bowl too many bouncers these days but I remember how it was then.'

Just as West Indian memories of Lillee and Thomson's onslaught in '75-76 died hard, Border's Australians would not forget what they had been through in '88-89. The ill feeling between the two sides would fester for quite a while. The next series, in 1991 in the Caribbean, would be just as ugly.

With the series decided in the first three Tests, the tenor of play changed for the final two matches. Unlike on that practice day in Brisbane when the West Indies stepped up a gear, in Sydney and Adelaide, they dropped back a cog or two. As far as they were concerned, the main contest was finished.

Yet again, Sydney's slow, turning pitch helped Australia to its only win of a series. The West Indies helped too. Manager Clive Lloyd reflected the mood of the team when he lost his cool before the match and complained about the poor quality of the Sydney Cricket Ground wicket. It was a ridiculous comment.

The SCG pitch might have been slow and spinner-friendly

Part of the job: despite a reputation to the contrary, Allan Border was always helpful and generous to the Australian press corps. Sydney, January 1989.

but it was consistent, unlike the MCG wicket. Essentially, the West Indies, remembering their defeat by Australia's spinners in Sydney in 1984-85, were upset because they thought their pace attack was being negated by unfair pitch preparation. But that preparation was the same as it had been for some time, and the West Indies would have known that before they arrived in Australia. What really worried them was that they had no Test-class spinner in their squad. So upset were they that Allan Border's modest left-arm spinners took 11/96 in the match, largely because the West Indian batsmen continually played too early at him and hit easy catches into a surprised and grateful infield. Australia won by seven wickets.

The most significant aspect of this match was that Australia brought in two new players, Queensland leg spinner Trevor Hohns and New South Wales left-hand opening batsman Mark Taylor. Both would be chosen for the Ashes tour that was now only a few months away. Taylor opened with Marsh, allowing Boon to drop to number three where, except for a brief period in 1992-93, he would bat superbly for at least the next seven years.

The fifth Test in Adelaide was drawn on a typically placid pitch. The cricket was subdued compared to the first three matches, although dissent at umpiring decisions by some of the tourists brought official complaints. For Australia, Dean Jones made 216, his highest Test score, while Merv Hughes made a courageous and undefeated 72. With the ball, Mike Whitney, the New South Wales left-armer took 7/89 and 2/60. Whitney went on to top the first-class bowling figures for the season and was bitterly disappointed at not being chosen for the Ashes tour. And although Jones batted superbly in Adelaide, that innings would be the first of several where he would frustrate the selectors by making runs late in a series after the main contest had been decided. By 1992-93 and the next home series against the West Indies, the selectors had had enough and dropped Jones for good from the Test team despite his average of 46.55 from 52 Tests and persistent cries of anguish from his fellow Victorians.

For Border, it had been a difficult summer. He had not reproduced his great batting feats in the Caribbean in 1984, but at least the final two Test matches had been less violent affairs than the first three. As well, Merv Hughes had grown in stature and Alderman was back and ready for a return to England, where he might well be as destructive as he had been in 1981. Lawson had recovered health and form after that broken jaw and, along with Alderman, would give the Ashes attack some experience. Taylor, despite a modest start against the West Indies, looked a quality player and was already considered the best slips fieldsman in the country.

Although pleased with the Sydney win, Border was not getting carried away with talk of any major renaissance. 'There are still things to improve,' he said. 'Every time we win a game or string a few good performances together, we follow that with a hiccup. So we'll just wait and see.'

What Border did not know was that England was about to do its best to surrender the Ashes and give Australia a handy shove over the final barren hilltop and on to a greener and more pleasant land.

THE PERFECT

11

TOUR

EADINGLEY, Leeds, Thursday, 8 June 1989. If one day
can be identified as the one that confirmed Australian
cricket's emergence from the dark days of the mid- to late
1980s, this was it. And fittingly, Allan Border, the long-suffering
Australian captain, led the way. Alongside him was Mark Taylor,
a steady left-handed opener in only his third Test match, his first
against England. Five years later, Taylor would succeed Border as
Australian captain, but on that grey day in Yorkshire, it was Border
who took control.

The captain came in to bat soon after lunch on the first day
of the first Test with Australia 2/57. Ten overs had been lost to
rain in the first session, but after lunch, the clouds began to lift.
At that scoreline, anything could have happened. Had the clouds
lingered and the English bowlers found line and length, Australia
could have collapsed. The game was delicately balanced.

David Gower had won the toss and sent Australia in because
of the wicket's reputation and the morning cloud cover. Determined
to rid the Australians of the 'Headingley Hoodoo', a clear-minded

Border had seen no demons in the pitch and had already decided to bat first were he to win the toss. The pessimist was determined to be positive. So with Taylor pushing, prodding and occasionally cutting and driving, Border attacked. For once, he was not reacting to a grim situation but trying to create a favourable one.

Gone was the apologetic leader of 1985 who seemed to accept defeat as the natural course of events – Border was having none of that this time. In the early weeks of the tour, he had been saying he wanted the Australians to thrash every county team they met and to play as aggressively as possible against England. However, he knew that the best way to get his team to play like that was to do so himself. The first day of the first Test was the time to start, so Border went for it.

To bat as he did, Border not only had to overcome the natural caution that affects every batsman on the first day of a Test series, but vivid and bitter memories of previous visits to Leeds. The Headingley pitch had a reputation as one of the most treacherous in the game. Once clouds obscured the distant, pale yellow sphere that passes for the sun in northern England, swing and seam bowlers ran amok. Yet it was not just the pitch but the whole ground which had a threatening aura about it. Australia had not won at Headingley since 1964, losing four and drawing two Tests. Most significantly, Headingley was where England came back from almost certain defeat to beat Australia in 1981 in one of the most famous Tests in history – Ian Botham's Test. That game had come to occupy a dark and dangerous corner in the collective psyche of Australian cricket. Mention of the word Headingley sent a shiver down the spine of every Australian cricketer, from Border to the slogger in the park.

From that '81 Australian team, only Border, Alderman and Lawson remained. Before the match, Border was convinced the younger members of the team would not be spooked by playing at this infamous ground. He told them at the team meeting the night before the match that he was going to go for his shots, that he was going to take on the England bowlers. Now he was doing it.

Border made 66 off 118 balls in what Martin Johnson in the *Independent* described as 'a champagne thrash'. It was not a typical Border innings. He did not hit everything in the middle of the bat as was his usual custom, but made as many runs from mishits and edges as good shots. There was little subtlety and no caution. Border hit nine fours, one five and one six. The latter came when he cut under a short ball from Phil DeFreitas. Border meant to

Champagne thrash: Allan Border attacks on the first day of the first Test of the 1989 Ashes series. His 66 set the tone for the rest of that historic series.

help the ball on its way to third man, but he had more adrenalin pumping through his veins than he realised and managed to lift it over the third-man boundary. When he saw where the shot had gone, Border glanced down at the middle of his bat, raised his eyebrows and nodded in approval. He had surprised himself with that one. Later, Border said that that six might well have had a very positive psychological effect on his teammates.

One for the purists: Steve Waugh crashes another elegant backfoot boundary during his brilliant 1989 Ashes series.

Magic bus: Allan Border and his brother John outside the Australian team bus after the fifth Test in Nottingham.

The captain's frenetic innings had set a pattern that persisted for the rest of the series. Border and Taylor added 117, Taylor ending the first day on 96 not out and carrying on to 136 the next morning. Dean Jones (76) played an unusual role, second fiddle to Steve Waugh who finally made his first Test century in his twenty-seventh match. Surging forward from the foundation of 3/207 which Border and Taylor had built on the first day, Australia ended the second at 6/580 with Waugh undefeated on 174. Australia went on to bowl England out in the fourth innings for 191 to win by 210 runs. The series followed a similar pattern, with Australia winning 4-0.

Looking back, teammates, commentators, past players and fans all agree that Border's 66 on that first day of the first Test was the most decisive moment of that famously successful tour. It was the innings by which Border stamped himself as a genuine leader. The mystery was why he had not used his formidable skills as a batsman to create more winning opportunities in earlier series. Even after that innings, he went back into his shell a little, although it should be said that his best days as a batsman had been during one of the bleakest periods in Australian cricket when adventurous batting was a luxury the team could rarely afford. After '89, Border was mostly content to play second fiddle behind maturing players such as Boon, Waugh, Taylor and Jones.

Greg Chappell considers that innings at Headingley a high point in Australian cricket's return to respectability. Chappell had played alongside Border in the latter's early career and saw him as a gifted player with a slight inferiority complex. Chappell thought that attitude held Border back from asserting himself more with the bat.

> Because of the way he is built and because of his temperament, Allan was always seen as a battler. He was so nimble but he didn't look nimble. The way he looked contributed to the way people saw him as a bit of a battler. And in a way that's how he saw himself. From early on I thought he looked so comfortable in the middle, but I can remember him saying things in the dressing-room that I couldn't believe, that I wouldn't even let myself think let alone say out loud. He wasn't that confident of himself, yet when he walked through that gate he was so determined and so single-minded that he was able to overcome that inferiority complex. And that's why his innings at Headingley in '89 was one of his better innings. Because he was creating a situation rather than reacting to one.

> That innings to me was the turnaround of Australian cricket at that time. We hadn't had a great deal of success, but it was a good side that was just starting to be competitive. The game was delicately balanced and Allan went out and played a very aggressive, very positive, terrific innings. For me, that set the tone for that series. Basically, it won the series for Australia. He didn't do that often enough.

That slight inferiority complex that Chappell saw in Border's attitude to his batting applies equally to his captaincy. Had he been one DNA molecule more reluctant to lead Australia, he surely would have resigned well before this tour. In his early years as captain, that hesitancy to grasp hold of the job meant that he was slow to come to grips with tactics and the subtleties of personnel management. In England in 1989, Border's captaincy, reinforced by the inside information he had gleaned from another thinly disguised spying mission with Essex the year before, took what Geoff Lawson described as 'a quantum leap'.

In England in '85, AB had been very unsure of himself as captain [Lawson said]. He didn't say much at team meetings and didn't talk much to his senior players. In '89 all that changed. There was a quantum leap in attitude and tactics. There was a deliberate change to play it tough on the field, not to chat with the Poms at all and to win all the county games. AB also used other people's ideas. After watching Graham Gooch at Essex, he had worked out the tactic of placing close fielders on the on-side to cut off Graham's favourite scoring shot early in an innings. When I suggested I might try bowling outside Gower's leg stump, most of the guys at the team meeting laughed. But AB remembered how I'd got Gower out like that in 1982-83 and he said, 'Yeah. Let's try it.' The '89 series was the first time AB realised you could set different fields for different batsmen, even unusual fields. It made a huge difference to the team.

Greg Chappell also noticed the difference from the comfort of his Brisbane lounge room. 'I can remember watching the first Test on television and saying to my wife: "Look at this. He really wants to do the captain's job now." The change in his attitude was obvious.'

The other noticeable change in Border from '85 to '89 was his attitude towards the England players on the field. He no longer chatted amicably with his opponents as he had in '85. Then, it seemed as if he were more comfortable with the Englishmen than with the team he was supposed to be leading and moulding. In '89, Border took a more ruthless line, one that surprised Gower.

The England captain wrote in his autobiography: 'He batted very well in '85, but was generally out of control as captain, and from the moment he arrived in '89 he set out his stall to be as mean as possible. He was mean to the opposition, to the press, and indeed to his own players. He sledged pretty fiercely, too, which is something that doesn't normally bother me too much, although on this tour it was hyper unfriendly.'

Gower might have overstated things a little there. Border was not mean to the press nor to his own players, just determined not to let anything distract him from winning the series. At times, a journalist or a teammate might have copped a serve from him but only because they had somehow interfered with his march towards the Ashes.

The change in Border's attitude to on-field relations stemmed from those criticisms Ian Chappell had made in the media after the '85 series. Chappell thought Border had sent the wrong message to his players in '85 by fraternising so amicably and in such a public manner with the Englishmen during play. Although not exactly conceding the point to Chappell, Border's attitude did change in '89, perhaps even more than Chappell's view required.

This was no temporary change either. To the end of his career, Border remained a fiercely determined and confrontational personality on the field. There were the occasional lighter moments, but essentially, Border became a distant, uncompromising figure to opponents once he walked through the gate. As Greg Chappell noted, Border had always succumbed to 'white line fever' when he batted. From '89, he brought that attitude to his captaincy as well.

Even as a young first grader for Mosman in Sydney, Border was not averse to an angry word or two with opponents. In an interview with Gideon Haigh in the *Australian* in 1994-95, former England all-rounder and Mosman captain Barry Knight recalled the young Border's aggressive attitude on the field on Saturday afternoons. Knight, a pivotal influence on the early Border, remembered how the young left-hander's regular suggestion as to how to break an annoying partnership was to 'bounce 'em'. Towards the end of his career, Border's Test team gained a reputation for sledging, which *Wisden* noted with strong disapproval in its assessment of the 1993 Ashes series. Most teams which played against Border in those later years made some sort of complaint about Australian sledging. No doubt many of those teams were guilty of the same sin, but by the end of his career, Border's side had begun to attract labels like 'the ugly Australians' and the captain himself was reported twice for dissent. This trend was the one major blemish in his years as Australian captain.

During Border's first summer in retirement from international cricket, one Brisbane player brought some humour to the sledging issue. The young quick had beaten Border in a club match and had whinged about luck denying him the prize wicket. Border replied with some succinct advice to the young bowler, who came back with: 'How many club games have you played?' Border was struck dumb.

In England in 1989, two factors encouraged Border to change his approach to captaincy, to experiment tactically and to impose himself upon his team and his opponents. The first was a speech Laurie Sawle gave before the team left Melbourne. Sawle had been appointed manager for the tour, although he had been as reluctant to do that job as Border had been to accept the captaincy back in 1984. Sawle, a shy man, saw an enormous job ahead of him with hours of public relations work and too many speeches. It did not appeal to him, but at the ACB's third request, he accepted. To its credit, the ACB knew its man. Like Border, Sawle rose to the challenge superbly.

The ACB reasoned that Sawle, as chairman of selectors, had been the architect of the rebuilding process that was now nearing its final test. He was the man who should be in England with Border and Simpson to see it through. So at a final briefing in Sawle's room at the Melbourne Hilton before the flight to London, the Colonel gave a rare speech. 'One of the things I had to say was that we could win the series, but that we needed to really rally behind AB, to make it an historic tour for him and for all of us. I told them we had to get behind AB and bring the Ashes back for him. I was trying to seal it all in as a unit with AB as the boss, the man at the helm.'

The second factor encouraging Border to make a real go of the captaincy was that it might have been his last chance. Had he lost that series, Border would have become the first Australian captain to lose three Ashes series. He'd shown himself to be a great batsman, but as a captain he had won one series out of ten. Poor team or not, another captain would have had to be found sooner rather than later.

As Ian Chappell noted in the *Bulletin* in early May: 'The kindest way you can put it is that AB's future will have to be evaluated as part of a major shake-up of the whole team. The England side is only very average, just as it was in 1985 and 1986-87 when they beat us. I'd be very annoyed if that happened again. I think a lot of people see this tour as Border's last chance.'

Another former captain, Bill Lawry, was even tougher in his expectations. Writing in Melbourne's *Sunday Observer*, Lawry argued: 'This tour will be Border's greatest opportunity to be in charge of a winning team against England. It will be his last chance against mediocre opposition to prove that, not only is he one of the world's best batsmen, but also a capable captain. If he can't win this series, then I think he should stand down.'

So for Allan Border, the 1989 Ashes series was just about do or die. Fortunately, from the first days in London in early May, the omens were favourable. It wasn't raining, for a start, and Lord's practice wickets were dry and available every day of that first week. The weather might seem a poor place to begin counting the blessings of that tour, but for an Australian cricketer, a miserably damp English summer can be deeply demoralising. The momentum gained in that first week of net sessions lasted another four and a half months. In many ways, this tour would turn out to be the perfect tour. Even Britain's notoriously nosy tabloid newspapers could not spoil the Australians' march across England.

Border had caused one major problem before the team left for England. He had banned the players' partners from staying at the team hotels until the final month of the tour. Most of the partners were unhappy, but Border stood firm, maintaining that this was the best policy for keeping the team together and concentrating on its cricket. From the excellent team spirit which developed, the policy must be deemed a success, however politically incorrect.

During that first week, several of the team spent an afternoon at a London studio posing for advertising photographs for tour sponsor XXXX beer. The pictures centred on Merv Hughes and his froth-covered moustache. The photographs were used on giant billboards all over Britain that summer and helped raise the profile of the touring team even higher than is normal for an Australian cricket team in England. If those posters encouraged the English players and public to think of the Australians as unsophisticated beer-swilling yobs, so much the better. What they learned from Headingley was that Border's team was technically superior to the local product in all departments and was prepared to play attacking, positive cricket.

Off the field, the omens continued to promise success. The team hotel, the Westbury in Mayfair, was a fairly ugly-looking brick building from the front but inside was a friendly, welcoming home base. The 1985 team had not been happy with its London hotel and there was general relief among the senior members of the 1989 party when the Westbury proved to be a major improvement. Again, it might seem a minor point, but homesickness can be a major problem on a four-month tour of England, and a touring team needs as many off-field things as possible to go well for its on-field efforts to be successful. Besides, English hotels do not always match up to Australian standards. For example, most hotels the team stayed at on this tour did not have air-conditioning. Normally that would not matter, but the summer of '89 was hot. Tempers occasionally frayed at provincial hotels when, after a long day in the field against an uninterested county team, the Australians returned to hotel rooms that were more like saunas than pleasant retreats from the rigours of constant cricket.

When away from London, the team travelled in a state-of-the-art bus complete with video screens, mini-bar and extensive menu. With XXXX ads plastered across the side of the bus as well as a sign declaring proudly that the occupants were the Australian Cricket Touring Team 1989, the players were often saluted as they travelled up and down the country's motorways. After the Ashes were regained with the win in the fourth Test at Old Trafford, the words 'Ashes-Winning' were added to the side of the bus.

Cricket matters began just as well. During that first week of net practice at the Nursery at Lord's, Border and Simpson assigned Terry Alderman to work in the same net with young Tasmanian pace bowler Greg Campbell, while Geoff Lawson worked with Hughes in the adjoining net. This sort of cooperation typified the tour, with each player a part of the whole.

Apart from the first county game against Worcestershire, Australia was never beaten in a first-class match. The New Road ground in that beautiful provincial city might be one of the prettiest in the world, but its pitch was a shocker. When the match finished in two days, Border refused to play a one-day game on the scheduled third day as the risk of injury was too high. Instead, the bus headed south-west to Somerset for an extra net session in better conditions. Border had his mind set on a successful tour and not even his personal bat-maker, Duncan Fearnley, Worcestershire's chairman, could distract him from what was best for the Australian team.

Steve Waugh's classical 177 at Headingley was his first Test century. He made many of those runs with elegant, straight-backed square and cover drives off the back foot, hit with awesome power. Wearing his beloved baggy green cap, Waugh looked like a throwback to cricket's golden age, a typically laconic Australian country boy with a simple, correct technique and a no-nonsense approach to the game. But this was a misreading: Waugh is in fact a street-smart character from the gritty western suburbs of the big city, Sydney. He does harbour passion and respect for the history

Master craftsman: Terry Alderman's superb swing and seam bowling destroyed England's batting during the 1989 series.

of the game and the players of the past, but there is steel in his soul. Steve Waugh is a tough competitor, shrewd, proud and uncompromising, not unlike another Bankstown boy made good – Paul Keating. Steve Waugh was just the sort of cricketer Border needed.

While Merv Hughes happily played the role of the beer-swilling Aussie clown and Terry Alderman the silent destroyer with his mastery of the English art of swing bowling, Waugh captured the imagination of the British public, even inspiring one

In control: Allan Border's approach to leadership and tactical planning took a 'quantum leap' during the 1989 Ashes series. Here he watches Graham Gooch batting in the nets at Lord's.

female fan to coin the term 'Waughgasm' to describe the thrill those classical cover drives gave spectators.

In the second Test at Lord's, Australia marked Border's hundredth consecutive Test appearance with a win by six wickets. Waugh made an undefeated 152 in the first innings, during which the renowned English photographer Patrick Eagar captured him in all his technically correct elegance. Waugh was stretched fully forward in defence, front knee bent, left elbow cocked, capped head right over the ball. It was a beautiful photograph that came

115

to symbolise the fine cricket the Australians played that warm northern summer. It also provided a stark contrast with the disarray into which the England team had quickly fallen, with Gower, its captain, a lost and uninspired figure, and most of its batsmen lacking the basic techniques needed to counter the clever, accurate bowling of Alderman, Lawson and company.

The win at Lord's, witnessed by the then Australian Prime Minister Bob Hawke, was followed by a rain-affected draw at Edgbaston in Birmingham. Dean Jones made merry in that third Test with a fine 157, and even the return of England's ageing hero, Ian Botham, could not halt the momentum of Border's team. At one stage, Jones surprised Angus Fraser by yelling at him as another four raced towards the mid-wicket boundary: 'Didn't you go to the team meeting? They would have told you you can't bowl on middle and leg to me.' Confidence is a wonderful thing.

After Edgbaston, Australia led 2-0 with three Tests left. A win in the fourth at Old Trafford would give Australia the series. And although England's lower-order batsmen fought hard to stave off that defeat, they were only delaying the inevitable. As the names of the 16 England players to tour the outlawed republic of

The Gower plan: Geoff Lawson takes David Gower's wicket in the fourth Test at Old Trafford. Lawson and Border's plan for Gower worked perfectly throughout the series.

South Africa were released to the media, David Boon swept spinner Nick Cook to the square leg boundary to post a nine-wicket win. On the balcony outside the visitors' dressing-room, the rest of the touring party rose to their feet as one, arms raised in triumph. The photographs of that moment replaced Eagar's shot of Waugh as the ultimate symbol of this perfect tour. For nearly 400 years, English literature had had its famous balcony scene, from Shakespeare's *Romeo and Juliet*; Old Trafford, on 1 August 1989, provided Australian cricket with its own celebrated version.

At his press conference after the win at Old Trafford, Border was strangely reserved in his moment of triumph. Five minutes after the end of the match, he spoke to Gower, offering commiserations to the devastated England captain. As well as the surrendering of the Ashes, the news had come through that nine players who had played under Gower in this series and three in this match were turning their backs on the England team and joining Mike Gatting's rebel tour to South Africa. Border was reminded of his bitter disappointment at the Australian defectors who let him down in 1985 and how the team that was left surrendered the Ashes during Gower's triumphant summer.

After speaking briefly to Gower, Border joined his teammates in a raucous dressing-room where Merv Hughes was spraying champagne and beer at anything that moved. Amid the mayhem, Border noticed his vice-captain, Geoff Marsh, open his locker, take out his baggy green cap and proudly put it on, Merv Hughes or not. In a corner, Alderman and Lawson avoided the mayhem, chatting quietly about how satisfying this win was after the humiliation of 1981. Soon after, Border, hair plastered down with Hughes's hair spray, faced the media.

> It was a mixed-feeling sort of day [he said]. Talking to David Gower straight after the game brought me back down to earth a bit because I have been in that position before. It does take the gloss off it a bit. I'm as proud as anything to be in this position and am going to enjoy and savour the moment for as long as I can, but I can relate to the other captain sitting in the dressing-room now feeling the weight of the world on his shoulders.

In later years, when Border's captaincy reverted to more of a safety-first policy, it seemed that he had never been able to completely shake off the memories of those early years when defeat and disaster were constant companions. Perhaps he had been

The balcony scene: as David Boon hits the winning runs the 1989
tourists celebrate the moment the Ashes return to Australian hands.

scarred psychologically by those bitter experiences and was never able to leave them behind. He had often talked to his closest teammates about the motivating power of the fear of failure. Perhaps that was it. Certainly, the way Border referred so sympathetically to Gower that day at Old Trafford offered an insight into his thinking. One way or another, in his moment of triumph and release, Border was still haunted by defeat.

The Australians went on to win handsomely at Trent Bridge in Nottingham in the fifth Test and to draw at the Oval in the sixth for that 4-0 margin. All along, they set record after record, some of which included:

• regaining the Ashes in England for the first time since 1934;
• the 4-0 margin equalled the results achieved by the legendary 1921 and 1948 Australian touring teams;
• Mark Taylor became the third highest scorer of runs in a series with 839 (only bettered by Bradman – twice);
• Steve Waugh became the third batsman to average more than 100 in an Ashes series;
• Terry Alderman took 41 wickets in the series to become the first player to take 40 wickets or more in two series;
• Allan Border moved past Viv Richards, Gary Sobers and Geoff Boycott and into second place on the list of all-time Test run-scorers;
• at Trent Bridge, Taylor and Geoff Marsh became the first openers to bat through a complete day's play in a Test in England;
• Marsh and Taylor's stand of 329 was the highest opening partnership recorded in a Test in England;
• scoring 400 or more in the first innings in eight consecutive Test matches.

Border's 1989 Australians left English cricket in tatters. The new regime of chairman of selectors Ted Dexter began the summer with talk of a return to Test match success and ended it in massive defeat. Australia used 12 players in the six Tests; England used twenty-nine. Ian Botham was shown to be a spent force in Test cricket. Gower, who fell to Lawson seven times in 11 innings, was not even chosen for England's tour to the West Indies the following February. He was replaced as captain by Graham Gooch, whose batting had been so destroyed by Alderman that Gooch asked to be left out of the fifth Test. Amazingly, England's selectors agreed.

For Border, Sawle and Simpson, the satisfaction was immense. Their perseverance in the mid-1980s had finally been rewarded. As Border said at Old Trafford: 'Three years ago we picked a group of young players – Steve Waugh, David Boon and Dean Jones among them. They've had stretches of looking the goods and then got back into problem areas. But hard work and sticking with the combination you believed was going to come through has borne fruit, especially on this tour.'

During the next few years, it became apparent that the England side Australia beat so convincingly in 1989 was the first of several pathetic England teams. Equally, Australia's performances in subsequent series showed that the euphoria surrounding the 1989 Ashes series was a little overblown. However, that was understandable. The 1989 tour had been touched by magic. Throughout those four and a half sunny, successful months, the dressing-room ghetto-blaster played the team's adopted theme song, a jaunty number by Roy Orbison, the chorus of which went 'Anything you want, you got it, baby'. It was that sort of tour.

Although Border and his team knew their efforts had been appreciated back home in Australia, they had no idea when they left Heathrow in early August of the size of the reception which awaited them.

AUSTRALIA'S

12

HEROES

'WHAT'S the reaction been like in the papers back home?' Allan Border asked the touring press corps a few days after the win at Old Trafford had regained the Ashes for Australia. Assured that front and back pages were full of tributes to his team, Border noted a little vaguely: 'Yeah. Apparently there's been a pretty good response.'

Although the reach of the global village comfortably spanned the distance from Manchester to Melbourne, it was still not that easy for Border and his touring party to fully appreciate the size of the reaction back in Australia. And Border would have been the last to have any real appreciation for it. He always saw himself as a cricketer only. The fame, the national respect and the adulation of the fans came with the territory but were not things upon which he dwelt. Unlike many sportspeople, Border had not covered the walls of his Brisbane home with photographs and memorabilia of his many triumphs.

Towards the end of his career, Border did seem to develop more of an idea of his standing, though even then, it was relatively limited. In 1993-94, his final home season as a Test player, Border had to be cajoled into having a large testimonial dinner in Sydney. He just never saw himself as anything other than a cricketer – a very, very good one – but just a cricketer. Yet, by the end of the 1989 Ashes series, Border had become a national treasure and a symbol of the sort of unpretentious Aussie battler which Australian popular culture loved to mythologise.

National hero: after the triumphs in England in 1989,
Allan Border became the most popular sportsperson in the nation.

121

The then prime minister, Bob Hawke, liked to promote himself in a similar light, and in 1989, he was still, like Border, a man of the people. Hawke's descent into tasteless self-promotion and well-paid media 'appearances' was still several years away. Not surprisingly, Hawke the cricket-lover led the tributes to Border's team.

In his official message to Border, Hawke said: 'Congratulations on your historic Ashes victory. The 1989 side has performed magnificently as individuals, as a team and as representatives of Australia. Your own leadership has been superb. I know of no Australian sportsman who has fought more courageously for his country or more rightly deserved this ultimate achievement for an Australian captain.'

The then Opposition leader, Andrew Peacock, had spent most of the previous night watching the last day's play at Old Trafford and was equally lavish in his praise. 'If we still had imperial honours, the first knighthood would go to Allan Border. It [the Ashes victory] certainly marks the turning point in the fortunes of Australian cricket.'

Peacock was right in implying that cricket would be boosted by the Ashes success. The number of children playing cricket rose over the next year in response to the success of the Australian team. The days of the battling skipper dragging his inept teammates along behind him were over, although 'Sir Allan Border' would never have sounded right.

A month after the sixth Test at the Oval, the '89 Ashes squad assembled in Melbourne for a black tie dinner in its honour in the grand ballroom at the Sheraton Hotel in Exhibition Street. During this spectacular and successful night, Hawke surprised the crowd by presenting Border with the Order of Australia. Hawke, who left a Cabinet meeting in Canberra to attend the dinner, broke protocol by presenting the award four months ahead of the usual day, Australia Day, 26 January. There had been speculation that Hawke might call an early election and his haste in honouring Border was seen by many as cynical politicising of the national awards system.

As the ensuing controversy developed, Border offered to return the award. 'Wear it with pride,' the prime minister advised.

The morning after the dinner, the players and their partners flew to Sydney for a parade along George Street, from Circular Quay to Darling Harbour. The players thought this a rather exaggerated gesture and expected a modest reception, but when they looked south down George Street and saw thousands on the footpaths waiting to salute them, they were stunned. One estimate put the crowd at 400,000 people. The ticker-tape parade was followed by a gala lunch for 1500 and, on the Saturday back in Melbourne, a motorcade around the MCG in front of 96,000 fans happy to expend a little of their nervous energy on cheering Border and company, before settling in to watch Hawthorn fight off a brilliant finish by Geelong in the VFL grand final.

The intensity of the week's celebrations showed Border that, all along, he had not suffered alone. Not only had the cricket public felt for him as he battled defeat after defeat in his early years as captain, cricket lovers had suffered too. The thrashing of the oldest enemy of all brought forth a massive expression of relief and joy. Publishers were hastily arranging for books on the '89 tour and at least five publications made it to the shops. If sport, like religion, is an opiate of the masses, this week of celebrations resembled a national overdose.

Welcome home: there is nothing like a win against the old enemy to cheer Australian hearts. Allan Border and Geoff Marsh enjoy Sydney's ticker-tape parade.

123

It was also a week that saw Allan Border's popularity peak. His relationship with the public formed during the dark days after he took over the captaincy, and firmed as the public responded to a captain prepared to reveal shortcomings and misgivings in those early confessional interviews, while still making runs on the field. When success at Test level came, in the form of a huge win over England, the relationship was consummated with some passion. It was also marked officially a few months later, on Australia Day, when Border was named Australian of the Year for 1989.

In an August edition of *New Idea* magazine, Border's wife, Jane, spoke about that award. 'I was very proud: proud for him because he put in a lot of time and effort with cricket. I think Allan epitomises Australians to a degree. He's honest. He's a bit of a battler. And he pulls through when it's tough.'

With the Australian of the Year award came a national tour during the winter of 1990 in which the Borders travelled the country meeting the people – from politicians at official receptions, to prime-time television chat-show hosts and battlers in flood-ravaged Queensland outback towns, to admirers at modest suburban club rooms. Here, the fare was a cold-meat selection and a casserole with rice served in the culinary equivalent of the approach adopted by England's bowlers the previous winter: the smorgasbord, or help yourself. The Borders took their place in the queue with no fuss, much as Allan had in England in 1989, waiting patiently until Taylor, Marsh and Boon had had their fill.

When, in August 1990, Border was made Mayor of Mosman for a day, in the Sydney suburb where he had grown up, it was a full year after the Ashes series. He noted that: 'The last 12 months have been phenomenal as a result of the Ashes and I still don't think all of the guys in the team realise how big the response has been.'

Yet if there was one thing that could bring the captain and his players back to earth after the 1989 Ashes series, it was the game of Test cricket. The summer of 1989-90 saw New Zealand play Australia in a one-off Test in Perth in November, before two Tests against Sri Lanka and another three against Pakistan.

The cricket did bring the players back to earth quickly, even if the press and the public stayed on a high for too long. Sections of the cricket press had begun pushing the line that this Australian team was the most successful in the world. Rod Nicholson in the Melbourne *Sun* argued the case by citing figures that showed Australia had won more games of cricket in the previous 12 months than any other team. The bare figures were correct, but the problem was that many of those games were World Series one-day matches – matches played in Australian conditions, in front of parochial Australian crowds and against teams which often found the World Series a tiresome interruption to the far more important Test series.

In fact, Border's team won only two Tests in the first seven that followed the '89 Ashes campaign, failing in three to bowl out the opposition when a win was there for the taking. Although the Australian players might have been suffering a letdown after the highs of '89, of the three opponents, only Pakistan could be considered high class. It was a poor start to this much-heralded new era, and a few clear-eyed observers were arguing that as glorious as the '89 Ashes win had been, it was achieved against a very poor England team. Australia's quality was not to be judged solely by its results against England.

That first match against New Zealand became Mark Greatbatch's Test when he batted for just under 11 hours to save the match for his team. Australia's selectors had not chosen a spinner and the resultant lack of variety proved costly. Strangely, Border bowled only five overs in New Zealand's second innings, when footmarks outside the left-handed Greatbatch's off stump could have helped the Australian captain's left-arm spinners.

The first Test against Sri Lanka was drawn but Australia won the second, the first Test match played in Tasmania. The match, played at the Bellerive Oval in Hobart, was marred by accusations by the visiting team that the Australians had indulged in some nasty sledging. Fair or not, the accusations added a sour note to the summer and were the first of a number of such complaints from opposition teams.

In January, Australia snuck home to beat Pakistan in Melbourne in the first Test of that series. The win was controversial as Australia took six second-innings wickets with leg-before decisions, five, including the last, well on the front foot, falling to Terry Alderman.

As with Australia's alleged sledging, complaints from visiting teams about Australian umpiring standards would continue for some time.

Worse followed when, after the rain-affected second Test in Sydney, the Pakistanis staged a walk-off in the match against Victoria when umpire Robin Bailhache ruled that spinner Mushtaq Ahmed had run on the pitch after a final warning. The Pakistanis pleaded ignorance of the final warning and, led by manager Intikhab Alam, walked off. Victorian Cricket Association (VCA) officials reached a compromise and the match continued. The VCA could have declared the match won by Victoria on forfeit. Such a decision would have been for the greater good of the game but would have no doubt created a major controversy.

Yet another tasteless incident occurred during the one-day series after Imran Khan, Pakistan's captain, was named as International Cricketer of the Year. In the *Sun*, Rod Nicholson had written a story saying the Australians were upset that Imran and not Dean Jones had won the award. The Australians considered the voting system prejudiced against them, but to complain to a journalist was hardly the proper way to air their grievances. When Imran took the field for the first World Series final, the large MCG crowd greeted him with sustained booing. This was grossly unfair on Imran as he had had nothing to do with the voting, and he soon had a T-shirt made bearing the slogan: 'I'm sorry I won the car.'

This incident was a reminder to some members of the divided Australian press that poor sportsmanship was not necessarily confined to the Indian subcontinent. To the other faction, the booing of Imran provided some rather unusual job satisfaction.

At the end of the season, Australia travelled to New Zealand for a one-day tournament followed by a one-off Test in Wellington which the home side won by nine wickets, inflicting Australia's first loss in 15 Tests.

Although the romance between Border's Australian team and its public thrived for quite a while after the highs of '89, life for the cricketers had readily returned to the tough grind that is Test cricket. The summer of 1989-90 had been frustrating, marked by bickering, a few unexpected failures and the realisation that a resounding win over England did not guarantee success against other teams.

Overall, though, the decade of the 1980s ended well for Border and his Australian team. They had travelled quite a distance from those grim days in the summer of 1984-85.

THE 80s

IN the 26 weeks from 14 July 1987 to 9 February 1988, Dean Jones flew 86,000 kilometres around the world in 32 separate flights, spent 140 hours in the air and countless more in airport lounges, taxis and buses. In between flights, he stayed in 28 hotels on three continents and managed to play five Test matches, three four-day Sheffield Shield games, 16 one-day internationals and a handful of other matches – all in the course of his job as a professional cricketer.

During the 1980s, the amount of cricket played worldwide increased dramatically thanks to the increasing influence of television. Along with the West Indies four-man pace attack, television came to dominate the game in the first post-Packer decade.

In an article in the *Wide World of Sports Cricket Yearbook 1990*, Richie Benaud described the 1980s as the decade of 'lights, cameras and action'. The reference to television was not there just as a sop to Benaud's employer and the owner of the yearbook, Packer's Channel Nine. The 1980s was the decade when television came to run the game as much or, as it often seemed in Australia, more than the game's officials. From the time Packer bought his way into Australian cricket in 1977, the game changed forever and in most of those changes, Australia led the way.

The 'lights' of the one-day game brought perhaps the most noticeable change and, although other countries were slow to adopt day/night cricket, it was soon obvious that it was the way of the future.

The 'cameras' continued to bring the play and the players closer. This not only made the best cricketers more famous than their predecessors, but it focussed much more attention on what they did in the heat of battle. By the end of the decade, with international cricketers fully professional if not exactly as well paid as other professional athletes, the pressure to perform brought on a deterioration in on-field behaviour. The 1980s continued the trend of the 1970s. Bowlers' appeals became more theatrical, umpire's decisions were not always accepted and the chat between opponents on the field was often more heated than the pleasant banter we are told occurred before the war. In this, cricket mirrored trends in other sports, especially tennis, which set the standard for boorish behaviour.

The debate still rages as to just how much behaviour has deteriorated since the late 1970s, but even those who enjoy and demand a little aggro in their cricket would have to concede that poor behaviour is definitely more obvious because of the television cameras. And if it is more obvious, it is more of a problem. The cameras will not go away.

Perhaps the major change in world cricket in the 1980s is covered by the third word in Benaud's catchphrase, 'action'. One statistic should be enough. In the 1970s, from 1 January 1970 to 31 December 1979, Australia played 83 completed Tests and 31 one-day internationals. In the 1980s, it played 97 Tests and 187 one-dayers. The massive increase in one-day cricket typified the 1980s.

Kerry Packer and his television network had a great deal to do with this major change in cricket programming. His introduction of day/night one-day matches during World Series Cricket years had been a success, and Packer insisted a similar emphasis be maintained when official cricket finally decided it had to negotiate with him.

Throughout the 1980s, Packer's Channel Nine and its promotional arm, PBL Marketing, pushed one-day cricket in all its advertising, often to the exclusion of Test cricket. To many cricket lovers, this was criminal. The ACB was not always pleased with this mania for one-day cricket, but it was hamstrung by contractual obligations and the power of PBL; as were some of Packer's commentators.

In January 1991, Rod Marsh, a veteran of 96 Tests for Australia and a leading player in Packer's breakaway World Series Cricket, was summarily sacked from Packer's Radio 2UE commentary team during the third Test. Marsh had offended his boss by making a derogatory comment about one-day cricket. This unfortunate episode ended well for Australian cricket. Suddenly free of his obligations to Packer, Marsh was on the open market and was quickly approached by the ACB's Graham Halbish for the job of running the Cricket Academy.

Whenever his contract for the television rights was up for renegotiation, Packer was able to insist on the formula of a three-team one-day competition with 12 preliminary games and a best-of-three finals series. Where those one-day games sat amongst the Test matches varied quite often until the ACB settled on the pattern that exists now where the one-dayers are played in two blocks – in December after the first Test and in January after the third. Most of the purists who prefer Test matches have learned to cope with this programming, even if that only means they know when to turn off their attention for a fortnight before another Test starts.

Whenever England toured Australia, they would complain about the amount of one-day cricket and travelling their players had to endure. During the 1990-91 Ashes tour, Doug Insole, the Test and County Cricket Board's (TCCB) tours chairman, noted that England's itinerary involved more cross-continent flights than the home team had to endure. But Insole knew why there was so much one-day cricket compared to the three one-day internationals England was scheduling at the time. 'There are commercial reasons why some things are done a certain way,' he said in a deftly managed English understatement.

England's complaints about the amount of one-day cricket played in Australia could be countered by the fact that its domestic scene is burdened with three one-day competitions; and its complaints about hectic scheduling in Australia could be countered by a brief look at Australia's itinerary for the 1989 Ashes tour, where innumerable county matches were squeezed in between the six Test matches. The provincial matches in England were invariably boring, lacklustre affairs and boredom is as much an enemy of the professional cricketer as constant pressure.

Boredom was a persistent problem for Australia's cricketers in this period, although it was more likely to be suffered at an airport or on a plane than in the middle of a cricket ground. Dean Jones had encountered the problem many times.

According to an article by Rod Nicholson in the *Herald* (Melbourne) in February 1988, Jones had spent those 26 weeks travelling from Melbourne to London to play in the Lord's Bicentenary match for a World XI captained by Allan Border, flown back to Melbourne to prepare to leave for the World Cup in India and Pakistan, then came home for a full season of Tests, one-day games and Sheffield Shield matches. He spent far more time in the air than batting, more time packing, travelling and training than playing.

> It does become tiresome after a while [Jones commented]. Even a trip to Sydney, which in flying time is only an hour, virtually takes a half a day by the time you pack, get to the airport and away at the other end to unpack again. The day/night games can be really tough. You don't get to bed until late – you need time to unwind no matter what time the game finishes – and then you must be up early to travel to the next destination. It is all part of the job, but it is a rather unglamorous part of it. After a while, you just get a sort of elongated jet-lag and it takes a fair bit out of you.

While England resisted the flood of one-day cricket, India, Pakistan and Sri Lanka took to it with relish. This had three major effects. The poor living standards in these countries meant that most cricket lovers could afford to go to only one or two days cricket, so they chose the game that would guarantee them action and a result. Consequently, crowds at Test matches dropped alarmingly as the 1980s drew to a close. That situation seemed to right itself a little in the early to mid-1990s when more attacking tactics led to more results in Test matches.

Another by-product of the rise of one-day cricket and the West Indies' dominance was a decline in spin bowling. With one-day cricket essentially a defensive game, boring medium pacers, mostly of limited ability and less spectator appeal, were favoured ahead of spinners. Pakistan's Abdul Qadir was a great enough leg spinner to resist the trend, but the worldwide decline in spin bowling slowed over rates in Test matches and reduced the variety of play. As the 1990s began, most of the great fast bowlers who dominated the previous decade were nearing the end of their careers; the dominance of pace was fading. The arrival of two fine leg spinners – India's Anil Kumble and Australia's Shane Warne – brought spin back into fashion.

The third consequence of the increase in the one-day game outside Australia was that every international team was playing much more cricket. Australia had introduced this emphasis on one-day cricket and could hardly complain about a similar increase when it toured overseas. The international program became crowded and one-off one-day tournaments to commemorate this or that were added to the more regular programs.

In all, international cricket became a fully professional circuit even if the programming was not fully coordinated. By the mid-1990s, the International Cricket Council (ICC) had still not been able to bring together all the senior playing nations to jointly program a circuit of Tests and one-day games. It had legislated for fines to be imposed for slow over rates – less than 90 a day in a Test – and although of limited effectiveness, this was at least a move in the right direction. As was the introduction in 1991 of ICC-neutral referees and, later, one neutral umpire at Tests and one-day matches and a third to adjudicate some decisions by video replay. One of the main jobs of the referees was to monitor player behaviour and impose fines for those who crossed the line. Although suffering teething problems, the system was a success as was the presence of neutral umpires, eliminating suspicions of home-town bias if not human error.

However, rules for one-day cricket varied from nation to nation and Tests were scheduled in an ad hoc manner. One idea floated at this time was for the ICC to coordinate a four-yearly cycle of Test series with points for home and away wins, draws et cetera, with the top two teams playing off in a series every four years for a World Championship of Test cricket. This would be decided in between the four-yearly World Cup tournament for one-day cricket. By 1995, such a program was still considered too difficult to organise, but it is an idea whose time might come.

Two other issues festered throughout the 1980s – the prevalence and effects of short-pitched pace bowling and the rightful place of South Africa in world cricket.

Although most people outside the West Indies agreed that the dominance of pace bowling slowed the game and lessened its variety, the ICC found it difficult politically to do anything about the problem. The West Indies perfected a game where four fast bowlers were used in rotation all day long with slow over rates to allow each bowler sufficient rest between overs. They also perfected a type of short-pitched delivery aimed between the waist and shoulders of batsmen, which was not strictly a bouncer but which made scoring difficult and injury likely. The constant physical threat often made Test series against the West Indies unpleasant affairs.

Any moves to force the West Indies to change their tactics were met with the argument that such tactics had not been questioned when England and Australia – the two white founding powers of world cricket – had strong pace bowling. After all, argued the West Indians, England – with Harold Larwood as the weapon – invented and unleashed Bodyline in the 1930s, and Australia – with Lillee and the frighteningly fast Jeff Thomson – battered England and the West Indies into submission in the mid-1970s.

The West Indian response to any suggestion of legislative action to curb their fast bowlers was that this was born out of jealousy and, quite possibly, racism from the white power block of England and Australia. This was not unreasonable, either: until 1993, England and Australia had a right of veto on major ICC decisions. With India and Pakistan gaining in stature in world cricket in the 1970s and '80s, the threat of a black-white split hung over cricket politics and change was therefore slowed by diplomatic compromises.

Racism was also the major factor in the South African issue. Banned from Commonwealth and Olympic sport because of its racist apartheid policies, South Africa had not been part of international cricket since the early 1970s. Desperate for some international matches to stay in touch with developments in the game, former Test captain Ali Bacher used what seemed to be an unlimited supply of cash to lure a number of rebel teams to the republic during the 1980s. The establishment banned these players who had turned their backs on official cricket, although in England and Australia there was always an underlying wish among most players and officials that politics be kept out of cricket and their white cousins in South Africa be allowed to play again.

Fortunately for the black people of South Africa, political powers above and beyond the parochial world of cricket dictated policy on this issue, and Australian and English cricket were forced to toe the line. Even so, the bans on the rebel players were neither fully enforced nor severe enough for some observers, and many of these 'rebel' players soon returned to Test cricket.

Before their return and the final ill-judged rebel tour by Mike Gatting's English team in 1990, Bacher damaged English and Australian cricket, particularly the latter during the early years of Border's reign as Australian captain. With genuine reform finally taking place in South Africa, and much of it in sport led by Bacher and his colleagues, the republic was readmitted to world cricket for the 1992 World Cup in Australia.

On the field, one team dominated the 1980s. Australia led the way in changing the programming and content of international cricket and, in a less direct way, also in the way the game was played on the field. After the 5-1 battering by Australia's pace bowlers in 1975-76, the West Indies went home and Deryck Murray and Clive Lloyd decided also to rely on pace, opting for a four-man attack that ruled the cricket world until 3 May 1995, when Mark Taylor's Australian team won the fourth Test at Sabina Park in Kingston, Jamaica, to take that series 2-1. The West Indies lost a series 1-0 in New Zealand in 1979-80, then remained unbeaten for 29 consecutive series, the most comprehensive domination of any period in the game's history.

In the decade, the results of the Test nations were:

Country	Matches	Wins	Draws	Losses	Ties	Win %
West Indies	85	47	28	9	–	55.29%
New Zealand	59	17	27	14	–	28.81%
Pakistan	80	23	44	13	–	28.75%
Australia	97	26	38	32	1	26.80%
England	103	20	44	39	–	19.42%
India	81	10	48	22	1	12.35%
Sri Lanka	29	2	11	16	–	6.89%

England's decline as a world power in Test cricket began, on paper anyway, after the 1985 Ashes win. In the second half of the 1980s, England won one Test series, in Australia in 1986-87, lost seven and drew one. The only nation it failed to lose a series to was newcomer Sri Lanka.

The dominance Border's teams enjoyed over England, which began in 1989, was maintained in 1990-91 and 1993 and continued under Mark Taylor in 1994-95. In fact, it became the most dominant period in Ashes history, with Australia going a record 18 Tests –

*The best of his era: West Indies' Malcolm Marshall was the
most successful bowler in world cricket during the 1980s.*

A great batsman: despite carrying a struggling team for much of the decade,
Allan Border was the most prolific batsman in the game during the 1980s.

from January 1987 to August 1993 – without a loss.

This success rate against England was also enjoyed by the rest of the cricket world. All sorts of reasons were offered for England's poor record, including myopic administration, the poor standard of England's domestic county championship, the mind-numbing repetition of six-days-a-week county cricket, too much one-day cricket between tired and uninspired county teams, the decline of cricket in the schools, the use of too many overseas players in county cricket, the use of too many overseas-born players in the England team and, last but not least, short-sighted selection. Whatever the reasons, theorising about them became a popular pastime for other countries who thoroughly enjoyed the chance to beat England at its own game.

Not surprisingly, the West Indies had three batsmen and three bowlers in the lists of the 10 best performers of the decade. Their opening batsmen, Gordon Greenidge and Desmond Haynes, were there alongside the great Viv Richards. Their fast bowlers were there naturally, led by the one their wicket-keeper, Jeff Dujon, and many of the world's batsmen rated the greatest of a great lot – Malcolm Marshall. Also on the list were Joel Garner and Michael Holding, but the only bowler to surpass Marshall's rate of 5.13 wickets a Test was Richard Hadlee with 5.45.

Dujon once said that Marshall was the best of the Caribbean dynasty because he learned from all of them and could adapt their various styles to the conditions. Marshall, the shortest of all the modern West Indian fast bowlers, took 323 wickets in 63 Tests in the 1980s at the brilliant average of 19.91.

Australia had two bowlers in the list – Geoff Lawson at nine and Dennis Lillee at ten. Lawson had done very well considering a severe back injury which cost him some 10 months out of the game. Lillee retired in 1984, but was so great a bowler that those four years were enough to earn him a mention in the top 10 of the decade. Such was the emphasis on pace and the quality of the pace bowlers around then that Pakistan's Abdul Qadir was the only spinner in this illustrious company.

Australia provided only one batsmen in that list, but at least he topped it. A.R. Border made 7386 runs from his 97 Tests in the 1980s at an average of 55.12. As well, he made 20 centuries, 40 half-centuries and chipped in with 115 catches. For two-thirds of the decade, he did all this in losing teams in which he carried an inordinate amount of responsibility, far more than any other cricketer on either list.

FEAR AND

LOATHING IN
THE CARIBBEAN

A FTER the success of the 1989 Ashes series, Allan Border could afford to look forward with some relish to his first defence of the famous little urn. After a few months off in the winter of 1990, Border was as hyped up as a kid with a belly full of lollies as the next summer approached. In his own words, he was 'so fit, it's a worry', and he considered Australian cricket 'on the threshold'.

Border's enthusiasm was inspired by the challenges of the next seven months. With the Englishmen arriving soon and a series in the Caribbean following, there was a chance Australia could return from the West Indies the following May with the Ashes and the Frank Worrell Trophy in its hands, the latter prize automatically bringing with it the unofficial title of the best team in the world. As well, Border wanted to improve his own batting, not only to satisfy his personal standards and to ensure that his march towards 10,000 Test runs would not take too long, but also to ward off the critics and the challenges from a talented generation of young batsmen flourishing in the Sheffield Shield.

*That winning feeling: Allan Border meets the press after
Australia wins the first Test of the 1990-91 Ashes series.*

England, under new captain Graham Gooch, arrived in mid-October promising a much tougher contest than in '89. But in the early warm-up weeks in Perth, Gooch suffered a badly cut hand at practice that kept him out of the opening Test. It was the first of numerous disasters that befell a team which lost the Test series 3-0, failed to qualify for the finals of the World Series and eventually won only one of 11 first-class matches.

For Australia, the news was all good. Bruce Reid was back from injury and took 27 wickets in four Tests at 16 apiece. Terry Alderman took 16 wickets and Merv Hughes 15 from four games each, while Craig McDermott charged back to the fray with 18 from the final two.

138

Experienced leader: after overcoming self-doubt early in his captaincy career, Allan Border developed into a confident, highly motivated leader.

Matthews did play all five Tests and made a fine 128 in Sydney among his 353 runs at 70.6. His bowling, however, was again modest. David Boon led the batting with support from Matthews, Border and, in the final two games, Mark Waugh. The younger of the twins replaced his older brother for the fourth Test after a long apprenticeship in Shield and county cricket. Steve took 43 innings to make his first Test century. Mark took a couple of delightful hours on the first day of his first Test match. His 138 was a gem, full of the grace and easy strokeplay the Adelaide crowd had hoped to see.

That Australia could bring in a batsman of such obvious class for his debut while England had to rely for runs on two veterans,

Gooch and Gower, nearing the end of their careers reflected the relative health of the two nation's games.

In 1988-89, the West Indies had toughened Border's team before it left for the '89 Ashes tour. This time, the pattern was reversed as England encouraged, falsely or not, Australian confidence before the toughest challenge: a tilt at the West Indies on their home turf. Viv Richards was nearing the end of a great career, as were Malcolm Marshall and Gordon Greenidge, but Richards promised that his team had a few more punches left. By the end of the series, Australia headed to Bermuda for a week of R & R well and truly punch-drunk – and still without the Frank Worrell Trophy.

After Viv Richards's burst at Bob Simpson at the end of the fourth Test in Barbados, the cricket boards of the West Indies and Australia parried statements and demands back and forth like seasoned diplomats going through a rough patch in relations. Despite the loss in Barbados, which ended Australia's chances of winning the series, the Australian players were able to see the more humorous side of the Richards-Simpson affair. Tapes of Richards's press conference became prized possessions and several players asked one of the Australian journalists travelling with the team for a private replay.

That born performer, Mike Whitney, spotted the most potential in the affair and, on a tape-recorder on which he was keeping a diary of the tour, Whitney copied the Richards tirade. Over the next day or two, he studied it closely, perfecting his already impressive Richards impersonation. A few days later, a team meeting was about to begin. Whitney, wearing a black stocking on his head and carrying a white handkerchief similar to the one with which Richards often wiped his sweating brow when under media interrogation, ensured he was the last to arrive. Simpson was just starting to address his troops when Whitney came in, held up an imperious hand and, in an impressive Antiguan accent with only the barest hint of Coogee, said: 'Hold it a minute. I got a few tings I want to say first.'

Whitney started on Simpson, performing word for word Richards's speech on the coach. Then Whitney went around the room, criticising Border for being a former great batsman who could no longer hit the ball off the wicket square, Boon for mumbling suspected abuse from under his helmet at short leg and even physio Errol Alcott for the cool way he sat at the end of the hotel bar smoking a cigarette, sipping his favourite white wine and soda and checking out the scene. It was a great performance, relieving a lot of tension and drawing forth a fine ovation. Only someone with Whitney's charm and natural performance skills could have pulled it off.

Apart from that amusing half-hour there was little to laugh about on this tour. The cricket was probably the most intense any of the Australians had ever played. They had gone to the West Indies saying in public that they believed they had a very good chance of winning. Richards and his team, realising they were facing a better-than-usual challenge, lifted after a poor showing in the one-day series. The intensity of the play, spiced by short-pitched fast bowling from both teams, spilled over into relations off the field and the series ended up a bitter, ugly affair.

On the field there was the infamous clash between two volatile, aggressive and proud characters, Desmond Haynes and Ian Healy, in which Haynes threatened Healy by walking behind the stumps towards the Australian keeper and lifting his bat menacingly. What lay behind this incident was that Healy had become increasingly angry at Haynes's sledging of Border. As had been their tactic for many years, the West Indies targeted the opposition captain, even such a tough campaigner as Border. The West Indies believed by now that their bowlers had Border's measure and so they attacked him verbally as well as physically.

In an article on sledging in the March 1995 edition of *Inside Edge*, Border made the point that the West Indies were as guilty as the Australians, just more subtle in the way they delivered their taunts. Border wrote: 'I've never made this comment public before but, in one Test, I heard this voice almost from my hip pocket. It was Desi at bat-pad – "Please, Curtly, take this man out, one good bouncer, that's all I pray for". He literally had his hands together. I never think anything of stuff like that. Have a dash at a West Indian, though, and they always seem to take major offence.'

After being hit in the face by a Courtney Walsh bouncer in an early tour game, Craig McDermott was labelled a coward by the West Indians, but the pace bowler responded by mixing it with the West Indians bouncer for bouncer.

The Australians became incensed when the West Indians failed to recall Dean Jones after he was given out run out off a no-ball that had bowled him in the second innings of the second Test at Georgetown, Guyana. Having heard the rattle of his stumps rather than the no-ball call, Jones left his crease to walk off and

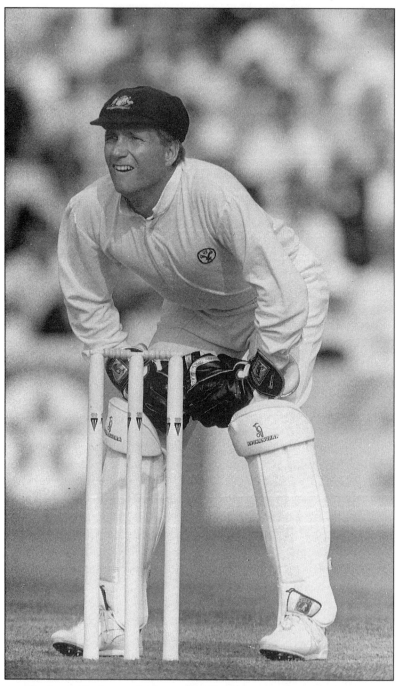

In the thick of it: wicketkeeper Ian Healy was as uncompromising a competitor as his captain and clashed several times with West Indian players.

could not recover it once everyone on the field realised a no-ball had been called and thought a run out was possible. Border, at the other end, shouted at Jones to get back to his crease, but Carl Hooper beat Jones and broke the stumps. Umpire Clyde Cumberbatch incorrectly sent Jones to an early shower.

The pivotal incident in the Test in Guyana was not Jones's run out on the fourth day, but Richie Richardson's brilliant 182 on the second afternoon and the third morning. Australia had made a slow but useful 348 in its first innings and Richardson had come in at 1/10 in the third over. This was a critical moment in the series.

During the first week of the 1995 tour to the West Indies, ABC Radio's Jim Maxwell asked Ian Healy whether he expected a decisive moment to arise in that series. 'There'll be a few,' Healy replied. 'You just have to recognise it. If you don't, the other team will take it.'

Healy was speaking from experience. He was behind the stumps in Guyana in 1991 when Richie Richardson seized the decisive moment of that series.

Australia had won the one-day series 4-1 and the first Test had been drawn after rain had ruined any prospect of a result. With Australia on the verge of a breakthrough on the second day in Guyana, Richardson followed decades of West Indian tradition: he launched a manic counterattack that swung the game and the series to the West Indies. By stumps that night, the total was 1/226 with Richardson on 114 and Haynes on 87. Richardson had scored 106 off the 41 overs of the final session. Eventually, the pair added 297, breaking the Australians' spirit.

Richardson's was a brutal assault, begun under pressure with the game in the balance – a great post-war innings. It was also the type of innings the Australians were never able to produce. Both Ian and Greg Chappell were there commentating for Channel Nine, and both thought the differing responses to the same situation from Richardson and the Australians exposed the marked differences in the thinking of the two teams.

Having seen the West Indies for a long time now [Ian Chappell said], I'm sure you can't beat them by sitting back and waiting for them to come off the rails. You've got to attack them – sensibly, and great captains know when the sensible time has come. When that opportunity is there, you have to attack, to push them off the rails. And under Border and Simpson, Australia never did that. We never

Reaching the heights: David Boon celebrates his tenth Test century, probably his best because it was made against the West Indies in Jamaica during a fiercely contested 1991 series.

took the West Indies on and there was never a better example of that than in Guyana in '91.

I'd never seen the West Indies so wobbly after that one-day series. Curtly Ambrose was the only bowler who had withstood the Australians' attacking batting and the West Indian fielding was abysmal. They were in disarray. To me that was the perfect time to keep the momentum going by attacking them again. I thought the Australians were very conservative in their batting in the first innings and it was almost as though Richie, having seen the Australians' attitude with the West Indies on the ropes, came out to bat thinking: 'Well, these bastards haven't taken the thing by the throat so I will.' That innings changed the whole momentum of the tour and that was the result of the conservative approach of Border and Simpson.

It was as if the Australians thought: 'Well, we might just have these guys. Let's see what happens from here.' You can get away with that approach against ordinary teams because they'll make mistakes. Against good teams you have to let them know you know they're wobbly.

That final point is perhaps the most telling. Ian Chappell showed in his captaincy, and continues to show in his commentary and articles, an appreciation for the psychological drama of Test cricket. There are times in Test matches when the tide of events can turn either way. The player and the team that can see that first, and then have the courage to announce to their opponents that they have seen it and are acting on it, usually prevail.

Chappell captained like that, but Border rarely did, which was why Chappell always considered Border naive tactically. Border did not need to grasp the moment against the poor England teams of the late 1980s and early 1990s. Against the West Indies, he could never quite bring himself to risk all and go for broke because the West Indies were capable of exacting the highest price.

One of the more colourful products of this tour was a book by a Sydney-based freelance writer, Roland Fishman, called *Calypso Cricket*. Fishman was an acquaintance of Greg Matthews who helped him gain more access to the Australian team than the regular press enjoyed. Fishman's book caused a minor storm by quoting married Australian players talking about their sexual adventures during the tour. I was one of several reviewers to savage Fishman because he never warned the players that everything said in his presence, even very personal chat late at night in a secluded bar, was fodder for his book. Those reservations aside, Fishman did gather some interesting insights, mainly from his conversations with players, press and television commentators.

In the book, Fishman recounts a conversation late in the tour with Greg Chappell where the latter gave his views as to what went wrong with the Australians' campaign.

> To succeed at this level you have to be prepared to take chances and fail [Chappell said]. We had our chances to win by playing positive cricket. We erred on the side of being too defensive and paid the consequences. We have to learn to be more positive and more aggressive. We took some options – particularly in Barbados [the fourth Test, before which the West Indies led 1-0] where we picked only three bowlers – a strategy which was designed to avoid losing rather than achieving a win. When you limit your chances of winning, you increase your chances of losing. I have the feeling they didn't really believe they could win the series.

Chappell was talking about that familiar 'fear of failure' that so motivated Border throughout his career and that he had discussed in a magazine article in the weeks before the 1984-85 season, the season that turned his cricket world upside down.

Chappell went on to discuss another familiar facet of the Border-Simpson era: the tendency of their team to fall victim to negative thinking, to blame outside factors for internal failings.

> I believe that they are a team that readily takes on the view that the whole world is against them, and that is very dangerous. They allow themselves to think that all the bad decisions are going against them and the whole world is their enemy, and so they withdraw into their shell. They don't mix with the opposition; they don't talk to the press; they don't talk to the television people. I think it breeds negative thinking which is so dangerous. If you expect the worst, that is exactly what you get. Negative thinking leads to negative results.

Fishman agreed with Chappell's point about the Australians retreating into their 'shell'. The press, usually the first outsiders to notice the early symptoms of this syndrome, and often the first to be blamed for something, call it 'the siege mentality'. Fishman had noticed that the Australians had begun the tour in a pleasant, friendly frame of mind but changed their mood as results on the field went against them. The press assured him this was not uncommon.

The after-play drinks both managements had agreed would happen more often than not fell away as relations deteriorated. After losing the one-day series and realising the Australians were capable of mounting a genuine challenge in the Test series, the West Indies' demeanour changed. They did not take kindly to being beaten and soon were not available for a few drinks after a day's play.

After winning the second Test in Guyana, the third was also drawn because of time lost to rain. The fourth in Barbados was won by the West Indies by a whopping 343 runs even though they were bowled out in the first innings for only 149. It seemed that every time Australia played itself into a strong position, the West Indies, like a truly great team which expected to win, was able to fight its way out of strife.

Australia, yet again, won a consolation victory in the fifth Test after the series had been decided. It was a win that proved two things. First, that the Australians could relax and play attacking cricket only when the main issue had been decided – perhaps it was easier because the fear of failure had faded. Second, when the Australians, led by centuries to Mark Waugh and Mark Taylor, batted with more dash in Antigua, they put their side in a winning position. But the lessons, such as they were, were learned too late.

For Australia, McDermott was superb, as fast and as formidable as any of the West Indian pace men. But the other Australian fast bowlers struggled. Alderman's selection proved as ill-judged as many critics had predicted, and Bruce Reid, on whom many hopes had rested, never seemed to recover mentally and, presumably, physically from an uncomfortable flight over which apparently aggravated his dodgy back. Of the batsmen, Taylor and Mark Waugh did well, while Boon made one century; Jones and Border only one half-century each. Steve Waugh, like Matthews and Whitney, played only two Tests.

At the final presentation ceremony in Antigua, the president of the West Indies Board of Control and a former great player, Clyde Walcott, mentioned his disappointment at the poor relations between the teams. In many ways, this series was a low point, possibly a fitting farewell to the old system in which umpires had to control player behaviour as well as everything else. Four months later, the ICC sent its first referee to oversee a Test match.

This series also said much about the Border-Simpson era. The Australians were talented, tough and feisty but unable in the end to back their ability with achievement as did the West Indies. Faced with the ultimate challenge in modern cricket, the Australians faltered, choosing caution when they had to dare to win.

As the respected West Indian journalist Tony Cozier wrote

in his report of the series for *Wisden Cricketers' Almanack 1992*: 'The main difference between the teams was in attitude. The Australians consistently erred on the side of caution; the West Indians, especially in adversity, chose the option of counterattack.'

That is the difference between a great team and a very good one.

TROUBLE

AT HOME

I T was an unusual sight. Alone with his thoughts about the coming day's play, Allan Border stood, bat in hand, on the Adelaide Oval pitch. He wandered up and down the wicket for a few minutes, distractedly inspecting its surface and hoping his bowlers could finish India off and so seal the 1991-92 Test series. It was Wednesday, 29 January 1992, Geoff Marsh's last day as a Test cricketer.

Border was the first man onto the field for the warm-up that final morning of the fourth Test. He had things on his mind. Coach and selector Bob Simpson had warned Border the night before that the selectors were about to drop Marsh and Mark Waugh. Early on the Wednesday morning, Simpson told Marsh and then Border that the decision was official.

It was 9.20 am when Border wandered out to the wicket square. The Indian team had not yet arrived and the ground was quiet and peaceful, empty except for a few ground staff, a couple of security guards and a few dozen elderly spectators following their time-honoured practice of getting to the ground early to secure

Good and faithful servant: the selectors' decision to drop Geoff Marsh during the 1991-92 series against India deeply angered the Australian captain.

their favourite seats. And across the other side, a man and a boy were setting up their sun-shade on the hill for what was to be a dramatic last day, on and off the field.

After inspecting the pitch, Border joined the first few players to follow him onto the ground. Not long after, Bob Simpson gathered the team together for the brief pep talk he gave them before each day's play. Instead of the usual resumé of the previous day's efforts and a rev-up for the coming one, Simpson shocked everyone by announcing that Marsh and Mark Waugh had been dropped for the fifth Test in Perth in a few days' time.

It was a risky move by Simpson. Marsh had been vice-captain

for years and one of the original members of Border's team when the long haul out of the depths had begun in the previous series against India in Australia in 1985-86. Marsh had asked Simpson to tell the team of the selectors' decision, but Simpson might have been better advised to hold off until the end of the Test match. He must have known there was a chance it would put the players off their game. India was 0/31 chasing 372 to win, unlikely given their uneven batting form that summer, but it was still a Test that had to be won by Australia. As it was, Border's side dropped several catches that day – Mark Waugh offending on one occasion – before winning by 38 runs.

The news of the selectors' decision hit the players hard. Jaws dropped; eyes looked down. The senior players were very upset. Their careers had coincided with Marsh's 50 Tests and they thought Waugh the most naturally gifted player in the team.

Simpson urged them to win the game for the two, but that sentiment had little impact. He then told them that he had done his best at the selection table to save Marsh and Waugh, but that in the end the panel had decided there had to be changes after a summer of scant progress.

Waugh, the selectors thought, needed a kick in the backside to force him to put more value on his wicket. Marsh, no matter how popular and pivotal a figure in the early days, was badly out of form. There had been talk during the summer that the selectors had become too conservative, that it was too difficult for talented young batsmen to break into the team even though it was widely felt that the Australian batting line-up was coasting.

Most of the players offered a sympathetic pat on the shoulder to the pair before they all lined up for a few fielding drills. It was a sloppy session. The usual noisy banter was missing and Waugh, a brilliant fieldsman, threw several wild returns to keeper Healy.

After a desultory net session, the players began to shower and change for the start of play. By this time, Border's mood had darkened. He could not accept the selectors' decision. About 10 minutes before 11 o'clock, the twelfth man, Paul Reiffel, emerged from the showers. He was the last out and was taking his time as he needed only to be changed and ready as his teammates took the field. Reiffel is a shy, self-effacing man. He was stunned at what followed.

'You better get your whites on quickly,' Border called across to Reiffel.

'What?'

'You better get your whites on quickly.'

'Why?' asked Reiffel.

'Because I fuckin' said so,' snapped the skipper. 'I'm staying in here for a while.'

Border was furious at the dropping of his old mate Marsh and he had decided to ring chairman of selectors Laurie Sawle to speak his mind. Simpson came over to Border to suggest he should lead his team onto the field.

'Fuck off,' Border said.

As Marsh led the team out to start the day's play, Border found Sawle's number and rang him from the dressing-room phone. Sawle was at home in Perth, settling in to watch play on television. He had noticed Border was not on the field and had assumed, like thousands around the country, that the captain was ill.

'As soon as I answered the phone I knew he wasn't crook,' Sawle recalled. 'He gave me a real rocket. I had to be conciliatory, but I had to be firm. He thought I could get the panel to reconsider, which I wasn't prepared to do. I told him it had been a unanimous decision. Eventually he accepted it but I wouldn't say he burst into laughter.'

Border finally called Reiffel in and took his place about 20 minutes after play had begun. After a tense struggle, Australia took its unbeatable 3-0 lead. Yet it was a subdued dressing-room that greeted India's Kapil Dev and Manoj Prabhakar when they came in to offer their congratulations.

Later, as the team packed up ready for its flight to Perth that night, Border told the players he was not coming. He was still fuming. As the players began to file out of the rooms to board the team bus, most walked over to Border, expressed their support for his stand and shook his hand.

It was only as the team headed out to the airport that someone remarked to David Boon that he had not led the team in its traditional victory song. 'Forget it,' said Boon. 'We made an executive decision. We'll sing it in Perth.'

Of the many 'dummy spits' his alter ego as 'Captain Grumpy' had perpetrated, this was a double-stunner from Border – first, refusing to take the field with the team and then refusing to travel with it as planned. Simpson addressed the team on the bus and told them Border was acting childishly. Again, Simpson had chosen the wrong words and the wrong time. His players were not impressed; their loyalty was to their captain, and they would not hear otherwise.

As soon as the story broke, critics began calling for Border's head. He had gone too far this time, they argued: insubordination, dereliction of duty, open criticism of the selectors. He had been in the job too long and, besides, the team had gone stale and needed new blood. There were also stories in the press saying the ACB was furious with Border and that he might be sacked. Border said he had had a prior commitment in Adelaide on the final night of the game, although later, the ACB's Graham Halbish said: 'It was agreed that it was best at the time for him to have 24 hours to himself.'

What the ACB, Simpson or manager Ian McDonald did not know for certain was whether Border would be on a flight to Perth the next day. David Boon was hurriedly given the vice-captaincy and was put on standby in case Border did not appear.

Sawle, a member of the ACB as well as chairman of selectors, looks back on the episode with no ill feeling and says the ACB would never have sacked Border, although it did expect him to return to the job promptly, which he did.

'One of Allan's greatest attributes – and it's to his everlasting credit – is his loyalty,' Sawle said. 'He was loyal to the point of being over-loyal. In that instance in Adelaide, he had around him a group of guys who'd brought back the Ashes, brought Australian cricket back to being highly regarded. Swamp [Marsh] as vice-captain had been one of his main people.'

Border later explained: 'You lose your right-hand man who's been an integral part of our resurgence over four years and it goes deeper than pure statistics. The guy just gives so much to the team on and off the field. He is a very valued member of the side and very close to me personally so it's a particularly tough one.'

The episode in Adelaide was not the only problem during what ended up being a difficult and somewhat unsuccessful summer. India offered only fair opposition, mainly because their batting was fragile and Australia's pace bowling strong. Australia won the first, second, fourth and fifth Tests, while India was robbed of a likely win in Sydney by rain.

This series was the first to be presided over by an ICC match referee and to include a new rule that limited bowlers to one bouncer per batsman per over. Although there were many reservations about such a strict limit on bouncers, the referee system worked well enough. Nevertheless, umpiring controversies marred the series. In Melbourne, the Indians were upset at several decisions, especially one in which Dean Jones appeared to be guilty of handling the ball or obstructing the field – or both. Then, in Adelaide, Australia was granted eight leg-before decisions to India's two. As *Wisden* noted in its series report, Indian complaints were not without reason. Sadly, former Indian captain and batting great Sunil Gavaskar criticised the Australian umpiring so strongly that some of the umpires instituted legal action against him.

Bruce Reid broke down again during the third Test, but McDermott, Hughes and Whitney prospered. David Boon led the batting, feasting as ever on his favourite opponents. Dean Jones struggled and could easily have been dropped for the fifth Test instead of Mark Waugh. Jones faltered against an in-form Kapil Dev who made up for reduced pace with skilful swing and seam and intelligent assessment of batsmen's weaknesses.

As they had been against class bowlers such as Richard Hadlee and the West Indians, Jones's technical and temperamental weaknesses were exposed by a world-class bowler. He saved his spot in the Australian side by making a century in the fifth Test. Again, he had played his best innings of a Test series at the end after the result had been decided. The Australian selectors noticed this and began to wonder whether Jones was really contributing to the team as well as his career Test average of 45 suggested. His days as a Test batsman were numbered.

Two gifted young cricketers appeared in this series. India's 18-year-old prodigy, Sachin Tendulkar, made two centuries and averaged 46 for the series. His magnificent 148 not out in Sydney made him the youngest player to score a Test century in Australia. Tendulkar's confidence, poise and balanced footwork spoke of a batting genius. When his Sydney innings ended, Merv Hughes ran across the ground and threw his arm around the teenager to offer congratulations and, it seemed, a joke. Tendulkar threw his head back and smiled broadly.

The other young player who made his debut in Sydney was a chubby, 22-year-old leg spinner from the St Kilda Club in Melbourne: Shane Keith Warne. Australia had not had a top-line leg spinner for many years and the selectors were desperate to find one before the West Indies arrived the following summer. Australian cricket was not going to lose to the West Indies again without knowing whether the cheeky blond had genuine talent. After only seven first-class games, Warne was chosen for his first Test. At that stage, he had taken five wickets in an innings once in a first-class match and never in Australia. In fact, he had not even managed it in first-grade cricket in Melbourne.

*India's aristocrat: the great all-rounder, Kapil Dev, still caused
the Australian batsmen problems during the 1991-92 series.*

*Batting prodigy: only 18 years old, India's batting genius,
Sachin Tendulkar, produced the innings of the 1991-92
summer with his 148 not out in the Sydney Test.*

The experience of bowling against batsmen raised on quality spin made Warne wonder whether he could make a go of Test cricket. In his two Tests that summer, he took 1/228. Critics thought he had been sent to the top too early and that his career had been badly damaged. Yet, despite those figures, Australian cricket's tradition of promoting youthful talent and fast-tracking wrist spinners would soon be repaid a thousandfold. No one knew it at the time, but in Warne, Australia had found a great spinner. Three years later, Tendulkar would be rated by many as the best batsman in the world; Warne, the best bowler.

The Border incident in Adelaide signalled a cooling in relations between the captain and the coach that would become apparent several times over the next few summers. This period was one of stagnation. The Australian batting was too conservative, as if the players had settled into secure jobs and were content to do just enough to stay employed. Relations between some of the leading figures seemed to be going stale. The team needed a lift.

A BAD

MONTH

THE 1992 World Cup was going to be the biggest, brightest and best yet. The fifth tournament was the first to be held in Australasia, the first to be played in coloured clothes with white balls, the first to include games played under lights and the largest, with nine teams playing a total of 39 matches, compared to the first event in England in 1975 when eight teams played only 15 matches. It was also the first World Cup to include South Africa.

In fact, the only exclusion from this huge party seemed to be one of the two host nations and defending champions – Australia. The home team won only four of its eight games and so failed to qualify for the semi-finals after enjoying years of success in its home-grown competition, the World Series.

The '92 World Cup has to be rated a success, yet Australia's role in it attracted a great deal of criticism. The opening dinner in Sydney was a shemozzle, held in a poor venue with an unimpressive guest speaker. The bits-and-pieces television coverage annoyed viewers; the apparently patriotic and chivalrous Graham

157

Gooch and Ian Botham walked out of a dinner in Melbourne when a local comedian dared to impersonate their Queen; South Africa was robbed of a reasonable run-chase in its game against England when the rules for rain interruption were exposed as unfair; and Pakistan captain Imran Khan took no little delight in calling this World Cup the worst organised of the five he had attended.

However, what pleased most of the visiting teams was simply that the hot favourites played so poorly. Australia was unable to adapt its highly regimented style of play to counter the unorthodox tactics of opposing teams who had obviously given the tournament far more thought than the home side. Here was further evidence that the Australians had become complacent, that the team had gone stale and needed revamping and that its leadership was too conservative.

The Australian team gathered in Sydney for the opening ceremonies and a warm-up match against the strong New South Wales team played at North Sydney Oval on Tuesday, 18 February. New South Wales was the best domestic one-day team in the competition, and although the match was friendly, there was an edge of rivalry. There was little affection between Bob Simpson and many people in New South Wales cricket, and thus something of a philosophical distance between the successful New South Wales set-up and the national team.

An example of that distance came to light after the one-off Test against New Zealand in Wellington early in 1991. Off spinner Peter Taylor played for Australia in that game, but a few days later was made twelfth man for New South Wales for the Sheffield Shield final against Queensland in Sydney; New South Wales preferred off-spinning all-rounder Greg Matthews. Strictly, it could be argued that young leg spinner Adrian Tucker took Taylor's place as New South Wales wanted variety in its spin attack rather than two off spinners. But it was still extraordinary that the nation's number one spinner could not command a place in the New South Wales team.

Geoff Lawson, the New South Wales captain and, at the time, probably the best captain in the country, had made little secret of his lack of regard for the Australian coach. The feeling was mutual. Most of Lawson's players knew that Simpson often criticised the adventurous, attacking style of play which, under Lawson and coach Steve Rixon, had taken New South Wales to the top in both limited overs and four-day cricket. New South Wales had set the agenda at state level and by 1994-95, every state but Tasmania had adopted a similar approach. As did the Australian team after one of Lawson's players, Mark Taylor, took over as captain from Border in 1994. In 1992, though, at a time when the Australian team under Border and Simpson seemed to be short of new ideas, the tactical freshness of the New South Wales team made for a striking comparison.

The match ended in an exciting tie, with New South Wales pride endorsed. The next day, the Australians flew to Auckland for a windswept warm-up game to be followed on the Saturday by the opening game of the tournament, against New Zealand at the angular Eden Park. Before that first match, Rod Nicholson, in the *Herald Sun*, broke the news that Simpson had just been reappointed Australian team coach for another two-year term. Simpson's contract was not due to expire until June so the news caught most people by surprise – as surprised as when, a few days earlier, Simpson had questioned Simon O'Donnell's contributions to Australia's previous one-day successes.

In his negotiations with the ACB, Simpson had argued that he and his team would not be able to concentrate fully on the World Cup while his future was in doubt. If only the players could have used that argument with the selectors. To the players and other close observers, it seemed ludicrous that Simpson's performance in the World Cup would not be taken into account when assessing his future once the existing contract had expired. International cricketers have the selectors' axe hanging over their heads all the time; their futures are judged largely on their recent performances. In this case, their coach successfully negotiated a cosier system. Perhaps it was just as well, too, given the Australians' form during the tournament.

Noisy, parochial Eden Park was full to capacity on the following Saturday as the gentlemanly John Wright and the bulky Rod Latham walked out to open the batting against every New Zealander's favourite enemy, Australia. At 2/13, New Zealand looked set to fulfil expectations by losing to the most successful one-day team in the world. Enter the captain Martin Crowe, who made 100 not out off 134 balls in a masterly display. Knowing that the short square boundaries would give him maximum value for cross-bat shots, Crowe was especially savage on any short deliveries. That innings was Crowe's only orthodox offering for the day.

With Australia chasing 249 to win, Crowe stunned his opponents and the crowd by opening the bowling with the modest

Simple, really: New Zealand captain Martin Crowe explains the unorthodox tactics that helped his team beat favourites Australia in the opening match of the 1992 World Cup.

off spin of Dipak Patel. He followed that by using his bevy of nondescript medium pacers in short spells, sometimes only two overs at a time. Although they all bowled in a similar style, the constant changing never allowed the Australians to settle into a rhythm. David Boon made 100 off three fewer balls than Crowe, but New Zealand won by 37 runs. The 1992 World Cup had begun with a major upset.

The win was a triumph for Crowe, who had masterminded the daring tactics, as well as for one-day cricket, which had become all too predictable under the measured game plan of the Australians. Crowe had done the tournament a favour by breaking the conventions, creating a debate about one-day tactics and throwing the competition wide open.

Crowe had also exposed the Australians. A combination of poor pre-tournament planning and preparation, a general lack of form and an inability to adapt to new tactics sent Australia into a tailspin. The tensions between Border and Simpson which had become apparent during the Test series flared under the pressures of failure in front of expectant home crowds.

New Zealand made its merry way into the semi-finals. Crowe often opened the batting with big-hitting, left-hander Mark Greatbatch, who set about thumping sixes from the first over as, thousands of kilometres away at another venue, the Australians were pushing increasingly uncertain singles.

After the loss to New Zealand, Border and Simpson along with Marsh – the selectors for the tournament – expressed faith in their previously successful tactic of building scores gradually, taking lots of singles and using the steady Marsh and the more adventurous Boon as contrasting openers.

Before the second match, against South Africa in Sydney, Border was guarded. He harboured too many memories of past losses to foolishly predict the next result, although he said he did not see any reason to radically alter Australia's tactics at that stage. 'Maybe we are predictable, but we've been successful. Until that changes, we'll keep doing the same things.'

Simpson had no doubts. 'We're not going to lose two,' he declared. The newly re-appointed coach would regret those words.

Australia lost to South Africa in the republic's first international match in Australia for 28 years. A one-run win against India in Brisbane gave Border's side some breathing space, but a loss to England in Sydney confirmed the pattern, even though the home side conceded tactical ground by opening the batting with Tom

Moody, a powerful hitter. In the end, the Australians did not qualify for the semi-finals, despite trying seven different batting line-ups in eight games.

After the loss to South Africa, Simpson was furious. As the squad members sat slumped in front of their lockers, he stood at the foot of a small set of stairs leading to the back changing-room and launched a strong attack on their performance. It went something like this: 'It's about time we had some home truths. I've saved all your careers at some stage and you owe me. You owe me better than this. You owe the people of Australia better than this.'

Not surprisingly, the players were not impressed with such a naked display of the coach/selector's power over them.

To the media, Simpson tried to save face: 'It's not our thinking that needs revamping. It's the fact that we've wavered from what's made us a great one-day side. One of the interesting things is that we've been done by two teams who have copied us totally and utterly.'

Like most of his colleagues, Patrick Smithers in the *Age* was bemused. Of Simpson's last comment he wrote:

> . . . He sounded like an old Russian party chief clinging to an outdated ideology. (Besides which, no one could remember Australia opening its bowling with a spinner or rotating medium pacers in two-over shifts, as Martin Crowe did in Auckland.) Simpson's response to Australia's woeful start to the tournament has been nothing short of bizarre. His statements detracting from Simon O'Donnell's contribution to the side look even more out of order now than they were at the time. How Australia could do with O'Donnell now. Australian policy seems to be based on a series of compromises between Simpson's essentially conservative thinking and the more dynamic approach of some of his fellow selectors.

Analyses and recriminations poured forth. Rod Nicholson of the *Sun* noted the burn-out some of the Australians suffered because of their crowded schedules, worsened in that summer by the ACB's contractual obligation to Channel Nine to continue its three-team World Series one-day competition before the demanding World Cup. Nicholson wrote of 'the fear of failure' and the insecurity that had begun to plague the Australian team after the dropping of Marsh and Mark Waugh during the summer and of Dean Jones during the World Series. 'The leadership is the burning question,' he wrote, addressing Border's position but not Simpson's.

Robert Craddock in the *Courier-Mail* saw things from a broader perspective. After Australia's win over the West Indies in the final match, he wrote: 'Criticism of the side's preparation does not reflect well on the performance of coach Bob Simpson who was recently reappointed for two years.'

From midway through the tournament, Simpson seemed to retreat to the background while Border did his best to explain the debacle to the cricket media. On top of that pressure, Border was annoyed about unfounded rumours that he was about to retire or, more fancifully still, be sacked. The several television crews which approached him unannounced at various airports to ask about retirement were met by 'Captain Grumpy' in full fury.

Anger at sections of the media was not restricted to the captain. The coach at one stage berated a photographer from the *Age* for the paper's use on its back page that morning of a smiling West Indian at training the day before.

In a column in Britain's *Today* newspaper, Ian Chappell called the Australians 'world-class duffers' and criticised Border's negative pre-tournament attitude and his delegation of leadership duties to Simpson. 'If you keep repeating that the World Cup will be hard to win and you don't deserve favouritism, someone is going to believe it.'

Then Chappell queried the team set-up in which Simpson had such influence.

The players bat, bowl and field . . . a coach's contribution in cricket is minimal. About the biggest effect the coach can have at that level is on the players' mental approach. By allowing a coach to perform some of his duties, Border has failed his team. It is the captain's job to lead from the front, especially when the team are struggling. If Allan wants to stay as a successful captain of Australia he has to grab the reins firmly in two hands, politely put Simpson in his place and get on with the job of leading his team back to their confident best.

Just why Border was never able to alter the team structure to reassert the primacy of the Australian captaincy and reduce Simpson's power, only he knows. Those close to him believe it is something that, in the end, he regretted not trying.

Border probably thought he had weakened his negotiating position to some extent by his reaction to Marsh's being dropped earlier that season. This was also the view of the pro-Simpson press, which seemed to have turned against Border. Simpson's reappointment ahead of schedule on the eve of the first World Cup match suggested the coach enjoyed strong support at board level. Yet, if Border had been more politically adventurous and it had come down to a political fight between the coach and the captain for the ACB's support, the board would surely have sided with Border.

The ACB greatly appreciated Border's loyalty and all the work he had done to rebuild the team. As well, sacking such a popular figure would have turned the paying public against the game's anonymous, grey-suited administrators, always easy targets in such a situation. Some senior board people might have viewed Border in a less complimentary way than the public, but they knew he deserved better than to be dumped while the coach carried on regardless. Of the two, Border had been indispensable; Simpson, an influential assistant.

As well, Simpson had always been a shrewd political operator with a fierce survival instinct, and, like all the players, Border knew this. If Simpson was to be shifted, it would take some doing. The pair was never close personally, with Border consistently describing their double act as 'a working relationship'. Border, never a political animal, seemed to have decided early on that he would concentrate on his batting and his team's work on the field – the things he knew best – and leave the rest to Simpson, the other selectors, manager Ian McDonald, the ACB and the fates.

Australia's fall from grace in the 1992 World Cup delighted the other cricket nations. Having had to come to Australia often and play what they considered was far too much one-day cricket, the likes of England were delighted the Australians had been embarrassed in front of their home crowds.

Under the headline 'Oz nightmare ends in a row', Britain's *Daily Mirror* noted:

> *No one has been left with more egg on his face than Australian team manager Bob Simpson, who had the arrogance to declare that Australia 'would not lose another game' following their first defeat by New Zealand. He has kept a remarkably low profile during the downfall of his team, apparently happy to allow skipper Border to take the brunt of the flak from a disillusioned Australian sporting public.*

As ever, Border coped with the attack as he played the world's best bowlers in a tough situation – standing his ground with honest

*Wear and tear: Allan Border shows the strain during
Australia's disappointing 1992 World Cup campaign.*

defence and commendable courage. Accepting his share of the
blame and hinting at the poor efforts of others, he told the press:

*New Zealand captain Martin Crowe sat down and really
worked it out pretty well, whereas we just didn't really prepare at all.
We had just been playing a particular pattern and we didn't really sit
down and prepare a strategy for the Cup – that is where Martin had
one up on us. We pushed the panic button with the team after our
first loss against New Zealand and never had a settled side.*

Although Border was prepared to concede the failings of the
World Cup campaign, Simpson has never wavered from the

comments he made after the loss to South Africa. He still believes it was the players' poor execution of a sound game plan which cost Australia the Cup, not the team's inability to adapt to new tactics from its opponents.

When I interviewed Simpson for this book, during the fourth Test against England in Adelaide in January 1995, he said of the 1992 World Cup:

> We played poorly. In retrospect we should have gone into a camp. At that stage, we were very confident of our one-day cricket. We were playing beautiful cricket. We'd been dominant in one-day cricket for about four years. We got into that competition and we did everything we said we wouldn't do. We lost totally our game plan. It was only towards the end that we started to play well. If we'd got to the semis, I'm sure we'd have won the whole bloody thing. Pakistan only got in because of a washed-out match against England in Adelaide. We just played poor cricket. Perhaps they [the players] tightened up.

New Zealand and South Africa were popular semi-finalists but not strong enough to beat the top two teams, Pakistan and England. The final was played in front of an official world record one-day crowd of 87,182 at the Melbourne Cricket Ground on 25 March. Imran Khan, playing in his fifth World Cup over 20 years, made a shrewd and steadying 72 off 110 balls, helping his side to 6/249. Although Pakistan's batting had been a combination of measured accumulation and brilliant late-innings stroke play, their bowling broke one-day convention by attacking full throttle for wickets rather than trying to wear down England's batsmen by concentrating on line and length.

There were three memorable moments which had the massive stadium roaring. First, leg spinner Mushtaq Ahmed tortured a confused Graeme Hick before finally trapping him leg before with a perfect wrong 'un. Then Imran brought his best bowler, Man of the Match Wasim Akram, back into the attack to end the middle-order resistance of Allan Lamb. From around the wicket and off his unnervingly short run-up, Akram bowled the ball of the tournament, a 'jaffa' which swung in late from the off then straightened back off the pitch towards the slips to bowl Lamb for 31. Next ball, Akram bowled Chris Lewis with a fast delivery which seamed in wickedly from outside off stump. It was great captaincy from Imran, brilliant bowling from a highly gifted all-

*Calm and confident: Pakistan captain Imran Khan
limbers up before the World Cup Final against England
at the MCG, 25 March 1992. Pakistan won by 22 runs.*

rounder and a final reminder that this World Cup had reconfirmed the value of attack in one-day cricket, as opposed to the approach that had reigned for the four years since the previous Cup – that of Australia's measured, safety-first game plan.

The day before the first semi-final in Auckland between New Zealand and Pakistan, and on the eve of a four-month break after 70 gruelling days of international and state cricket, Allan Border told Malcolm Conn of the *Australian* of his concerns about the balance in Australia between one-day cricket and Test cricket. 'I think they [the public] are getting force-fed that the one-day game is the one to watch rather than Test matches. We've got to make sure we keep Test cricket fresh and promote it properly. Certainly from the players' point of view it's the game we want to play, but the public really like the one-day stuff. As long as we can keep both in equilibrium that would be ideal.'

Border was concerned that the promotion of cricket in Australia concentrated far too much on the one-day game with few attempts to market the more subtle joys of the Test match.

Essentially, this was a hangover from the World Series Cricket revolution of the late 1970s. Under the terms of its agreement with the ACB, Kerry Packer's PBL Marketing dictated the promotion of the game in Australia, pushing the cheap thrills of one-day cricket to the almost total exclusion of Test cricket. Border was not the only person worried by this trend. It would not be until the ACB-PBL deal ran out in March 1994 that the ACB took over the marketing of the game and promptly began to correct the imbalance.

Although Border was taking a commendably broad view of the game's health when he made those comments, he was also speaking from the heart. In the summer of 1991-92, Australia had played 10 World Series games and eight World Cup matches, and by the end of the latter tournament, many people in Australia, from the captain down, had had quite enough of one-day cricket.

CHANGE

AT LAST

T HE tour to Sri Lanka in August-September 1992 was an odd mixture. Several landmarks were created, some careers took significant strides, while others, despite good performances on the tour, went backwards when the player returned to Australia.

This tour marked a turning point in Shane Warne's career, and for that alone, must be considered significant. Greg Matthews played superbly with both bat and ball to be Australia's best player of the tour. He made five half-centuries in the series from number seven and his partnerships with Allan Border and Ian Healy saved Australia several times. Matthews also offered crucial encouragement to Warne.

Australia's tense victory in the first Test in Colombo was the first Test win on the Indian subcontinent by any of Border's teams. The tour to India in 1986 produced one tie and two draws, and the one to Pakistan two years later produced a loss and two draws. It was a poor record for a team some thought the most successful in the game. In fact, the poor record in India went back further than 1986: the win in Colombo was Australia's first on the subcontinent for 23 years.

In the third Test, Border finally made his twenty-fourth Test century, his first for four long years, during which time he had made 21 half-centuries – no big scores but the usual consistency.

Dean Jones made the other century of the Test series and topped the averages with 276 runs at 55.2. Yet it was not a convincing performance as Jones profited from missed stumpings and dropped catches. The third Test at Moratuwa in the second week of September was the last of his career. Steve Waugh, not chosen for this tour, replaced Jones in the next home series against the West Indies.

It seemed that at least some of the luck that blessed Jones in Sri Lanka was meant for his roommate Mark Waugh, who became the sixth player to suffer the indignity of four straight ducks in Test cricket; the others were not specialist batsmen. In keeping with the mixed consequences which flowed from this tour, Waugh's career was not damaged by these lapses, while Jones's run-scoring failed to save his.

Having finally recognised Geoff Marsh's decline and the need for fresh batting talent by dropping Marsh during the previous Test series against India, the selectors marked time by leaving his opening spot all but vacant on the tour to Sri Lanka. Victoria's Wayne Phillips replaced Marsh for the final Test of the series against India and then, used and abused, was discarded. Western Australia's Tom Moody was chosen as the second opener for Sri Lanka, a surprise to all, including Moody, who found out only the day the team left Darwin for Colombo. Moody must have wondered what was being done to his career when he saw the first of many green, seaming pitches in Sri Lanka. Of all tours, this was not one on which to be opening the batting.

Phil Wilkins proposed one scenario in the *Sydney Morning Herald* in late August when he wrote that: 'The door is temptingly ajar. If Australia's gamble on Tom Moody as Mark Taylor's new opening partner fails in Sri Lanka, Marsh will be the first Test choice ahead of young bloods such as Justin Langer and Matthew Hayden with David Boon implanted at No. 3.'

Although that theory might have been favoured by the more conservative selectors, it did not come to pass. The need for change was too great, especially with the West Indies coming for a series in Australia. Boon was moved up the order to open while the selectors waited for the appearance of a genuine opener.

Marsh's absence did produce one positive if belated decision from the selectors. Mark Taylor replaced Marsh as long-term vice-captain. Although Marsh had been Border's loyal deputy for some time, many observers thought Taylor should have replaced him sooner. Marsh was never seen as a future Test captain and, with Border's retirement drawing closer, it was odd that the selectors did not elevate their most favoured successor sooner than they did.

These decisions marked this period as one of change, however hesitant. A new team was being fashioned.

In the fourth innings of the first Test at the Sinhalese Sports Club in Colombo, Sri Lanka needed 181 to win in 58 overs. At 2/127, the home side was cruising until Aravinda de Silva made a fatal mistake. The gifted but hyperactive stroke player had blasted 37 from 32 balls before he tried to loft McDermott over Border at mid-on for the second time in the over. Border ran some 25 metres with the flight of the ball and held an excellent catch. That wicket began a collapse that saw the last eight wickets fall for 37 and Australia win a nail-biter by 16 runs.

Matthews made 6 and 64 and took 3/93 and 4/76 to be named Man of the Match. His major contribution off the field came on the fourth night when he shared a meal with Warne. The young leg spinner had worked hard on his fitness after those disappointing Tests against India, but returned figures of 0/107 in Sri Lanka's first innings. Carrying a Test average of 344 at the time and seriously doubting whether he would ever be able to make a go of Test cricket, Warne was losing confidence rapidly. The ever-optimistic Matthews spotted this and, sensing he and Warne would have important work to do the next day, encouraged his young teammate to believe in himself.

'Go down fighting,' Matthews told Warne. 'If it bounces twice, who cares? If you're spinning it hard, you're a chance.'

It was typical, positive thinking from Matthews and, the next day, Border must have sensed the change in Warne's attitude. With Sri Lanka needing 36 to win with four wickets in hand and Matthews tying them in knots at one end, Border called across to Warne, 'Warm up. You're on next over.'

Border's confidence and Matthews's advice paid off. Warne's thick fingers ripped the ball and he ended the match by taking 3/0 off his final 11 deliveries. Australia had won under intense pressure and Warne had taken a long stride forward.

The world's best batsmen were about to confront a Warne

The brotherhood of spin: Greg Matthews' advice and encouragement in Sri Lanka in 1992 helped the young Shane Warne overcome self-doubt at a crucial point in his career.

very different from the one the Indians had encountered. Sadly, one man who had championed the cause of leg spin for decades would not see Warne's rapid rise. Former great leg spinner Bill O'Reilly died on 6 October, six weeks after Warne's work in the first Test in Colombo. The 86-year-old O'Reilly, whom Bradman considered the best bowler he ever faced, watched Warne's Test debut in Sydney that summer and liked what he saw. Yet not even O'Reilly could have imagined how quickly Warne would develop in the following 12 months.

Patrick Smithers wrote of Matthews in the *Age*:

> *The part he has played in Warne's development should not be overlooked, either. Matthews has taken Warne under his wing from the start of this tour, encouraged him on the field and talked him through the bad times. Matthews described the win as a great day for the 'brotherhood' of Australian slow bowlers. Significantly he did not talk about his own seven wickets, but the 10 he and Warne took.*

Smithers reported that Matthews, thrilled by the best match contribution of his chequered career, thanked Geoff Lawson 'for the latitude he had given him', Taylor for their work together over the winter, his wife, Jillian, and Border – 'for just meeting me halfway'.

Encouraged by New South Wales selector John Benaud and state captain Lawson, Taylor had helped Matthews organise a chat with Border in the early days of the tour. Significantly, it was not

Border who initiated the much-needed heart-to-heart. Still, the pair tried to patch up a shaky relationship for the good of the team. After finding some middle ground with his captain, Matthews thrived.

Before the tour, Border had honestly assessed his team's overseas record and disagreed with its most ardent media supporters when he ranked Australia below West Indies and Pakistan in a putative worldwide order of merit. It was an admission that, despite the handsome series wins against England in 1989 and 1990-91, Australia's overseas record was poor. Even after Taylor's side beat the West Indies 2-1 in the 1995 series in the Caribbean, Australia's less-than-satisfactory efforts overseas, particularly on the Indian subcontinent, were cited by the West Indians as evidence that claims to the title of world Test champions were premature.

When Border discussed these figures at the start of the tour to Sri Lanka, Australia had won 11 and lost 27 Tests abroad since Ian Chappell had retired as captain 17 years earlier. The only series wins were in New Zealand in 1977 and in England in 1989.

'The West Indies are still top of the tree,' Border said, 'and I suppose the Pakistanis are vying for that top spot. I suppose the rest of us are pretty clumped together.'

No evidence has emerged that Border was accused of disloyalty for stating the obvious so honestly. Of winning overseas, Border said:

> I just think it's a true measure of a side's ability. It's all very well to play well in Perth or Brisbane or Sydney all the time, but you want to be winning games away from home. Winning in England is one thing, but the subcontinent has been a traditional graveyard for us, so we've got to try and lift the way we play. Being a good cricketer is being able to adapt to all conditions. The West Indies have done it, and that's why I still believe they're the best side.

Although Border's teams tried to adopt a more positive attitude to touring the subcontinent than the almost ritual whingeing of previous teams, they still found it hard to play their most positive cricket there. England was easy – mediocre opposition, a familiar culture, friendly crowds and dry summers (well, in '89 and '93 anyway) – but the subcontinent was truly foreign. In all, Border took three teams there to play a total of nine Tests. Australia won one, the first in the 1992 series against Sri Lanka, lost one, tied one and drew six. It was not a terrible record, but it was hardly an improvement on previous Australian teams.

DOING

BUSINESS

ON the morning of a World Series match against the West Indies at the Melbourne Cricket Ground in the late 1980s, Australian team manager Ian McDonald faced a huge problem. His captain was threatening to refuse to play.

Allan Border was upset that some of his players had been fined for wearing non-authorised clothing in a photograph that had been used on a poster. At times, the ACB would sign deals with sportswear manufacturers compelling its players to wear that particular product. Sometimes, these agreements conflicted with personal deals players had signed with rival manufacturers. As well, cricketers can be fussy about their gear. Tell a fast bowler to wear boots he does not like and you will find yourself in trouble.

Border's fierce loyalty to his team was well known in ACB circles, and this time, he told McDonald he was going to stand up for his players' rights. If the matter was not resolved, Border, for one, was going to refuse to take the field. A big crowd was expected that day. McDonald, as he often did in such sticky situations, rang ACB chairman Malcolm Gray, who happened to be in Lorne, a few hours' drive south-west of Melbourne. Gray had planned to arrive at the game well after the start of play, but at 6 am McDonald's call woke him. The chairman knew who would be on the line.

'Malcolm, we've got a problem,' said McDonald.

Over time, that phrase became a running joke between the two officials. It was code for one thing: the skipper was upset and some diplomatic discussion was required. Gray hopped in his car and headed back to the city.

The crowd of 60,000 at the MCG that day had no idea that before play, Gray and Border stood in the dark, concrete caverns underneath one of the giant grandstands trying to come to a compromise. In the end, Border won some ground and, soon after, walked out into the sunlight to toss the coin and get the match under way.

Border always saw himself as a player first and foremost. As captain, his players were the most important people in his working world. Like most cricketers, he didn't trust officials and often kept a professional distance between himself and those with whom he had to deal.

Border often caused consternation at the ACB. For one thing, he hated official dinners. So many people interrupted his meal with requests for autographs that what might have been a relaxing evening ended up a trial. There were times when he simply refused to attend. At other times, when the pressures of the captaincy and the constant travelling got to him and his mood dipped, he might disappear for a while, go AWOL or lock himself in his hotel room, the 'bat cave', as cricketers call it.

At these times, McDonald covered for Border. Often, the manager would ring Geoff Marsh, David Boon and Dean Jones and tell them to grab an armful of beers and go and talk to the captain. On most occasions, the three managed to soften the skipper's mood.

Sometimes, after a bad day in the field, Border would not want to attend the compulsory press conference. On a few rare occasions, the vice-captain was called in. More often, McDonald would manage to get the skipper off his dressing-room bench and into the media throng. Once there, of course, Border would be fine. As soon as he began to talk about the game that was his life, the words flowed. Often, it was the journalists who called a halt.

At times, tempers in the dressing-room flared and angry words cut short the usual banter. McDonald often was on the receiving end, but the manager knew that was part of his job and he could always manage a laugh about it later over a well-earned drink in the hotel bar. McDonald also had a much better idea than most of the intense pressures which can bear down on the captain of the Australian cricket team.

At times, the dressing-room resembled a hothouse – cricket gear and bags strewn all over the floors, clothes hanging from every available hook, the phone ringing, fans waiting at the front and back doors for a word with their heroes, emotions overheated by the claustrophobic atmosphere and the pressures of expectation. There were always a couple of players fighting insecurity, a cricketer's constant companion, worried about a loss of form or another injury. It was no wonder Merv Hughes's ability to maintain a sense of humour and elicit a few laughs from the others was so highly valued, although there were times when even Hughes knew that it was best to keep quiet.

In the second half of Border's decade as captain, there were many grand times behind the dressing-room door, when victory celebrations became the norm rather than the rare events they had been from late 1984 to early 1989. From the first week of that Ashes tour in '89, the team spirit was very good. The once disparate collection of individuals had blended into a tightly knit unit with a recognisable identity.

Whatever the prevailing mood, the touring caravan, at home or overseas, lived under pressure. And no one was under more pressure than the captain. It did not take long for Mark Taylor to learn this after he took over from Border in mid-1994.

'Since I got the job as captain,' Taylor told a journalist during the tour to Pakistan in the spring of '94, 'I've had about a million different things to do and I expected it to be like that. Once it's happened it made me appreciate how good a job AB did for so long. It can be pretty hectic.'

Allan Border's greatest attribute as a cricketer, apart from formidable talent, was his fierce determination. It was the quality that had kept him in the captaincy through circumstances which would have broken lesser characters.

ACB officials deeply appreciated Border's loyalty, his single-minded pursuit of excellence and the years of hard work he had put in to rescue Australian cricket. They also knew that when the skipper was upset at some administrative act, they would be confronted by one very determined man. Former ACB chairman Malcolm Gray has great respect for Border's contribution:

*Allan played an exceedingly important role in restoring Austra-
lian cricket. He was a fantastic captain in very tough times. He was
tremendously single-minded. And he was a great team man. He loved
the dressing-room and he didn't particularly like authority. Sure, he
could be exasperating at times, but he had a very difficult job. He
always had the good of Australian cricket at heart and he always
treated me and the position of chairman with respect. He never held
grudges.*

Although in the early years of his captaincy Border occasionally
frustrated the ACB, and a few teammates, by showing little interest
in off-field matters, he began to play a more active role in his later
years. One long-running issue that finally inspired him to action
was that of player payments.

While in Sri Lanka in 1992, the Australian players called a
meeting to discuss an old problem – money and, specifically, their
contracts with the ACB. The players thought they were not being
fairly rewarded for the increased amount of cricket they were being
asked to play nor the higher levels of fitness they were expected
to maintain.

Scores of footballers were receiving better payments than the
best 20 or so cricketers in the country. Cricket was still the number
one national sport and attracted big crowds and television audiences
which were the envy of other major sports. The game was a popular
and profitable exercise. The income from the sale of television
rights had to be substantial, although a well-kept secret. The
revenue from the merchandising of products associated with the
national team was a growing business, but only PBL, which had
the rights to the merchandising, and the ACB knew how much
income that business generated. Little of it went directly to the
players whose names and likenesses adorned most of the products.

The meeting in Sri Lanka was for players only. They had not
told coach Bob Simpson about it. Simpson had his own contract
with the ACB and his salary was another well-kept secret. Although
supposed to be confidential, the base salaries of most players leaked
out.

The Australians had had a similar meeting in Goa in India
soon after the 1989 Ashes win, and Border promised to lobby on
their behalf. As a result of that meeting, the Cricket Committee
(which included Border and captains or representatives from each
state team but not the full national side) met before the first Test
against Sri Lanka in late 1989. Simpson was at that meeting.

177

The main issue for the players was the poor amounts some members of the '89 Ashes squad had been offered. Border had signed a lucrative deal that, according to Geoff Lawson in his autobiography, *Henry*, saw Border's pay increase to double that of the next best-paid players. But the new opening batsman, Mark Taylor, after a brilliant Ashes series in which he scored 839 runs, the next best Ashes aggregate to Bradman's in 1930, was offered the lowest level of contract.

Astute and attacking: Geoff Lawson's captaincy of NSW and his battles for better wages and conditions made him an important and controversial figure in the game.

Discussion at the Brisbane meeting was amicable enough, but the next day Terry Brindle in the *Australian* and Rod Nicholson in the *Sun* broke the news that the Australians, 'easily the highest paid cricketers in the world' according to Nicholson, wanted more. England's players were comfortably better paid than the Australians, as were many overseas professionals playing county cricket in England. Lawson believed there had been a leak from the meeting although all who attended it had agreed to keep it confidential. The articles painted a picture of greedy, rich Australian players wanting even more, while the Sri Lankans struggled on a pittance. Comparing the Australians' pay with the Sri Lankans' was, of course, irrelevant and unfair.

Nicholson took a similar stance after I reported in the *Sunday Age* the 1992 meeting in Sri Lanka and the subsequent negotiations back in Australia. He said that Border earned about $500,000 in

1991. This was quite probably correct, except that Nicholson failed to mention that only half at most of that amount was paid by the ACB. The rest came from Border's own contractual agreements and his non-cricket work, and it was the same case with other players. Nicholson wrote that below Border, the next nine were on $100,000 excluding match fees, tour fees and other ACB payments. In fact, the $100,000 would have included all those payments.

Nicholson's estimates were about double what the players were actually being paid by the ACB. And at that time, there were at least 30 Australian Football League (AFL) players earning $100,000 or more a year, and doing so without having to spend months overseas, away from home and family. The thirtieth best cricketer was probably earning about $30,000 from the cricket authorities, if he was lucky, and that would have included corporate sponsorship money from his involvement with his state team, money which obviously did not come from ACB coffers.

Although it is always difficult to compare earnings from one sport to another, it is worth noting that in 1992, the AFL Players' Association thought the 300th best footballer in the league should have been earning a minimum of $25,000 a year. The ACB had 23 players on its contract system and the lowest paid of those was earning little more than that proposed wage for the 300th best AFL footballer. The 300th best cricketer would have been playing first grade at a suburban ground, and probably paying for the privilege.

During earlier pay-rise negotiations, Allan Border had been less than enthusiastic. He simply did not see most off-field aspects of the game as his responsibility. Just as he had delegated various cricket jobs to Simpson, which captains before him had performed themselves, Border did not relish getting into financial negotiations with the ACB. But in 1992, he decided to push hard on behalf of his players.

Border was happy with his own contract and was not lobbying for an increase. This time, he was using his bargaining power as Australian captain and as one of the most respected and popular sportspeople in the country to improve the lot of teammates as well as Sheffield Shield players who maintained that competition as the best of its type in the world. Essentially, Border wanted more of an idea of the size of the financial cake and whether the players were receiving their fair share, especially given the strict limits on their ability to earn income from outside ventures. The players strongly suspected their wages fell below that fair share.

One prominent sports agent certainly agreed with them. In the *Sunday Age*, Frank Williams, Melbourne manager of IMG, the powerful worldwide sports agency and promotions company, estimated that Allan Border was worth $10,000 a match instead of the $3750 a Test and $1250 a one-day international all players were then receiving. At that rate, Williams thought Border ought to have been paid $500,000 just for playing. In 1991, players, including Border, who appeared in every Test and one-day game were paid match fees of $43,000. 'For the amount of sponsorships and people Border attracts to the game, plus the rights for the game's huge television coverage,' Williams said, 'I'd say Border would be one of the few sportspeople who are grossly underpaid.'

And at that time, Border was happy with his earnings! Even allowing for a little managerial exaggeration on Williams's part, Australia's cricketers were certainly not overpaid.

Back home in Brisbane from Sri Lanka, Border spoke to his contacts in other sports, notably Rugby League, and prepared a written proposal which he submitted to the ACB. Although nervously conceding in private that he had never done anything like that before, Border's proposal was well received at ACB headquarters where it was seen as thorough and fair.

Nicholson had written that Border's lobbying 'caused a bewildering shake of the head'. In fact, it achieved considerable success. While the team was in New Zealand in March 1993, the ACB announced it would pay the 1993 Ashes tourists a base fee of almost $50,000 – double what it had paid the 1989 tourists four years before. With sponsorship, the tour fee was close to $70,000, an improvement, though still not big money for four and a half months away from home with very few free days.

The overall review the ACB promised in March continued, with payments becoming increasingly performance based. By 1995, regular members of the national team were earning about $200,000 a year from the ACB. This represented a 185 per cent increase on the estimated $70,000 players earned in 1984, the year Border became captain. In the same period, average yearly earnings of adult Australian males increased from $20,280 to $36,920, an increase of 82 per cent.

On those figures, Australia's cricketers won significant pay rises over the decade of Border's captaincy. But those bare figures do not take into account increases gained by other sportspeople nor the general commercialisation of sport.

As well, Test cricketers enjoy minimal job security. Lose form and your place in the team, and you lose all match payments. Over a year, including an overseas tour, that could add up to a loss of at least $50,000. Suffer a serious injury in the line of duty – as most of Australia's senior fast bowlers did in the Border era – and your income could be halved or worse. In contrast, Super League, the breakaway Rugby League group formed by Rupert Murdoch's giant media company, News Ltd, was offering an injured player 100 per cent of his salary for the year in which he suffered the injury and 50 per cent of the remainder of his contract should he be unable to resume his career.

From 1994, the ACB, under Graham Halbish and Alan Crompton, began consulting the players on a regular basis, even inviting them to ACB meetings, a practice which would have outraged their predecessors. The ACB found that Allan Border had not been especially interested in such administrative affairs, although his involvement did increase in the later stages of his career. Mark Taylor, on the other hand, was a willing and constructive participant, as were several of the other leading players, and this further encouraged the board to adopt a more open attitude towards the players.

Taylor even managed something of a coup when he convinced the ACB to allow each player his own hotel room. From 1986, the captain and vice-captain had single rooms while the other players shared in pairs. Border, Simpson and manager Ian McDonald had tried but never been able to persuade the ACB to be more generous. Perhaps Taylor contrived for Halbish or Crompton to share a room for a night with Tim May, the team's most notorious snorer. Certainly, the ACB recognised the players' need for privacy given the busy schedules of the modern game.

How long this more expensive arrangement will last might depend on the ACB's search for a new major sponsor. From 1972, cricket's number one sponsor had been tobacco company Benson and Hedges, a name that was closely associated with Australian cricket for two decades. Despite widespread concern about tobacco products and government moves against the industry, the ACB ignored the dictates of political correctness and stood firm in its relationship with its generous sponsor. But changing community standards led eventually to federal government legislation which banned sponsorship by tobacco companies of Australian cricket from the end of the 1995-96 season.

From late 1994, the ACB began courting major corporations

in search of one prepared to match the estimated $8 million per year Benson and Hedges was believed to be contributing by the mid-1990s. The search was proving difficult. Benson and Hedges was the largest sports sponsorship in Australia but, although this confirmed cricket's pre-eminence, the marketplace had tightened. There were fewer dollars available and more sports chasing them.

At least the ACB could offer prospective sponsors the image of a young, dashing and successful team. The victory by Mark Taylor's side over the unofficial world champions, the West Indies, in May 1995 was perfectly timed.

Although the ACB in 1995 was a more conciliatory employer than its counterpart of 1985, and so enjoyed better relations with its players, life for sports administrators was in many ways more complex than it had been a decade earlier. More intrusive involvement from corporate sponsors, especially those who signed leading players to private endorsements, the increasing number and power of personal managers who organised those deals, the growth in sports unionism and more complex legal arrangements added to the problems. And when Murdoch's News Ltd raided Australian and then world Rugby League, as Kerry Packer had raided cricket in 1977, administrators realised their hold on the sport was not necessarily as secure as they had assumed.

Throughout his time as a senior player and then as captain, Allan Border had never shown any inclination to assist in the formation of a players' association. Ian Chappell had offered to help Kim Hughes and Border form one not long after the World Series schism was healed, but the captain and vice-captain were not interested. Later, Geoff Lawson tried to resurrect the idea but again Border was not prepared to support such a move.

England's professional cricketers had long had an association which fought for better wages and conditions. And most major sports in Europe had formed similar organisations by the mid-1990s. That trend came to Australia from 1993 onwards as more and more sportspeople formed their own unions. Players in the two largest professional team sports apart from cricket, Rugby League and Australian football, formed players' associations. Later, other Australian sportspeople began joining a new union, the Media, Entertainment and Arts Alliance (MEAA). Everyone – officials, players and spectators – agreed that sport was entertainment and therefore sportspeople were entertainers. Undoubtedly, they were also employees. Yet while many athletes began joining unions, cricketers, in particular, were left behind.

The MEAA wanted to enlist cricketers, but attempts at a meeting came to nothing. When News Ltd split Australian Rugby League early in 1995 with a raid on players and clubs that exceeded Packer's revolution, the new Super League looked likely to change the structure of sport in Australia. News Ltd created Super League because it wanted the game for its new pay-television services in Europe and Asia, and it paid big money to secure as many of the best players as possible, at times signing whole clubs en masse.

Super League offered its players a package of extra benefits that treated them as valued employees. It was a change that had occurred a decade before in the United States and Canada. Players had been trying for years to win many of those benefits from the Australian Rugby League, but old habits died hard in the corridors of sporting power. Super League's added benefits included generous superannuation, comprehensive health care cover for players and their immediate families, a percentage of gate takings, a 50 per cent share of revenue from the sale of merchandising products bearing their names or likenesses and job training for life after football.

Admittedly, News Ltd could call on massive financial and logistical support for this scheme, and its proposed commitment to the grassroots of the game is yet to be tested, but such a major step forward in player payments and conditions was likely to have an effect on all sports, cricket included.

By mid-winter 1995, Steve Waugh and Ian Healy were leading another push for better wages and conditions, backed by two of the architects of Kerry Packer's World Series Cricket revolution of the 1970s – Austin Robertson (manager of Border and Warne) and John Cornell. Amongst a range of claims, the players wanted at least a doubling of their salaries. As well, they had instituted discussions with the MEAA and were finally considering following thousands of other Australian sportspeople in joining a union. Again, these were major changes in attitude and philosophy which had come about in the first 12 months of Mark Taylor's reign as captain.

In this environment, the ACB will not be able to sit back and merely watch its successful team move towards the turn of the century. Pay television, in particular, looks set to change for ever the nature of world sport. In June 1995, the Seven network paid an estimated $200 million for free-to-air and pay-television rights to AFL football for a five-year period. One would expect cricket, as by far the most popular television sport every summer, to command similarly large fees for its broadcasting rights in what is now a far more competitive broadcasting climate. And if the nation's best cricketers begin to think that their status and income are falling too far behind those enjoyed by players in comparable sports, Mark Taylor will probably be forced to call a few more team meetings like the one in Sri Lanka in 1992.

NOT QUITE

GOOD ENOUGH

W HENEVER the West Indies were on their way to Australia for a Test series, trouble seemed to brew in the home camp. Perhaps it was the memory of past bruises – to individual bodies, fragile egos and the collective psyche – or the tremblings of recent trauma syndrome in the back of the mind.

The summer of 1992-93 began with widespread mutterings about the stagnant condition of the Australian cricket team, continued with the leading protagonists sniping at each other and ended with savage defeat in a three-day Test in Perth. The West Indies had gone within two runs of their first series defeat for 13 years, but five days later went home with the Frank Worrell Trophy in their kit bag. Allan Border's last chance to beat his fiercest rivals had failed.

Most of the early debate centred on the conservatism which seemed to have taken hold of the Australian team, particularly in two areas – selection and tactics. By keeping the 'door ajar' for Geoff Marsh, the selectors had strengthened the view that they were showing too much loyalty to players who had been Border's stalwarts in the early days but who were no longer the best people for the job. This was a carry-over from the period when Laurie Sawle, chairman of selectors, had brought consistency and stability to selection. But those were different times, a period when playing talent was low and those with some ability needed to be carried while they learned Test cricket. Loyalty to players who had served the team well was commendable, but there was also a need to assess all team members dispassionately. This was only fair on younger players doing consistently well at Sheffield Shield level.

After some conservative declarations and generally cautious batting, observers had begun to worry about the lack of adventure in the Australian team's tactical approach. The previous summer Australia had beaten a fairly poor Indian team 4-0. Yet, despite the impressive-looking margin, many people had expected more of a thrashing.

Statistics were published which confirmed the critics' concerns about Australia's slow batting. The figures revealed that since Australia's win in England in 1989, it had been the slowest scoring side of the established Test powers. Australia had made its runs at 2.87 per over, only better than Sri Lanka and New Zealand. Not surprisingly, West Indies topped the list with 3.3, followed by India at 3.16, England 3.04 and Pakistan 2.9. As well, the figures showed that three of the 11 slowest Test hundreds scored by Australians had been made against India the preceding summer – two by Boon and one by Taylor. Given India's mediocre bowling attack, this supported the view that the team needed to play with more urgency.

Before the Test series against the West Indies began, Norman Tasker in the *Bulletin* summed up the mood.

> *First, there is the perception that selection is too stick-in-the-mud; that it offers plenty of stability but no adventure; loads of security but no opportunity. Some say the Australian team has become something of a retirement village in which those who have been there the longest have the most secure tenure of all.*
>
> *Secondly, there is the question of attitude – that the team has been shaped to fear defeat rather than cherish victory and that the outlook is stoic and steadfast rather than aggressive and imaginative.*
>
> *At the centre of it all is Bob Simpson, the former Australian captain, who has been team coach since 1986 and a selector as well for the last five years of his term. He wields enormous influence.*
>
> *Simpson was a conservative, if courageous, captain in his day.*

He took control of a shell-shocked Australian team in the mid-'80s and there is no doubt he helped them gather discipline, pride and success. But six years on, those who are lining up the guns against him might say that too much of the caution he displayed as captain has lived on in his role as coach and selector, and that he simply has too much say in getting the people he wants in the Australian side.

The performance of the Australian team under Mark Taylor in the Caribbean in 1995 proved that the criticisms Tasker set out were correct.

Essentially, in the early 1990s, the Australian team did stagnate. When Taylor took over, two things changed. First, he brought more imagination and adventure to the captaincy, especially by aiming to score 300 runs in a day's play (a rate of 3.3 runs an over). Second, with the support of the ACB, Taylor ran the team his way. Simpson, having been encouraged to stand down as a selector soon after Taylor's appointment, was relegated to the role of assistant to the captain rather than the highly influential role he played under Border. These were major changes and it was no coincidence that so soon after they were introduced, Australia finally beat the West Indies – and away from home at that. In the summer of 1992-93, however, the Australians were still battling each other as well as trying to cope with their old phobias about the West Indies.

The first Test in Brisbane was a close contest until a fourth-innings collapse by the West Indies had them facing defeat. Australia was denied several leg-before decisions on the final day and tempers frayed. West Indies survived by two wickets and were able to head for a fortnight of World Series matches during which they would try to recover the form and direction which had been missing in Brisbane. Australia, having given ground to the critics by dropping Dean Jones to twelfth man and introducing the talented Damien Martyn, lost a perfect opportunity to win the first Test of a series, and so put pressure on a West Indian team that was in transition under new captain Richie Richardson.

Australia's frustration at umpiring decisions on the fifth day led to Border and Merv Hughes being reported and fined. Border chose not to attend the post-match hearing, an error of judgement for which he later apologised. Given that the hearing was in front of International Cricket Council (ICC) match referee Raman Subba Row, the ACB was embarrassed by Border's action. Subba Row fined the captain $2000; and Hughes, $400.

The work ethic: David Boon and Dean Jones in the nets
before the start of the 1992-93 series against the West Indies.

The other embarrassment for Australia was a controversial incident in which the Australians were given a stumping decision by umpire Terry Prue when television replays showed that keeper Ian Healy did not have the ball in his hand when he broke the wicket. The batsman, Brian Lara, was on 58 at the time and involved in a partnership of 112 with Keith Arthurton, who went on to make 157 runs. Lara's departure was a blow to the West Indies' chances of building a substantial first innings lead; Healy's involvement a concern for Australian cricket.

To his credit, Lara accepted the decision with good grace, although behind the scenes, the West Indies were very upset. Although he protested his innocence, Healy's standing was affected. He had already gained a reputation for over-appealing and been involved in several ugly on-field clashes. This latest incident effectively ended any hopes he had of succeeding Border as captain.

The temperature was about to rise again in the Australian camp when Border criticised the team's preparation for its first World Series Cup match of the summer. Australia lost by nine wickets to the West Indies in Perth, prompting Border to publicly comment that the team should have practised on the Friday as well as their usual session on the Saturday before a Sunday game.

'It's just not good enough and we've got to, in my view, approach these things a little bit more professionally. Obviously I've got to have more input of what I think.'

Practice arrangements were normally organised by captain and coach, so Border's comments were a thinly disguised criticism of Simpson. The trouble in the camp which had surfaced the summer before was still simmering. The ACB, through a statement from team manager Ian McDonald, sided with Simpson. Border's attempt at self-assertion had been answered so promptly and so strongly that there was no question which side the ACB was backing. Soon, some sections of the press began questioning whether Border should continue as captain.

Border missed the next four one-day matches with a hamstring injury. While he was out of action, his critics pounced. Ian Healy had captained the previous season's Australian XI in a four-day match against the West Indies in Hobart. His opposing captain that day had been Desmond Haynes, his old foe from the 1991 Caribbean tour. Not a lot was said during that toss of the coin.

Healy's appointment for that match inspired Rod Nicholson and Terry Brindle to propose the keeper as a strong candidate for captain should Border go. Healy's appointment for the same match in 1992-93 furthered the speculation, but the Lara stumping controversy a week later stopped that campaign. By the end of Australia's fifth one-day game, on 15 December in Melbourne, Mark Taylor was back in favour as the leading candidate.

Although vice-captain since the tour to Sri Lanka, Taylor's chances of becoming captain were thought to be diminished by the fact that he had never been able to win a permanent place in the one-day team. This was a furphy. The selectors' priority was Test cricket, and if Taylor were the best man for that job, he would be given it. The one-day situation would be sorted out later – as it was. Still, with Border out injured, Taylor took the opportunity to show he could play well in one-day cricket. He also used the opportunity to give Simpson and the team a hint of how he would approach the captaincy.

After that first loss to the West Indies in Perth, the two sides met again on a damp Sydney pitch on 8 December. This was Taylor's first game as captain.

The team's normal pre-match routine was a warm-up jog, stretching exercises, a brief fielding session, a pep talk from Simpson then a quick knock-up in the nets. As the coach took up position in mid-field, the players began to gather around. But as Simpson was about to speak, Taylor held out his arm.

'Just a minute, Simmo,' he said. Taylor then said his piece before motioning the players to the nets. Simpson, left stranded, called them back and, in different words, repeated Taylor's instructions. More than a few players were impressed by the changed routine.

Taylor turned the rain-shortened game with four fine catches at first slip and won the Man of the Match award. It was an impressive debut – on and off the field – and a preview of his approach once he took over from Border.

With Healy out of the running at this stage, Rod Nicholson began pushing Taylor's case for the captaincy in his articles in News Ltd's five metropolitan daily papers. After Taylor led the Australians to a win over Pakistan in Adelaide five days after the Sydney game, Nicholson wrote that: 'The more that Taylor and the Australian team succeeds, the more pressure there is on Border to retain his position as captain and his place in the Test team.' Nicholson also noted that: 'Taylor again showed a liking and responsibility for the task at hand, and was not bashful when it came to declaring his desire to retain the job at a time when Border is out of favour with officialdom.'

Border might have been out of favour with some officials, but the ACB was certainly not contemplating a change in captain. As for his deputy's alleged unabashed desire to stay in the job, even Taylor baulked at that. Other press reports of Taylor's comments included his remarks that the team was looking forward to Border's return. Worried that Nicholson's story made it look as if he was pushing himself for the top job, Taylor conferred with Border and team management before clearing up the matter with the press corps the next day.

Relax man, relax: Ian Bishop accepts his captain Richie Richardson's advice after a torrid net session the day before the dramatic fourth Test in Adelaide.

Nicholson's suggestions that a push for a change in captain had begun might have been an exaggeration, but Taylor's success in the Caribbean in 1995 prompts the thought that he might have been able to halt the stagnation that afflicted the team in the final years of Border's captaincy. To do so, however, Taylor would have had to redefine Simpson's role. He did manage this after he took over in 1994, but in 1992-93, Simpson's standing with the ACB was still high, and it is doubtful whether back then Taylor would have been able to muster the support he needed to reduce Simpson's influence.

As Richie Benaud noted at the time, the West Indies must have been laughing themselves silly at all the in-fighting in the Australian camp. Yet the visitors failed to turn this situation to their advantage in the second Test in Melbourne, which followed the first batch of one-day games.

Border and Mark Waugh made centuries in the first innings. It was Border's first at home for five years and a rather satisfying reply to his critics. Waugh's century was made with some thrilling but unorthodox stroke play. In an attempt to break the hold of the West Indian fast bowlers, Waugh backed away to the leg side to give himself room to hit over the slips and gully region. He was criticised by West Indian and Australian commentators for a lack of courage, but praised by others for trying something different, a counterattack which brought him a hundred and helped Australia to a win. Simpson supported Waugh's tactics.

Set 359 to win on a wearing pitch, the West Indies succumbed to the master plan Australia had been developing for several years: a quality leg spinner bowling the West Indies out on a fifth-day pitch. Shane Warne took 7/52 and Australia led 1-0 after two Tests.

The third match in Sydney belonged to the lively Brian Lara and a dead pitch. Australia batted first to make 9/503, with Steve Waugh making his first century against the West Indies and Boon, Matthews and Border reaching 70. Border's twenty-first run took him to 10,000 Test runs, an achievement matched only by India's Sunil Gavaskar.

A massive run-chase on a ground they mistrusted only a few days after losing in Melbourne provided the West Indies with their toughest challenge in Australia since Greg Chappell's team won the first of a three-game series in 1981-82. With occasional showers holding the pitch together and turning the ball into a cake of soap for the bowlers, Lara and Richardson added 293 for the third wicket. Richardson made 109 and said later that he could hardly remember the innings, so enthralled was he with Lara's brilliant batting at the other end. Lara's first Test century in his fifth match ended when he ran himself out for 277, the highest score in Australia versus West Indies Test cricket.

So to Adelaide, with Australia leading 1-0 after three games. As we saw earlier, the West Indies avoided a series defeat by one run in that fourth Test. Such a close result sapped the emotional energy of the Australians. The momentum had swung dramatically behind the visitors. In the fifth Test in Perth, Man of the Series Curtly Ambrose blew Australia's challenge across the Swan River and off into the Indian Ocean. On a fast, green pitch, Ambrose took 7/25 and 2/54 and West Indies won by an innings and 25 runs in less than three days. Border made his first pair in 138 matches and he and Hughes were again reported for dissent, this time receiving a severe reprimand.

While discussing the in-fighting amongst the Australians that season, Richie Benaud had ended his column on 16 December in the *Herald-Sun* with a warning: 'The ultimate irony would be if, in the season where the Australians have their best chance in 16 years of beating the Caribbean champions, they should have to limp away from the final Test victims of the cruel accident of shooting themselves in the feet.'

And that is pretty much how this difficult season ended. The wounds in the feet came not just from the in-fighting but from the loss of focus in the field on that final day of the first Test in Brisbane and a general fear of the power of the West Indies. Before the fifth Test, Allan Border said he was pleased with the selection of young players such as Justin Langer, Damien Martyn and Jo Angel. 'First-year players haven't got the recent trauma syndrome. They go out there and play naturally and Damien is a perfect example of that.'

No doubt the West Indies saw this mention of 'recent trauma syndrome' and decided to update the condition one more time before they left Perth for home at the end of the fifth Test. By the time the two teams met again, Ambrose would be recovering slowly from a shoulder injury, Richardson from emotional and physical fatigue and the Australians, under Taylor, would be confident of inflicting a little recent trauma syndrome of their own.

THE BORDER

GANG

WHEN the 1989 Australians arrived in England, they were given the familiar tag of 'the worst ever' Ashes touring team. By 1993, even the most patriotic of English supporters knew better than to jump again to that conclusion. The arrival of Border's 1993 squad was noted by the production of a widely available T-shirt which summed up the local feeling. 'The Border Gang' T-shirt depicted as wanted men the Australian captain, David Boon, Merv Hughes and the new pretender, Shane Warne.

The inclusion of Warne was a rare example of English prescience. The people who ran cricket in England had not taken Warne's bowling very seriously, an error which later proved costly. Apart from the old, unfunny convict joke, the T-shirt was an accurate summation of Border's intentions. This team had come to do another four months' marauding across England, thrashing the county teams, laying waste to the national side and, of course, winning the little urn which contains the Ashes.

All of this was achieved in an aggressive style similar to that

Trump card: Shane Warne during the 1993 Ashes series.
His first ball, which hit Mike Gatting's off stump after
pitching outside leg, has been called the ball of the century.

adopted on the '89 tour. Australia won the one-day series 3-0 and the Test series 4-1. Australia used 13 players in the six Tests; England 24 under two captains. The series win was Border's third straight success against England, and his last. He had retired by the time England returned to Australia in 1994-95. His Ashes record as captain was 12 wins, three losses and seven draws from 22 matches since the start of the 1986-87 series. Since the turnaround in '89, Border had won 11 Tests and lost one in 17 games. In England in '85, Border had wondered what the future held and whether he would survive it as captain. In '93, he led a team that contained the future.

There were two defining moments in the '93 series. The first came with Shane Warne's first delivery in Ashes cricket, bowled to Mike Gatting on the second day of the first Test at Old Trafford in Manchester. Many English players and commentators knew of Australia's high regard for their new, 23-year-old, blond-haired, blue-eyed glamour boy. However, English cricket happily dismissed Warne and his off-spin partner, Tim May, even to the extent of encouraging groundsmen to prepare spinning pitches for the Test series in a bid to blunt Australia's perceived superiority in pace bowling.

Warne had had an excellent short tour of New Zealand before the Ashes tour. Australia had not played particularly well, drawing the three-game series 1-1. Apart from Warne's superb 17 series wickets at 15.05, the only other highlight came on 26 February, the second day of the first Test at Christchurch, when Border slightly mishit off spinner Dipak Patel to backward square leg to break the ultimate batting record: Sunil Gavaskar's world record Test aggregate of 10,122 runs. Border said later he would have preferred to break the record in Australia, but after a long wait, he had finally made it to the peak of a famous mountain.

Still, on that short tour of New Zealand, Warne's bowling was the most significant aspect. His accuracy was stunning, his overs costing less than two runs apiece. Warne seemed to be breaking new ground, becoming the first leg spinner in the history of the game to combine the accuracy of a finger spinner with the side-spin, dip and swerve of a prodigious wrist spinner. The New Zealanders had been mesmerised by Warne's accuracy and variety, their feet anchored behind the crease like all modestly talented batsmen confronted by high-class spin bowling.

Early on that tour of New Zealand, Martin Crowe had smashed Warne out of the small Pukekura Park in New Plymouth during a warm-up match. Worcestershire and England's Graeme Hick had done the same early on the '93 Ashes tour in his county's match against the tourists. As happened in New Zealand, English concerns about Warne were cast aside after Hick's assault. What few if any English people realised was that Border had told Warne not to bowl anything at Hick but his standard leg break. The variations – the big-spinning leg break, the bouncing top spinner, the savagely skidding flipper, the floating zooter and the wrong 'un – were to be saved for the Tests. Amazingly, England fell for the trick and only realised what they were up against when Gatting pushed forward to that first ball from Warne and had the top of his off stump hit by a leg break that spun from well outside his leg stump.

Gatting, a fine player of spin, was stunned, and his teammates, with the exception of Graham Gooch, never recovered from the psychological blow. As John Thicknesse wrote in the 1994 edition of *Wisden*: 'Thanks to TV, Warne's first ball in Ashes cricket, which bowled Mike Gatting at Old Trafford, may become the most famous ball ever bowled . . . As it was the ball was unplayable and, by impressing the bowler's capabilities on England, it had a profound impact on the series.'

Warne went on to take 34 wickets in the series at 25.79, a tally bettered only by one other leg spinner – Arthur Mailey, who took 36 wickets in five Tests in the 1920-21 series.

The second defining moment, amongst many contenders, came at Lord's when Michael Slater reached three figures for the first time. As he ran off down the pitch to register a hundred in only his second Test, Slater kissed the badge on his dark green Australian helmet. The gesture was not only a reminder of the Australians' commitment to the national game and the team cause, but of English cricket's decline.

Had an Englishman managed somehow to score such an exhilarating century, he might have kissed a white England helmet with or without badge, or a dark blue England helmet with or without badge. Opener Mark Lathwell would have kissed his Somerset helmet as he did not see fit even to wear one of England's several designated helmets. Still, when his selection for the first of his two Tests that summer was announced, Lathwell told the press he was not sure whether he was ready for Test cricket. It is unlikely any of the new young batsmen in the Australian touring party would have even entertained such doubt, let alone expressed it so publicly. Lathwell lasted two matches, made a top score of 38 and displayed all the footwork of a drunken elephant.

The entertainer: Michael Slater injected some much-needed fire into the Australian batting when he made his debut in England in 1993.

Slater carried on to an effervescent 152 in a stand of 260 with Taylor. After Australia piled on 4/632 declared, England's morale was shattered and Merv Hughes, Warne and Tim May completed the rout. Australia won the second Test by an innings and 62 runs with a 10-man team, having lost only four wickets in the match. Craig McDermott had been rushed to hospital on the second day with severe stomach pains caused by complications from earlier surgery and Australia was left a bowler short for all of England's two innings. It did not matter.

Michael Slater's rise to the Test side had been rapid. In the 1992-93 first-class season, he had made 1019 runs at 59.94 with such style, swift footwork and attacking flair that the selectors were forced to overlook several more fancied players and include Slater as one of three specialist openers in the '93 touring team.

Although Boon, in Geoff Marsh's absence, had opened in the home series against the West Indies, Border and Simpson had said in New Zealand that they wanted Boon to return permanently to number three. Matthew Hayden, Queensland's prolific left-hander, demanded a place on weight of runs, although there were misgivings amongst some selectors that his heavier footwork would be exposed by English conditions. With Boon not considered as an opener, Slater was chosen as the third specialist. This meant that Boon had effectively taken a middle-order spot which might have gone to either Justin Langer or Dean Jones; neither made the team. Slater jumped ahead of Hayden early in the tour and since then has never been in danger of losing his place. The selection of Slater, which produced animated debate at the selection meeting, proved a triumph.

Intelligent, articulate, enthusiastic and a dashing stroke-player, Slater is exactly the sort of player Test cricket needs. In many ways, he quickly came to symbolise the change in the Australian team's personality in the final years of Border's captaincy and, most significantly, during the first year of Taylor's reign. The steadier Marsh typified the cautious approach of Border and Simpson who, in many ways, moulded Marsh to their requirements. Slater took over that spot and stamped his own personality on it from the start. As much as Warne, Slater personified a revamped and refreshed Australian team which was leaving behind the somewhat dour play of the early 1990s.

Slater's run of success was not without its problems, most significantly in the one-day game where he was dropped from Australia's 1993-94 World Series after only three matches. While the selectors tried in vain to find places for Taylor, Dean Jones and Matthew Hayden in an already crowded batting line-up, the gifted Slater was overlooked. The selectors wanted to give Hayden some senior recognition as reward for the mountain of runs he had made in the Sheffield Shield. The problem was that Hayden was more of a four-day specialist, whereas Slater was an entertainer, an extrovert perfectly suited to a more exciting brand of one-day cricket. It seemed a harsh judgement on Slater, although it should be said that at the time, Slater's fielding was not brilliant. That soon changed, as did Slater's one-day career.

Taylor and Slater averaged in the low 40s in the '93 Ashes series, while the middle order – Boon, Mark Waugh, Border, Steve Waugh and Ian Healy – averaged more than 50 runs. Boon made up for not scoring a Test century on the '85 and '89 tours by making three in this series, while Taylor made two and the others one each. Border's was his second double and Healy's his first in Test cricket. Healy had a superb tour: his wicket-keeping to Warne and May was brilliant and his 26 dismissals were a record for a Test series in England.

Of the bowlers apart from Warne, May enjoyed his best series, seamer Paul Reiffel bowled well in his two Test appearances and Hughes covered for McDermott's absence with a performance which was highly courageous, even by his high standards. By the end of the series, Hughes's knees were giving way and in many respects, he never recovered from that tour de force. Seven months later, he played what was surely his last Test for Australia, against South Africa in Cape Town. In that period after the Ashes tour, Hughes fought a losing battle against fitness and, it seemed, enthusiasm as if the burdens he carried in England in 1993 sapped his large body of its remaining energy.

In his 53 Tests, Hughes took 212 wickets at 28.3, dismissing a batsman every 58 balls and averaging four wickets a Test match. At the end of his final Test, Hughes was seventh on the list of Australian wicket-takers and his average of wickets per match was bettered only by Dennis Lillee, Graham McKenzie and Clarrie Grimmett. Hughes also averaged 16.65 with the bat and took 23 catches in the out-field with a very safe pair of hands.

Throughout his career, Hughes readily accepted Border and Simpson's demands for hard work. He improved his cricket steadily from start to finish, convincing all those who originally doubted his ability. He was often at his best, as in England in '93, when his team needed him most. At times, Hughes might have crossed the line that separates aggressive behaviour from the outright boorish, but to the end, he was a passionate and committed cricketer whose courage and sense of fun brought people through the turnstiles and earned the affection and respect of all those who played with and against him.

With his handlebar moustache, stubble and series of bizarre hairstyles, Hughes was never mistaken for an intellectual. But he was a sharp operator as well as a smart cricketer. In England in '93, his broad girth inspired crowds to chant 'Sumo, Sumo' whenever he was in the play. Spotting the chance for a financial killing, Hughes had hundreds of T-shirts made and augmented his tour fee quite nicely. Merv Hughes was a key figure in the Border era.

For England, the '93 series was another disaster. Before that summer, Gooch's team lost all three Tests in India and a one-off Test in Sri Lanka. After losing the fourth Test against Australia, England began its ritual blood-letting with Gooch's resignation. Mike Atherton, at 25, brought a little more imagination to the captaincy as well as a victory in only his second match in charge, at the Oval in the sixth Test. After that game, England's chairman of selectors, also known as the supremo, former captain Ted Dexter, also resigned. Although Dexter had introduced some badly needed reforms at the lower levels of the game since taking up the position before the 1989 Ashes series, he had failed to improve the performances of the national team and so had to go.

Gooch's resignation, despite his fine batting, drew attention to both the attrition rate of England captains and the longevity of Border's reign. The fate of the two nations' cricket teams was reflected in the fates of their captains. As Border's reign settled down and Australia's rebuilding process began to bear fruit, England's cricket fell further into chaos. From 1984 to 1994, Australia had one captain, Allan Border. In that time, England had eight and, at the time of writing in the southern winter of 1995, Atherton's hold on the job was anything but secure.

To emphasise Border's phenomenal strength of will in surviving so long in a job he never wanted and never really thought himself suited for, the eight England captains who battled against and occasionally contributed to their team's decline tossed coins with six Indians, seven New Zealanders, six Pakistanis, four Sri Lankans and five West Indians. In all, while one man led Australia, the other six Test-playing nations used 36 captains.

In 1984, Laurie Sawle, the chairman of selectors, thought

that one of the prerequisites for Australian cricket's emergence from such a serious slump was for the selectors to find a long-term captain for the Australian team. Although it took some effort to convince him that he should accept the job, Allan Border more than fulfilled Sawle's expectations. Border never missed a Test as captain after his appointment in December 1984. Despite countless broken and chipped bones on his hands, Border kept his appointment for the toss of the coin. And through it all, he kept his Test batting average above 50. In one-day cricket, he captained Australia in a record 178 matches, many as draining for a captain in a few hours as a five-day Test match. For a reluctant leader, it was a mighty achievement.

As Thicknesse noted in his summary of the 1993 Ashes series for *Wisden*, Border's behaviour on that tour and at other times had been cause for some concern. His fear of failure and hatred of losing occasionally pushed him over the line into unacceptable behaviour. He had twice been reported by umpires for dissent and his team developed a reputation for verbal abuse of opponents. Early in the '93 tour, Border showed how determined he was to repeat the successes of 1989 when he smashed down his stumps after being bowled by a full toss in a one-day game against Middlesex at Lord's. Thicknesse wrote:

> That he will be remembered in England with respect rather than affection stemmed from his condoning, not infrequently his participation in, the sledging of opponents and umpires during play, in open violation of the International Cricket Council's code of conduct . . . Despite all of that, and the promise of England's win at The Oval, the figures of the last three series were conclusive – England 1, Australia 11, drawn 5. Nobody could question that Border was the man Australia had to thank for that.

STALEMATE

V ISITING cricket teams and their supporters do not come to the Wanderers Stadium in Johannesburg to be entertained; they come, as far as the locals are concerned, to be beaten. And the locals come to gloat. Known as the 'Bull Ring' because of the ferocity of its parochial supporters, the Wanderers is a tough place in a tough city.

By the end of the second day's play in the first Test in March 1994, Allan Border looked like he had had more than enough of Johannesburg and its famous Wanderers ground.

South Africa had made 251 in its first innings and Australia had worked its way from 3/70 to 3/136 before the visitors began to self-destruct. First, Mark Waugh was run out in a mix-up with Border and then, six runs later, Border was out in the same way. Two wasteful run-outs ruined Australia's first innings and, in the end, contributed significantly to the loss of the match. That evening, Border was fuming. When he led the team onto the field in the last session, he left his teammates metres behind, strode to first slip, folded his arms angrily against his chest and waited for his players to assume their fielding positions. An hour after stumps, his mood had not improved.

Geoff Lawson and I were in South Africa together on a supporters' tour, and a short while after play that day, were sitting at a terrace bar a couple of kilometres from the ground. We'd been taken to the bar by two local businessmen we'd met that day at the cricket. A couple of beers on the way home seemed a good idea after another dramatic day's play in the hothouse atmosphere of the Wanderers. Halfway into our second beer, someone at a nearby table called out, 'Look, it's the Aussies.'

There on the road in front of us was the Australian team bus waiting at a set of traffic lights. About 10 of the squad were sitting at windows along the left-hand side of the bus with a perfect view into the bar. For us, it was like looking at a line of portraits in an art gallery. Some of the players waved casually to the locals before becoming more animated when they spotted two familiar faces in the crowd. Michael Slater responded most warmly: he and Lawson were from Wagga Wagga and Slater played with the University of New South Wales Cricket Club, Lawson's Sydney club. Merv Hughes started clawing at his window as if desperate to get away from cricket and relax for a while. In the middle of the row was the captain. Border did not even turn his head to see what the commotion was. He just sat there, glaring straight ahead with the blackest of black looks on his face. The skipper was in one of his moods.

If the 1989 Ashes series and the celebrations that followed were the peak of the Border years, the season of 1993-94 was the lowest point since the early years. The romance of the middle years had worn off. This was a long, bitter summer full of controversy, criticism, tough cricket and constant speculation about when Border would retire. A poor first-up performance in the cauldron of the Wanderers, after a difficult domestic season, sent Border into a mood swing that affected him for the rest of that tour.

The summer began badly when Australia could not force a win in the first Test against New Zealand in Perth. Australia's slow batting on the fourth day and Border's decision to set New Zealand 303 to win off 65 overs on the fifth day were widely criticised. New Zealand held the Trans-Tasman Trophy, so Australia had to win the three-match series to regain the title. The visitors' captain and best batsman, Martin Crowe, had suffered a knee injury and would be batting on one leg in the second innings. The New Zealand bowling, modest at best, was also affected by injuries. Despite these advantages, Australia's second innings dawdled meaninglessly on the fourth day. With wickets in hand, the Australians added only 89 from 28 overs in the final session when quick runs were needed to set up a push for victory on the fifth day. Mark Taylor and David Boon seemed to lose all purpose and urgency.

After a couple of seasons when the Australian batsmen had attracted criticism for slow play, this sort of cricket heightened the pressures on Border and his team. At a time when crowds at Tests around the world were dwindling, it did little to promote the traditional form of the game.

In his column in the *Sydney Morning Herald*, Geoff Lawson commented:

> *Border has shown no willingness to take risks through his reign, which is fine if you are always playing the game from behind as Australia did for much of the 1980s. But when the players are there to make quick runs and bowl sides out on all types of pitches, those resources must be used to the maximum. To hear Michael Slater criticised for having too many shots in his kitbag of talents shows a total lack of understanding of the direction Test cricket must take to survive – the Waugh brothers to flail if necessary, Boon and Taylor to stabilise if required, Border to rescue. Make the runs faster and you give yourself more time to win. If that means giving yourself more time to risk losing, then so be it. The fear of failure/losing is the major inhibition to exciting Test cricket – or any standard of cricket for that matter.*

Like Ian Chappell, Lawson was well qualified to make these criticisms as he had been an adventurous, attacking captain of New South Wales in the late 1980s and early 1990s. Unlike Chappell, Lawson had never led a Test team, but the odds are the aura and history that surround Test cricket would not have dampened his style too much. Lawson's approach could be traced back to Chappell's time as Australian captain and before that to Richie Benaud's days as a dynamic and imaginative captain of New South Wales and Australia. Again, the conservative, safety-first approach of Border and Simpson was at odds with the more adventurous tactics normally associated with Australian cricket and most recently employed by New South Wales.

Simpson confirmed the Australians had been below par in the first Test, although he noted that 'any declaration is always a matter for the captain to decide'. In the *Australian*, Mike Coward, after berating the team for its careless attitude to the welfare of Test cricket, wrote: 'Given the Australian players are underpinned by a host of professional advisers and consultants it is astonishing to think they must be cajoled into attaining the level of intensity required for Test match competition against NZ. Not for the first time this year it seems they are struggling to come to grips with the complex games of the mind which accompany any Test series.'

Although Australia thrashed a disintegrating New Zealand team in the remaining two Tests in Hobart and Brisbane, the public disquiet prompted by the poor showing in Perth set the tone for the summer. Again, there were calls for change, for new blood in the team. Again, a resounding win in England was followed by criticism back home from a public and media impatient for more substantial achievement.

That Border was 38 and near the end of a great career also encouraged the public to look to the future. The question of when Border was to retire dominated the summer. In 1993, many of the great names of the 1980s had retired – Viv Richards, Gordon Greenidge, Jeff Dujon, Ian Botham, David Gower, Imran Khan and Dilip Vengsarkar. Border had already said that he wanted to do one thing he and his generation had never managed: to play a Test series in South Africa now that the reforming republic was back in the family of Test-playing nations. As well, he had expressed reluctance about touring Pakistan in September-October 1994. It seemed 1993-94 would be his last summer of Test cricket in Australia; and the third Test in Durban in March 1994, his final appearance in the baggy green cap.

Border made his twenty-seventh and final Test century in Brisbane against New Zealand and was given a warm, affectionate farewell by the crowd, which had adopted him as its own back in 1980. At every ground that summer, crowds assumed they were seeing the last of Border as a Test player and they responded wonderfully well. When he left the field after being run out for four in the third Test against South Africa in Adelaide, he waved his bat to all parts of the ground. It seemed to be the final farewell.

During the season, Border agreed to a tribute celebrity match played at the Gabba and to a large black-tie dinner in his honour in Sydney on the night before the third World Series final against South Africa. After speeches by Richie Benaud, Sunil Gavaskar, Greg Ritchie and comedian Andrew Denton, Border, a reluctant public speaker, began eloquently enough. But soon the idea of giving a formal address marking the end of his career got the better of his emotions. Suddenly, the speech was over and Border was off the podium and heading towards the sanctuary of his table down on the floor with the rest of the crowd.

Although the season showed all the hallmarks of a farewell summer, Border could not quite bring himself to make the announcement. He would complete the tour to South Africa and see how he felt. In general the public and most past players polled by newspapers thought he deserved the good grace to be allowed to choose his time. He had given such long and loyal service and been such a great player that Australian cricket owed him as much. However, one sour note threatened to spoil that chorus of farewells.

After a storm-ravaged draw in Melbourne in the first Test against South Africa played in Australia since 1963-64, Border's team was set 117 to win the second match in Sydney. They failed by six runs and South Africa achieved a dramatic, courageous win and a 1-0 lead in the first of two consecutive three-game series.

The jittery way the Australians crumbled on that last day in Sydney provoked further demands for change and had editorial writers calling for Taylor to replace Border as captain for the tour to South Africa. In a leader in the *Australian* on 20 January, the paper said:

> *Border's contribution over the years has been immense. Nothing can detract from what he has achieved, especially during and after the tumultuous World Series revolution when, virtually on his own, he restored stability and credibility to Australian cricket. Border's place in history is secure. He is a giant of the game, a saviour of Australian cricket. But it is time to admit the truth: there is a fundamental problem with the Test team. It is not performing to potential. The leadership is too cautious and, in some cases, too negative.*

Border was besieged at airports around the country by television crews demanding to know when he was going to retire. At times, he lost his temper with this incessant questioning. The old nickname, Captain Grumpy, was resurrected. The pressure was building.

A predictable call for Border to stand down came from former great Australian left-hander Neil Harvey. A few years before, Rod Nicholson of News Ltd newspapers had instigated a practice of quoting Harvey as saying Border was finished as a player.

This time Harvey chimed in again: 'He's finished. I go back

to my time as a selector when we dropped Bill Lawry from the Test team when he was skipper. The same time has arrived for Border.'

What Harvey failed to mention was that the dropping of Lawry was a sad chapter in Australian cricket history, an example of the bad old days when players found out about selections from the media, not from the selectors. Harvey and his fellow selectors might have been justified in dropping Lawry as captain, but his replacement, Ian Chappell, while no great fan of Lawry's leadership, has always maintained that at that time, Lawry was still a world-class opening batsman and deserved to stay in the Australian team.

Fortunately, the ACB had moved on from those insensitive days and was not about to throw Border aside. To his credit, Border had declined to comment on Harvey's petty criticisms, but by 1993-94, he had had enough and eventually offered a possible reason for Harvey's campaign:

> Every year for the past three or four, someone drags Neil Harvey out of the woodwork to have a go at me. I really don't know why he has a go at me. Perhaps it's a jealousy thing. I am happy with what I have achieved and I am pleased to be still around and scoring runs. I used to have a lot of time for Neil Harvey. I admired him as a player and he was a selector when I first came into Test cricket.

Many people in cricket circles noted that, by most criteria, Border had replaced Harvey as the best Australian left-handed batsman since the Second World War. John Benaud showed in a column in the *Sun-Herald* before the start of this summer that since the 1990-91 Ashes series, Border had been Australia's next best-performed batsman after the formidable David Boon. In that period, Boon was arguably the best batsman in the world, while Border had performed better than the other established middle-order players such as Mark and Steve Waugh and Dean Jones, and newcomers such as Damien Martyn and Justin Langer. As a batsman, Border was still worth his place in the Test team.

As for the loss in Sydney, Border was as honest as ever. 'Ninety-five per cent of the time the batsmen do a tremendous job, but we are letting ourselves down in these tight ones. You get into situations and you almost expect to lose. I don't think I've won one of these games. That's the disappointing thing for me. That's a very bad attitude to have. We have to back ourselves more.' That phrase 'almost expect to lose' showed that Border's career-long fear of failure was still affecting the team psychology.

The player most affected on that final day in Sydney was 22-year-old Damien Martyn. A highly gifted, attacking shot-maker, Martyn froze out in the middle when the pressure of being the only specialist batsman left to take Australia to victory proved too much.

Border had been bowled by Allan Donald in the first over of the day and promptly sank into a bad mood. As the wickets fell, he remained up the back of the dressing-room and did not give Martyn any advice on how he should approach such a pressure situation. From the way he batted, Martyn's dilemma was not improved by any advice from his coach. The young batsman's failure that day set his career back a long way.

The loss of this match not only reflected badly on Border's leadership but on Simpson's inability to improve his team's approach to such run-chases, surely one of his main jobs as a former Test batsman who had by then been its coach for seven years. After all, apart from Border, Simpson had been coach when every one of the batsmen who faltered in Sydney had joined the team. Yet while Border copped all the criticism and faced calls for his replacement, Simpson's role was only rarely questioned. Simpson's major influence – as coach, tactical adviser and selector – escaped the attention of the leader writers.

The *Australian's* editorial noted that: 'The tradition of Australian cricket is that the captain is held accountable for poor performances.' True, except that the appointment of a coach-cum-selector had been a departure from that tradition. Australian teams had never had a full-time coach/selector before Simpson.

During a post-mortem into the Sydney loss on ABC Radio, Tracey Holmes noted that the coach's voice seemed to disappear from public debate at certain times. One of those times was definitely not the glorious aftermath of Australia's series win in the West Indies some 17 months after the loss to South Africa in Sydney. After the win in Jamaica, Simpson's voice was heard loud and long, thanks to an extraordinary article he wrote for the *Sydney Morning Herald* in which he took a great deal of credit for that historic victory. So much credit, in fact, that he failed to mention Mark Taylor's brilliant captaincy or the foundation built by Allan Border.

However, Simpson's role in the loss to South Africa in Sydney obviously did not concern the ACB. It was about to reappoint him for another two years.

Simpson's summer was not without its irritations. A few days before the first Test in Perth against New Zealand, Malcolm Conn had taken a different view of Simpson's role from that of Conn's predecessor on the *Australian*, Terry Brindle. Conn began his feature: 'When Bob Simpson was appointed coach of the Australian side in 1986 he said he wanted to make the position redundant, then proceeded to build an empire.' Conn went on to detail some of Simpson's politicking, his provocative dealings with the media and his touchy relationships with his players. While referring favourably to Simpson's work in restoring credibility to the Australian team from the mid-1980s, Conn wrote: 'But Simpson's unquestionably positive role as a practice captain who demands discipline and hard work and his valuable early support for captain Border, has been negated by his conservatism as a selector and tactician and his strong political desires to control all in his world.'

Simpson's desire to control his world was no more evident than in a bizarre controversy surrounding a comment in one of Dean Jones's columns in the *Sunday Age*. Jones had not played a Test since the tour to Sri Lanka three years earlier but he had fought his way back into the one-day team. He knew that some decent performances in the World Series in 1993-94 could win him a ticket on the plane to South Africa later that summer. Jones was reinstated to the one-day team for the match against South Africa in Brisbane on 9 January. He made 98 and won the Man of the Match award. Australia won the game.

In his column the following week, Jones wrote: 'Coach Bob Simpson was not there. That made the atmosphere more relaxed, with Allan Border telling us to to be positive and play our shots. I'm sure that helped me.'

By 'wrote', I mean that Jones dictated those comments to me over the phone and I formed them into the article. This had been our practice for some two years. Jones had never asked for faxes of the articles to be sent for checking nor had he ever complained about my interpretations of his comments. In fact, Jones had never been happy when another *Sunday Age* sportswriter had to do the column when I was unavailable. As for the controversial comment, I thought that Jones was expressing what almost every employee in Australia feels when his or her boss is away for a while.

An ACB official had faxed Simpson a copy of the column and after he rejoined the team in Perth a week after the Brisbane match. Simpson confronted Jones and threatened legal action unless Jones withdrew his comments. Jones's teammates were amazed. They told Jones the comment was accurate in that the team had been more relaxed in Simpson's absence. Some even offered to support Jones should the matter end up in court.

When the press found out about this confrontation, I checked with two sources who confirmed that Simpson had threatened legal action against Jones, then withdrew it a few days later. When questioned by the press about the issue, Simpson denied the legal threat; Malcolm Conn quoted him in the *Australian* as describing the claim as 'an absolute lie'. Of the column, Jones said his comments had been misinterpreted; Simpson said that 'it was a total misquote. He's totally retracted it and is highly embarrassed by the whole thing. It wasn't him.'

Jones was in a difficult situation. Simpson's dual role as coach/selector meant he had some say in whether Jones was chosen for the tour to South Africa. Jones felt he had little choice but to avoid any controversy and to side publicly with Simpson. Privately, the pair was hardly on friendly terms and their difficulties erupted into a shouting match at practice at the MCG on 20 January, the day before the first World Series final. Eventually, Border had to come between coach and batsman, pointing out that he and his team did not need this problem the day before an important match.

Several months later, after Jones's announcement in South Africa that he had retired from international cricket, he admitted in his book, *Deano: My Call*, that Simpson had indeed threatened him with legal action. 'Once I said in an article in the *Sunday Age* that the team relaxed when he wasn't around – and he jumped on me very quickly. It was meant innocently enough – when the cat's away and all that – but Simmo took strong objection to it and said I'd better retract the statement if I didn't want to be sued.'

That the coach of the Australian cricket team could threaten one of his players with a law suit over what was, at the very worst, an innocent and mildly critical comment and still be reappointed soon after, with glowing endorsements, by the sport's governing body was extraordinary. This was hardly the sort of mature, professional conduct which the ACB and Simpson had been trumpeting for years as the hallmark of the modern Australian cricket system. That the same man also remained a selector confirmed the failure of the ACB to look to the well-being of its team as well as its refusal to listen to the views of its senior players, including its captain, and of some of the most respected past players in the country.

Even the non-political Border had registered his disapproval

of captains and coaches being selectors in his book, *Beyond 10,000*,
published at the start of this difficult season:

> *Troubled players need a captain's ear and vice-versa, and there
> would be a certain reluctance to confess if the player feared it might
> damage his selection prospects.*
>
> *That's why I don't think the coach should be a selector, either.
> Consultant yes, because there has to be feedback on team direction.
> But I think on the whole to have a captain or a coach on the selection
> panel leaves the process too open to compromise, and that would be
> a weakness when the really tough decisions have to be made.*

It does not come any clearer than that.

Despite mounting evidence that the Australians' performances
had reached a plateau, the ACB, presuming the captain would
retire soon, judged that Simpson's reappointment would ensure
precious continuity.

A month after his reappointment, Simpson's position began
to decline. The ACB did not approve of the lack of leadership
displayed by the coach during the sledging controversies in
Johannesburg. During the winter which followed that tour, Simpson
was persuaded to stand down from the selection panel, and during
the following season, his role inside the dressing-room was redefined
and reduced by the new captain Mark Taylor with the support of
an ACB which finally began to pay heed to the views of its senior
players. Continuity was no longer such an important factor.

Australia squared the series against South Africa in Adelaide with
a strong 191-run win. During that match, Allan Border became
the first player to score 11,000 runs in Test cricket. So much for
the good news. The bad was that the two running controversies
of those years grabbed most of the attention. Australia's umpiring
standards came in for further criticism from South Africans upset
at decisions by Darrell Hair, and player behaviour was again
criticised.

The latter issue came to a head in Johannesburg on the third
day of the first Test, the day after Border's grim ride in the team
bus. For no apparent reason, Border decided not to introduce his
best bowler, Shane Warne, until South Africa had reached 1/123
off 43 overs. Warne spent most of the Sunday morning stationed
in the deep near two stands full of aggressive white South Africans.
At times, he joked with the crowd, at other times, he returned a
little quiet abuse of his own. When he bowled Andrew Hudson in

Trouble in the Bull Ring: *Tim May ducks for cover as*
Merv Hughes confronts an abusive spectator near the
end of the first Test in Johannesburg, March 1994.

that long-delayed first over, Warne lost his cool and gave Hudson
an awful, ugly 'send-off'. ICC referee Donald Carr fined Warne
1000 rand ($450) and Merv Hughes the same amount for sledging.

After those fines were imposed, Simpson announced that no
further action would be taken by team management. Team
management, Dr Cam Battersby and, apparently, Simpson might
have considered the matter closed; the ACB did not. It was not
Simpson's role to make managerial statements and his comment
embarrassed the ACB, which had recently announced a crackdown
on such behaviour.

Warne and Hughes's outbursts caused fierce reaction back in
Australia, where the simmering issue of the team's behaviour,
described by Ian Botham a few weeks before as the worst of all
Test teams, boiled over into severe criticism of the Australian side,
particularly its captain and coach.

During the home season, Border had offered his usual defence:
'I think it is a media build-up. In seven or eight hours' cricket,
you might get two minutes of blokes having a go at each other.
As soon as something happens, television flashes to my face or the
batsman's face and they highlight things that are not any big deal.
The players don't worry about it.'

The Australians certainly felt they had been unfairly criticised
for their behaviour, believing they did openly what others did

*Lost in thought: Allan Border seems to be contemplating his future while waiting
for the presentations to begin after the third Test in South Africa in 1994.*

surreptitiously. The Australians had been annoyed with some of
the comments made by their opponents that summer. According
to the Australians, in the Brisbane Test, New Zealand's Chris
Cairns had arrived at the wicket and quietly told Warne he was
going to belt him out of the park. When Warne dismissed Cairns
soon after, he gave the batsman an obvious send-off which attracted
widespread condemnation. Similarly, the Australians felt that South
Africa's Brian McMillan, in particular, had had plenty to say and
not received any attention.

Yet even if there were a perverse honesty about the Australians'
sledging, Border could not simply blame television. The cameras
were a fact of life and would always be attracted to any dramas
during play. Besides, some of the aggressive behaviour of the
Australians, and others, was obvious to spectators at the ground,
not just those watching on television. And, as Simpson said in a
speech at a dinner in Johannesburg to welcome the Australians to
South Africa: 'Unfortunately, with television and reporting in
many ways, too much is being made of it [sledging]. Some of the
greatest stories have come out of sledging. Too much obvious
sledging, however, is not good for the game.'

Most of Australia's umpires felt that the Australians under
Simpson and Border had been too loud in their disapproval of
umpiring decisions. One, Steve Randell, had actually reported the
Australian captain twice for dissent. Most of Randell's colleagues

supported his stand. This problem, like sledging, eased after Taylor became captain.

Back at the Wanderers, things deteriorated further when, on the final afternoon of the match, Hughes lost his temper at a spectator who abused him from outside the players' race. Hughes's reaction, thumping the fence with his bat, was shown on national news bulletins back in Australia.

After Carr's fines in Johannesburg, the press called for strong ACB action to back its new policy announced in Adelaide a few weeks earlier. ACB chairman Alan Crompton and Graham Halbish flew to Johannesburg and imposed further fines of $4000 each on Warne and Hughes.

Trevor Grant in the *Herald Sun* thought this action too weak and argued that the two players should have been suspended. Pat Smith in the *Age* was similarly critical: 'The ACB stands accused of cowardice at worst, dithering at best, for not taking strong action with players and team management years ago.' Smith also dismissed Border and Simpson's defence that Test cricket was a tough sport with the telling comment that: 'Tough cricketers would have scored 117 in the last innings of the Sydney Test to beat South Africa; would have made the 186 for victory in the last innings of the Adelaide Test against the West Indies last summer.'

Writing from South Africa, Mike Coward in the *Australian* said of the ACB:

> *Hopefully, they will have also demanded that coach Bob Simpson, arguably the most political figure in the Australian game, fairly and responsibly represent their interests in the future. After all, they are paying his substantial salary and, despite the misgivings of some of their number, they recently reappointed him for another two years.*
>
> *To this point Simpson has not kept his promise to restore traditional standards of behaviour to the Australian team.*

Coward then suggested the ACB launch an investigation into the team's poor performances overseas. Certainly, this series, especially the dramas of Johannesburg, added weight to the view of Coward and other commentators that under Border and Simpson the Australians too quickly lost their cool in foreign parts. That was definitely the case on that Sunday in Johannesburg. As he had been on the bus the evening before, Border was remote from his team on the field that day, and South Africa was able to bat itself into a strong position thanks to a century from Hansie Cronje and unusually sloppy play from the Australians. With Border in a funk and Taylor absent from the match through illness, the team lost its way.

To their credit, the Australians rallied from the defeat and controversies at the Wanderers to win in Cape Town and have the better of a dull draw in Durban. In the nine Tests that summer – three against New Zealand and six against South Africa – Warne had taken a staggering 51 wickets at 18.59. Australia had certainly found a powerful new cricketer.

To his credit, Warne rose above the traumas of Johannesburg, and throughout the tour, gave generously of his time in visits to townships where he thoroughly enjoyed meeting and coaching hundreds of enthusiastic black and coloured children. His on-field behaviour after the Wanderers Test match was exemplary.

But overall, two 1-1 results from two three-game series was not satisfactory against a team only recently returned to full international competition after more than 20 years in political and sporting exile.

Throughout the Tests in South Africa, Border seemed unusually distant. At times, Taylor appeared to be guiding him, offering him ideas and keeping the team running properly. Although he had still made no official announcement, even Border knew that his final innings of this series, in hot and steamy Durban, might be his final appearance for Australia in a Test match.

Australia made a modest and relatively slow 269 in its first innings at Kingsmead, Durban, before South Africa effectively killed the game with a reply of 422 which greedily consumed 832 minutes and 205 overs. It was a pointless exercise that rendered Border's last Test match a disappointing non-event.

On the fifth day, Border joined Mark Waugh with the score at 4/157, only four runs into the black. A few quick wickets and Australia might have been in danger of losing the match and the series. Although it was not quite a crisis of 1985 proportions, it was a situation which suited Border's back-to-the-wall temperament, or at least it suited Border to think so.

Throughout their 140-run partnership, the gifted and graceful Waugh made batting look simple, while at the other end, his captain battled hard against good bowling, particularly from a very fast Allan Donald, who seemed intent on becoming the last bowler in Test cricket to take the prized wicket of Allan Border. In the Australian dressing-room, Border's teammates watched closely,

The end: Allan Border leaves the ground after what proved to be his last Test innings – 42 not out at Kingsmead, Durban, 29 March 1994.

suspecting that they were witnessing the end of an era.

The Kingsmead crowd was a little restless. Although the South Africans had only just resumed their part in the history of Test cricket, they had observed Border's career from afar and knew something significant was happening. From carefully selected vantage points, photographers and television crews waited to record the end of a great career.

Out in the middle, Border refused to give an inch, still placing the highest price on his wicket. Several times he said to Waugh, 'There's no way I'm getting out here. It might be my last dig.'

To the final curtain, Border occupied centre stage. At his peak, he had dominated that stage, occasionally destroying bowlers as all great batsman should. But more often, circumstances forced him to restrain himself, to play within his capabilities to save his side from another loss. By the time his teammates had developed enough to win more than lose, they did the dominating while Border played a lesser role, guiding by example rather than leading from the front.

With Australia safe from collapse at 4/297, Kepler Wessels and Border agreed to call a halt. Waugh ended on 113, Border on 42. By the time his captain neared the boundary, Waugh had fallen a few respectful metres behind. As the South Africans, further away, moved to the left towards their dressing-room, most looked across to watch Border's final moments. Although a few photographers stayed close to him, continuing to the last the intense media scrutiny which had followed him throughout his captaincy career, Border was a solitary, dignified figure, hair and shirt plastered down with sweat, eyes straight ahead, no grand gestures.

For the crowd, Border must have seemed like the embodiment of the era of Test cricket their government's racist policies had denied them. In the two decades South Africa had been exiled from world cricket, Border had played all of his world-record 156 Test matches. In that time, international cricket had changed from a part-time sport to a full-time profession, and no cricketer had been more professional, more committed and more durable than Allan Border.

END

OF AN ERA

M OST international cricketers enjoy their golf, but few can have spent as much of their spare time walking the golf courses of the cricket world as Allan Border. Generally, Border used golf to take his mind off cricket. But on Wednesday, 11 May 1994, as he played a round with an old mate at the exclusive Brisbane Golf Club, he could not avoid thinking about cricket – specifically, his immediate future in the game. It was during that round of golf that Border finally decided to announce his retirement. As ever, he was reacting instinctively to what he saw as enemy forces attacking him.

As far as Border knew, he and the ACB were preparing for a full national press conference for later that week, but Border, annoyed by suggestions in the media that he had been 'gumming up the works' by delaying his announcement, lost his cool and reacted in his usual feisty manner.

The week before, Border told chairman of selectors Laurie Sawle that he intended to retire, but asked Sawle to keep it in confidence until later the following week. Border was due to have

Father figure: Allan Border's proud son Dene at the 1994 Allan Border Tribute Dinner in Sydney.

skin cancers removed from his face and wanted to fully recover before facing the nation's media. Sawle kept his word and, although ACB chairman Alan Crompton and CEO Graham Halbish had been warned by media manager Ian McDonald to be ready for an announcement at any time, they did not know for sure whether Border was even going to retire. In the morning of Tuesday, 10 May, McDonald issued a statement to the media saying that the Border question was irrelevant to that day's press conference, which was called as a matter of course to announce details of the ACB meeting.

Two factors complicated the situation. First, it was known that during the meeting the ACB had interviewed four senior players – Taylor, Boon, Healy and Steve Waugh. When news of these interviews spread, the public assumed the players were being interviewed for the captaincy. This upset Border as it seemed the board was preparing for a retirement he had not yet announced. The board had been considering candidates for the captaincy for some time and it was simplistic to think it would make that appointment on the results of one set of interviews.

The second complication was that everyone was waiting for the announcement of the team to tour Pakistan in August and September. It had already been postponed once to give Border time to make his decision and public impatience was growing. At the press conference after the board meeting, Crompton and Halbish

*The Big Four: Mark Taylor,
David Boon, Steve Waugh and
Ian Healy (clockwise from top
left) were called to an
important meeting with the
Australian Cricket Board
in May 1994.*

221

faced the inevitable questions about Border's decision. Although they denied any impatience, they had to admit that the naming of the team to Pakistan had been delayed until Border's announcement.

When Border read reports in the morning press of the ACB press conference, he interpreted comments by reporters that he was 'gumming up the works' as criticism from Halbish and Crompton. Having already told one board member, Sawle, that he would retire, Border became upset at what he thought was publicly expressed impatience from the board's two most senior officials. After weeks of speculation, Border decided over a few beers with his mate at the nineteenth hole to make the announcement that evening. The mate happened to be Channel Seven reporter Pat Welsh.

Although the board tried hard all that afternoon to contact Border to assure him he could still have as much time as he wanted to announce his decision, Border, face still affected by the skin cancer operation, spoke his mind to Welsh on an exclusive story on Channel Seven news that evening. Heavies at Channel Nine, the cricket station, were not amused. Border told Welsh:

> I'm going to retire, and it's done with a heavy heart. It's taken me a lot of weeks to come to this decision but I was under the impression I had those weeks up my sleeve to make what to me was the most important decision of my life. I'm basically fed up with all the innuendo. I'm just disappointed by some of the comments made by Graham Halbish and Alan Crompton, saying I'm gumming up the works when they knew full well there was a decision being made tomorrow at a national press conference. I don't know what the agenda is but it's very disappointing. It's a tough decision for me. It's like a part of me has died by making this decision to retire.

Typically, Border was the ultimate players' man to the end, suspicious of officialdom, fearful of a hidden agenda that did not exist. Had Sawle broken his confidence to Border, the confusion could have been avoided. Had the ACB realised the question of Border's future would certainly be raised at its post-meeting press conference, it could have called off the conference, merely issuing a press release saying the announcement of the team for Pakistan was imminent. But that would probably have failed as well. Border's future was the topic of the day, and one way or another, the media would have hounded those involved until they received an answer.

In essence, the mess was a result of the ACB's desire not to rush their captain, Sawle's honesty and Border's reluctance to leave a game that had been his life for so long – hardly major failings. Border's teammates were surprised by the sorry business as they had fully expected him to retire soon after returning from South Africa. Towards the end of that tour, the captain was so weary from 15 years of international cricket that he had even wanted to avoid playing in the one-day matches that followed the third Test in Durban. When he returned home and contemplated life after Test cricket, he began to have second thoughts.

Still, it was appropriate, if embarrassing and inconvenient for the ACB, that Border left the game in a huff – passionate, bucking against administrators – the players' traditional foe – enjoying a good stoush right to the end and still only vaguely aware of his high stature in the game.

Inevitably, Border's many admirers in the community thought the ACB had treated their hero shabbily, pushing him into retirement before he was ready. The board just had to wear that; there was little it could do. Admittedly, some members of the ACB thought that the team needed a change of leader, that it had been stagnating a little in recent times. During the previous few years, the ACB had suggested to Border that it would be happy if he decided to stand down from the captaincy but continue as a player. Despite the views of people such as Neil Harvey, Border was still performing well enough to retain his place in the team as a batsman. But Border wanted to play on as captain and there was no way a grateful ACB was going to force its loyal captain aside. In hindsight, his final years might have been less taxing mentally had he chosen to relinquish the captaincy a season or two before retiring.

A few days after the mix-up over the announcement of his retirement, all was forgiven. Border conceded it had been an innocent if somewhat clumsy mix-up and that the ACB was not acting on any hidden agenda. He said he planned to play the domestic season with his beloved Queensland in the hope of helping the state to its first Sheffield Shield win. He also said he hoped he would still be offered that job as the ACB's roving ambassador. The job had never been in doubt.

Although the ACB's meetings in Melbourne with the four senior players had not been interviews for the captaincy, they were an important landmark at the beginning of the post-Border era. Facing the full ACB board of directors – 14 state delegates and several

A heavy heart: Allan Border explains the most important decision of his life – to retire from international cricket.

senior administrators – was a rare experience for an Australian player. Bill O'Reilly would not have believed it: O'Reilly had been one of five players called in to a meeting with several board members in January 1937 when, in a roundabout way, their fondness for late-night carousing was raised and their commitment to their new captain, Don Bradman, questioned. The players called the board members' bluff and nothing came of the confrontation. The 1994 meeting was far more constructive.

Among a range of issues discussed, the ACB representatives asked the four whether they thought Bob Simpson should retain his role as selector as well as coach. Most commentators had been critical of this dual role for many years, but it was only in recent months that the ACB had begun to examine those criticisms. When the four senior players, interviewed separately, expressed the opinion that Simpson's role as coach had been hampering the smooth running of the team, the ACB decided a change was needed. Five months later, Simpson announced he was standing down as a selector.

The ACB had been impressed with Mark Taylor's vision for the post-Border Australian team, and when it chose him as the new captain, it gave him the traditional full mandate to run the team as he saw fit. It also agreed to his condition that he be chosen for an extended period in the one-day team. With Simpson no

The new captain: Mark Taylor's impressive performance at his first press conference as Australian captain offered a taste of things to come.

longer wielding so much power as a selector constantly present in the dressing-room, Taylor assumed more control over day-to-day matters than Border had ever sought to exercise. Although Simpson had never seen any problems with his dual role and had in the past lobbied to retain it, he had little choice but to accept the new arrangement.

To his credit, Taylor promptly accepted his mandate, initiating changes which confirmed that a new man was in charge. Politically, within and without the dressing-room, Taylor acted shrewdly. Even before he led his team onto the field in a match, he showed the qualities of a natural leader.

Border had always advised Taylor to be his own man should he be given the top job. With Taylor, that was never in doubt. While Border took a long time to think of himself as a captain and had only accepted the job because his country's cricket needed its best player to come forward, Taylor was from the start an eager, talented and confident leader. He knew he had inherited a strong, disciplined and increasingly attacking team and he was determined to take it to new heights.

The winter of 1994 was not just a winter of change and rebirth in Australian cricket. In the northern hemisphere, the West Indies' left-hander Brian Lara was rewriting the records; first, by breaking Sir Garfield Sobers's 36-year-old world record Test score

of 365 not out with a flawless 375 against England in the fifth
Test in Antigua in the third week of April, two weeks before his
twenty-fifth birthday.

The Trinidadian then left for England, where he continued
his stunning form, making six centuries in seven innings, culminating
in his second world record, this time for a first-class score of 501
not out for Warwickshire against Durham at Edgbaston on 6 June.
These astounding feats lifted Lara to megastar status thanks to the
spread of cricket telecasts throughout Asia via pay television. The
best thing about Lara's rise to prominence was that he scored his
runs with a flowing bat, playing glorious, graceful shots and taking
risks. He was a worthy successor to the great Sobers.

In India, the precocious Sachin Tendulkar had been joined
in that Test team by his boyhood batting partner, Vinod Kambli,
while young leg spinner Anil Kumble had quickly developed into
a world-class bowler.

Spin bowling was back in fashion, the dominance of pace
was fading and more Test matches were ending in results. The
game seemed to be in good shape. Even England looked to be
progressing. Mike Atherton, the young captain, managed to lead
his team to a 208-run win against the West Indies in Barbados in
April 1994. England lost the series 3-1, but did salvage some pride
towards the end. In that win, opener Alec Stewart made centuries
in both innings in a remarkable exhibition of courage and skill.

In Australia, the ACB was free of its long-time relationship
with Kerry Packer's marketing arm, PBL Marketing. The board set
up its own marketing division, and although many people were
sceptical about how well administrators could handle such a task,
the ACB deserved praise and encouragement for taking control of
the game.

The benefits of this new arrangement were soon obvious
when the board announced it would promote Test cricket as an
entity on its own rather than allow it to be swamped by all the
mindless razzamatazz for one-day cricket, which had typified cricket
promotions in Australia under PBL. At times in the past, the
ACB's wishes about how the game should be marketed had been
ignored by PBL, whose sole purpose seemed to be to fill grounds
at one-day matches. The ACB was determined to restore some
balance in promotion, realising that cricket's health depended to
some extent at least on the survival of Test matches.

With players like Warne, McDermott, Slater, Greg Blewett,
Michael Bevan, the Waughs and the popular veteran figure of

Boon, the ACB knew it had a highly marketable Test team which, under Taylor, would play attractive, attacking cricket.

Warne's influence in all of this cannot be overestimated. What Lara did for batting, Warne did for spin bowling. In 10 Tests in 1994, he took an amazing 70 wickets at an average of 18.3 apiece. Although he was a fine one-day bowler, the public soon realised that they could watch only 10 overs' worth of him in a one-day game. In Tests, though, they could watch him torment batsmen for over after over, hour after hour. Warne's role in showing the public that Test cricket was the form of the game where the subtle arts of slow bowling could best be seen and understood helped the traditional form of the game enormously; as did his image as the blond, good-looking, modern, fun-loving larrikin.

That such a contemporary, youthful figure practised leg-spin bowling, one of the game's oldest and most subtle crafts, a craft many thought close to extinction, revitalised the game. You only had to hear the buzz of expectation that raced around grounds when Warne was warming up for his first ball of the day to realise Australia had produced another great cricketer.

The realisation that in Warne Australia now had a bowler capable of being the first to reach the milestone of 500 Test wickets inspired the public as well as major international companies who signed Warne to lucrative contracts to endorse products such as sports footwear, casual fashion wear and the latest in sports-oriented soft drinks. The profile and earning capacity of Australia's young cricketers took a major step forward with Warne's arrival, as evidenced by gifted 20-year-old Tasmanian batsman Ricky Ponting's signing of what was believed to be a five-figure, three-year contract with giant United States sportswear company Nike, sponsors of Warne and Michael Slater.

The meeting between the ACB and those four senior players was not a one-off event. Under Halbish's administration, the ACB was keen to establish closer links with the players, to consult with them before making decisions that would directly affect their professional lives and to keep them informed of the reasons behind administrative decisions. Although Border became more involved in this side of the captaincy in his later years, the ACB found Taylor more receptive to this approach.

Before the tour to Pakistan in the spring, the team gathered in Adelaide for a camp that included media training, testing of a new, tougher fitness regime devised by Simpson and physiotherapist

Errol Alcott and advice on coping with the perceived traumas of touring Pakistan. This time the advice included material on the culture, politics and social mores of the Islamic republic.

Nine days after Border's unorthodox announcement of his retirement from international cricket, the ACB confirmed that Mark Taylor was the new Australian captain. At a pleasant press conference at the headquarters of the New South Wales Cricket Association in central Sydney, Taylor pledged to build on the foundation laid by Allan Border, to control his players' on-field behaviour, to try to improve the team's poor record in overseas series and to play positive, aggressive cricket. It was a smooth, flawless performance from someone at ease in his new job. Taylor, surrounded by smiling, relaxed officials, began his career as Australian captain in impressive style. He wanted the job and that was the best possible start.

In his first year as Australian captain, Taylor would lead Australia on the toughest tour of all, a three-Test series in Pakistan, followed by his first defence of the Ashes and then by the modern game's greatest challenge, a series against the West Indies in the Caribbean. A win there would mean that Taylor and his players would end that year with strong claims to being the best Test team in the world, the one achievement which had eluded Allan Border.

BEYOND

BORDER

BEFORE the start of the 1994-95 season, Rod Marsh wrote a thoughtful introduction to the 1994 edition of the *ABC Australian Cricket Almanac* in which he argued the need for Test cricket to provide more entertainment. After suggesting the ICC call all Test captains to a meeting to 'impress upon them the necessity of making Test cricket more entertaining', Marsh cited New South Wales as the leader in this area in recent years.

The former captain, Geoff Lawson, can take much of the credit for this positive approach [Marsh wrote], although I'm pleased to see Mark Taylor and Steve Waugh have continued the tradition, almost as if their state's enterprising attitude was ingrained in them. What a pity that all the other states don't play their cricket in the same way.

Marsh's article was prophetic in two ways. First, the other states did begin to adopt the New South Wales approach, and soon the number of outright wins in the Sheffield Shield competition rose dramatically, so much so that in 1994-95, 25 of the 30 games ended in uncontrived outright results.

Unexpectedly, New South Wales finished second last on the points table that season, with Steve Rixon struggling to balance his coaching commitments with his sports-clothing business, and a batch of inexperienced young players failing to cover the lengthy absences of the team's internationals. Lawson's appointment in June 1995 as Rixon's replacement suggested New South Wales was determined to regain its standing as the most adventurous team in Australian domestic cricket.

Second, when Taylor, a product of the 1980s version of New South Wales cricket, took over the captaincy from Allan Border, he brought a more adventurous attitude to the team, starting with a policy of trying to score 300 runs in a day's play.

As Ian Chappell noted after Australia's history-making series win in the Caribbean in 1995, Taylor's more attacking approach to Australia's batting was the most significant factor in that win, despite the fact that Australia's best batsman in the series, Steve Waugh, tended to play a more controlled game than Taylor, Slater, Mark Waugh and Greg Blewett. The crucial difference was in attitude. Taylor's Australians showed they were prepared to play the way they wanted, not the way their opponents were trying to force them to play. This is the essence of any sporting contest.

Given the fact that coach Simpson was present during all of Border's stint as captain and Taylor's first year, it might be fair to assume that the captains were totally responsible for the way their teams played, that Simpson had little impact on tactics. But this conclusion ignores Border's willingness to delegate much of his off-field role to Simpson, as well as the latter's record as one of Australia's most conservative captains. That the team began playing in a more relaxed, imaginative and adventurous way stemmed largely from the fact that Taylor began his captaincy by changing the way the team was run. Taylor quickly reasserted the prime position of the Australian captain.

Border, the reluctant leader, needed Simpson's help and so allowed his coach a large say in how the team was run. Taylor, a natural leader in the Benaud-Chappell-Lawson mould, did not need and did not want a powerful coach heavily involved in the day-to-day workings of his team.

Ian Chappell sees this as Border's greatest failing. 'The strongest criticism I have of Allan is that he allowed a coach, no matter who it is, to gain control of an international team. You cannot have conditional leadership.'

When the team began its first campaign under its new captain, in Sri Lanka and Pakistan in the spring of 1994, Taylor took charge of practice sessions, ran team meetings, pre-planned the tactics that would be discussed at those meetings, gave team talks before play, dealt with players in one-on-one talks and reduced the amount of training on long tours. He even began giving his pre-play talks in the dressing-room to the 11 involved in the match, while Simpson was still out on the ground hitting catches to the reserve players.

The changes were immediately obvious to the press travelling with the team, and both the *Australian*'s Trent Bouts and the *Age*'s Greg Baum commented on them.

In his wrap-up of the series, Baum wrote: 'Taylor immediately embraced the peripheral elements of the job that Allan Border eschewed. He established first that he was in command of the team, changing its dynamics so that coach Bob Simpson – who had a Machiavellian reputation in the Border era – was returned to the teaching role that was his original brief.'

Bouts wrote: 'Perhaps the most significant and perceptible sign of Taylor's determination to be his own man has been the dilution of Bob Simpson's role: the coach now suggests where once he directed ... The two work together well enough but it is not the partnership it was with Border.'

Unfortunately, these changes did not bring immediate success. Australia lost the series in Pakistan 0-1, which meant that the victory in Colombo in '91 was still the only Test won on the Indian subcontinent since Greg Chappell's team beat Sri Lanka in 1982-83.

In the first Test in Karachi, Australia almost broke that long drought but, in the end, lost by one wicket in agonising circumstances. A great last wicket stand of 57 between Inzamam ul-Haq and Mushtaq Ahmed dragged Pakistan across the line after Australia looked set to win comfortably. Off the final ball of the match, Pakistan needed three to win, Australia a wicket. Bravely, Taylor had left only one out-fielder on the on-side, and Inzaman accepted the challenge by coming down the pitch and trying to swing Warne to the leg boundary. The ball spun a long way, beating the bat, the stumps and, to Australia's great cost, Ian Healy's gloves. The result was four byes and a win to Pakistan in one of the great Test matches.

Although this was the third close loss for Australia in the previous 18 months, Taylor was able to maintain optimism and morale. This was no mean achievement given that in Karachi, he

*Near miss: Shane Warne, Inzamam ul-Haq and Ian Healy
watch as the last ball of the first Test in Karachi in 1994
goes away for four byes to give Pakistan the match.*

had dropped several catches at first slip and, worse still, made his first pair in a Test. It was a very poor start to his captaincy. But the Australians had played very well in that first Test and were able to continue that form in the remaining two drawn games. It was a series of the highest quality played between two talented teams ranked alongside each other as the only genuine challengers to West Indian supremacy.

Only after the Ashes series which followed in Australia did Phil Wilkins in the *Sydney Morning Herald* reveal accusations that a Pakistani player had offered substantial amounts of money to Warne, Tim May and Mark Waugh to help Pakistan win the Test series. The money was alleged to have come from the massive illegal cricket gambling industry that flourishes in India and Pakistan. The *Age* named that player as Pakistan captain Salim Malik, who played brilliantly in the series, compiling 559 runs at 93.17 an innings.

The bribery allegations became a major scandal throughout the cricket world, apparently confirming rumours that had been whispered in press boxes for years. Although the ACB informed the ICC of the allegations after the end of the third Test, the news took seven months to leak out. Later, the ACB sent depositions from the Australian players involved to the ICC, which were then passed on to the authorities in Pakistan, but the ACB declined a request from the Pakistan Cricket Board (PCB) to send the three players there to present their evidence at the PCB's formal inquiry.

At the time of writing, it seemed likely that the PCB would be left to deal with the problem. Its stand that Australia had yet to prove the allegations suggested that there would be no conclusive outcome to the affair. Earlier, widespread allegations about Pakistani ball-tampering had been dealt with by the ICC by the simple measure of instructing umpires to inspect the ball between overs. Allegations of illegal gambling, match-fixing and player corruption presented far more difficult problems for cricket's administrators. Given the huge amounts of money said to be involved in this illegal industry, a murky cloud of doubt was likely to hang over cricket on the subcontinent for some time.

Although all the evidence pointed to another one-sided Ashes series, Mike Atherton's team arrived in Perth in October 1994 breathing fire. Loaded with a contingent of blustering if not blistering fast bowlers rather than the usual skilful seamers, England promised a spirited challenge. Its batting would be bolstered by the inclusion of two former captains in their late thirties, Graham Gooch and Mike Gatting. Their role with the bat was to counter the threat posed by Shane Warne and, in the field, to avoid the ball as often as possible.

That two of England's squad, Martin McCague and Craig White, were born in the United Kingdom but grew up and learned their cricket in Australia, with the support of national and state academies, suggested English cricket still favoured pragmatism over pride. The Australian players, having learned all about national pride from Border, considered the two as traitors.

Michael Slater set the tone for the early part of the Test series by square cutting the first ball of the first Test in Brisbane behind point for four. The bowler, the consistently disappointing Phil DeFreitas, looked stiff, cold and underprepared for a Test match as he jogged in to bowl. His condition mirrored that of English cricket. Slater's shot and the philosophy behind it reflected the vigorous health of the Australian game in the mid-1990s.

Australia won well in Brisbane and Melbourne, Warne maintaining his mesmeric hold over the England batsmen with hauls of 3/39 and 8/71 in Brisbane and 6/46 and 3/16 in Melbourne, with the last three wickets coming from the final three balls of the second Test. Warne ended a brilliant 1994 with Australia's ninth Test hat-trick. The eighth had come three months earlier when Warne's Victorian teammate, Damien Fleming, did the trick in the second Test against Pakistan in Rawalpindi, his Test debut.

After the loss in Melbourne, English cricket sunk to unexplored depths with two losses in two days to a team of teenagers representing the Cricket Academy, coached by Rod Marsh and captained by his son Daniel. Admittedly, these games were organised more as practice for the England team than as an examination of the state of English cricket but, as a public relations exercise, the tourists' desultory form against a team of naturally talented and supremely confident, aggressive young Australians was a disaster. The British tabloids sunk the knife with relish.

England rallied in the third Test in Sydney, a dramatic draw that swung one way then the other before rain and gloom had their way. The Man of the Match was England's Yorkshire pace bowler and tailend slogger, Darren Gough, a cheeky, fresh-faced young cricketer full of passion, pride and joy. With Gough leading the way and the damp conditions limiting Warne's influence, England finally achieved the intensity of purpose required for Test cricket. But by then, England was down 0-2 with two Tests to play. Australia, under Taylor, had retained the Ashes.

When Gough suffered a broken bone in his foot during a World Series game in Melbourne and was forced to fly home, England's tour sank into chaos. Reserve players were flying in from wintry England, from an A team tour in India and from club cricket in Sydney. Atherton's team then suffered the further humiliation of failing to qualify for the World Series finals, which were contested by Australia and a new team, Australia A.

The Australia A team was made up of the best young fringe players from around the states and was designed, at Channel Nine's insistence, it seems, to ensure public interest in case England, the game's most consistent underachievers, and Zimbabwe, cricket's newest fully fledged international team, failed to perform up to standard.

The A team idea attracted a great deal of criticism. It was seen as an insult to the concept of international cricket where each country produced one team to represent it in any genuine international competition. Even Mark Taylor expressed his disapproval of having to play against fellow Australians in front of home crowds who cheered for the underdogs against the senior Australian team. Although all these criticisms were valid, the A team idea succeeded with the public, who delighted in being able to watch new players competing at a very high standard.

The most notable by-product of this venture was the emergence of South Australian opening batsman Greg Blewett. With Steve Waugh unable to bowl because of a shoulder injury, the selectors began searching for a possible middle-order batsman who could bowl in one-day games. Blewett won a place in the A team for the second batch of World Series matches as an all-rounder, and although his bowling was useful, his batting was a revelation. He came into the Test team for the fourth and fifth Tests in place of Michael Bevan, whose excellent form in Pakistan had disappeared. Batting at number six, Blewett made a century on debut in Adelaide and followed up with another in Perth.

Thanks to some remarkably cool-headed batting under pressure from Steve Waugh, Australia won the best-of-three finals series in two games, although both matches were tense and tight. Although the A team was relegated for the 1995-96 season to a single day/ night one-day match against the West Indies, the ACB had shown a preparedness to experiment, which deserved more credit than it received, although the influence of television in the decision to

The final farewell: during his first season in retirement Allan Border
visited each Test match ground to say goodbye to the public
which supported him through the bad times and the good.

field the A team was a matter of some concern.

England rallied well to win the fourth Test in Adelaide, with Gough present by fax if not in the flesh. With the prospect of a drawn series should Australia lose again in Perth in the fifth Test, Taylor did the rallying this time and Australia crushed England to end the season on a successful note. As England hobbled home to try to sort out another mess, Australia crossed the Tasman for a one-day series to commemorate New Zealand's centenary of cricket before heading off to the Caribbean in search of the ultimate victory.

At the start of the 1994–95 summer, Allan Border had amazed his Queensland teammates with his enthusiasm at pre-season training. Border had never pretended to like the physical preparation needed for modern cricket, but his pride and competitive spirit had never allowed his standards to slip. Even at the end of his international career, he was always one of the better performers at pre-season fitness trials. During the winter of 1994, his training was inspired by a major unfulfilled goal: helping Queensland win its first Sheffield Shield. Border's other unfulfilled ambition, playing in a winning Test series against the West Indies, was now beyond reach, but a Queensland Sheffield Shield was still there to be won.

The burly opening batsman, Matthew Hayden, led the fitness runs with the oldest member of the Queensland squad, Border, a

A strange feeling: Allan Border poses in his Queensland colours before the start of the 1994-95 season, his first since retiring from Test cricket.

few metres behind. In the words of one observer, Border trained 'like a kid'.

Some eight months later, Border was again acting 'like a kid', this time perched on a bench in the Queensland dressing-room at the Gabba, a can of beer in his left hand, his right arm around a teammate's shoulder, singing victory songs as if he had just played his first season of state cricket. The Australian team was already in the Caribbean, but in Australia there was only one cricket story: after 69 years, 62 seasons and many stumbles at the last hurdle, Queensland had won the Sheffield Shield. And Australian sport had lost one of its greatest stories – its longest and most famous losing streak was over.

From cab drivers in Cairns in the far north to Border's teammates in the dressing-room, every Queenslander agreed that Border's presence in the side for a full Shield season added the mental strength Queensland had always lacked when the Shield was to be decided in the final one or two games of a season. This time, Border's legendary determination and pride carried the team through to the ultimate prize. That determination was best illustrated when he batted in Melbourne against Victoria in a crucial game in February after suffering a broken bone in his forearm. He carried the injury for the remaining two games of the season and, as usual, never complained. His young teammates were inspired.

In 11 Shield games that season, Border topped Queensland's batting averages with 911 runs at 65.07. His last innings, in Queensland's win in the final over South Australia by an innings and 101 runs, ended two runs short of his seventy-first first-class century.

Fittingly, Border played in the first Sheffield Shield game played under lights, a day/night fixture against Western Australia at the WACA in Perth. All six state teams played in one day/night Shield game in 1994-95 in what was another example of the ACB's new-found willingness to experiment.

Border's time during this summer was not solely devoted to Queensland's quest for the Sheffield Shield. His job as a roving ambassador for the ACB had become so demanding that, by mid-season, he had rarely slept in his own bed. In the end, he asked the board to cut back his commitments. The ACB asked him to attend each Test match so he could be driven around the grounds to receive a formal farewell from the public. And throughout that season, he often spent time on the phone to his former Australian teammates, particularly Shane Warne, for whom Border had become hero, mentor and surrogate big brother.

Throughout his career, Border had never tried to exploit his huge popularity as an Australian icon for commercial gain. He had 'written' four best-selling books and was working on another during the winter of 1995. He had done a few television commercials. But these projects were a mere sideshow given his achievements and national and international popularity. To the end, Border preferred doing rather than basking in glory. Unlike many sportspeople of even modest achievement, Border had not covered the walls of his Brisbane home with photographs and memorabilia.

Still, the Border name was revered throughout Australia and promised to be a good earner. Hunter Valley winemakers Tyrrell's, a sponsor of Australian cricket, decided to produce a shiraz from its 1991 vintage, said to be its best since 1965, in 11,174 numbered and individually packaged bottles. This project may have been inspired by the sale of the same number of replicas of the bat Border used to score his 11,174 Test runs. The bats came complete with timber cabinet, brass plaque, personal signature and signed certificate of authenticity – all for $550. If all were sold, the income would total more than $6 million. Obviously, Border would not receive all of that money, but the project represented a useful retirement bonus. Even before that project, Allan Border must surely have been the first Australian cricketer to become a millionaire from cricket alone. Another first and another example of how Border's era was the one which took Australian cricket from semi-professional status into the modern world of full-time professional sport.

Before the Shield final, Border said he thought it unlikely he would be able to find sufficient enthusiasm to play another season. In the afterglow of victory, he was not so sure.

So long as I don't feel I'm excess baggage, I'll consider playing. I just enjoy the game so much I'm reluctant to draw the curtain. I've always said I'll be a long time retired. It's mainly a question of whether I can get myself up and do all the hard lead-up work that's necessary in the off-season. But the rewards are great. This year has been very special for me. It's hard to put it into a pecking order with the Tests but this [the Shield win] is simply not going to happen again. It's unique. And back-to-back Shields sounds pretty good.

The temptation to play on proved too great and in July it was confirmed that Border would play for Queensland in 1995-96. After the Shield final, Border left for a brief golfing trip to the United States with Dean Jones before the pair joined the commentary team of Galaxy Pay TV's PSN network for coverage of the last two Test matches in the Caribbean. Border always said he never saw himself moving into the role of media critic after retirement. His commitment to the dressing-room and the team ethic was too strong, his aversion to seeking unnecessary public exposure too ingrained. Galaxy had to work hard to convince him to sign. In the end, he agreed, and that typically reluctant decision gave him the chance to see first-hand the closing of a 10-year cycle of struggle, slow improvement, eventual success and finally, in Kingston, Jamaica, in early May 1995, the ultimate achievement: an Australian victory over the West Indies in a Test series.

THE BEST,

AT LAST

T HE most significant image from Australia's 2-1 win over the West Indies in the Caribbean in 1995 was surely that of a helmeted Steve Waugh face to face with an angry Curtly Ambrose on the first day of the third Test in Trinidad. Here were two of the modern game's fiercest rivals, personally and nationally, in full confrontation.

Despite a wickedly damp and green pitch, Waugh was staging a one-man rearguard action, holding his own in very difficult conditions against the most feared bowler in the world. Ambrose, after a poor start to the series, was beginning to look his old, menacing self, assisted by a poor pitch. After another dangerous delivery, a frustrated Ambrose stood hands on hip and glared down at Waugh. Given the state of the wicket, Waugh thought Ambrose had nothing to complain about and told him so. The giant fast bowler, always a brooding presence on the field, objected and strode down to within a metre of the batsman. Waugh stood his ground, feet spread stubbornly, looking confident and defiant. At one stage, Waugh tapped the side of his helmet as if to say, 'Do

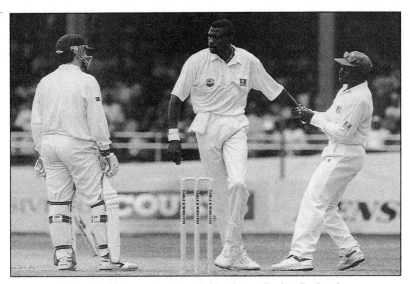

Irresistible force meets immovable object: Richie Richardson
drags Curtly Ambrose away from Steve Waugh during
a tense moment of the 1995 series in the Caribbean.

your worst, pal. This time it won't be good enough.' Ambrose was not used to such insolence.

Here was the ultimate image of the decisive change that had come over Australia versus West Indies cricket since the 1992-93 series in Australia. At last, the Australians had overcome West Indian intimidation, the factor that had forced the West Indies' opponents for more than a decade to believe they were inferior. In the end, it was always the fear and loathing of the West Indies' pace attack that hammered teams into submission. Led by Steve Waugh, the batsman, and Mark Taylor, the captain, the 1995 Australians refused to be intimidated. At times, Taylor and Slater would surface after ducking another bouncer and grin through their helmet grill down towards the frustrated bowler. No batsmen had ever tried that approach before.

If Ambrose had been able to break Waugh in that innings in Trinidad, the balance of the series might have swung towards the West Indies. But Waugh prevailed. While he went on to make the only half-century of that third Test and then an epic double century in the fourth to seal victory for Australia, Ambrose's threat faded. As the Australians' game took the long-awaited next step to a higher level, the West Indies' long-suspected decline was confirmed. The balance of power in world cricket had changed, for the time being at least.

After losing the early one-day series, Australia's campaign appeared near collapse when its two leading fast bowlers were lost through injury. Craig McDermott badly twisted an ankle on a jog back to the team hotel and took no further part in the tour. His likely new-ball partner, Damien Fleming, was the other casualty, a shoulder injury ending his tour.

After those setbacks, a mentally suspect team would have given in, but Taylor's side was different. The Australians still believed they were the better team. Taylor, through one-on-one chats, inspired the remaining pace bowlers – Paul Reiffel, Glenn McGrath and Brendon Julian – and encouraged the batsmen to think and play positively, not to fear failure. And although his slips catching had fallen away in Pakistan six months earlier, on this tour Taylor caught brilliantly, as did the other players.

No Australian team can have fielded better than Taylor's in the West Indies in 1995. Fielding is as sure a sign of confidence as there is in cricket. Australia's fielding in this series offered stark evidence of the improvement from the grim days of the mid-1980s when catches were more often spilled than held. This fielding performance was Simpson's greatest achievement as coach. And although players such as the Waughs would have been great fieldsmen anyway, Simpson's emphasis on fielding drills throughout his tenure greatly helped the rebuilding process and deserved praise. Excellent fielding had, though, been part of Australian cricket throughout its history.

Australia beat a disunited and sluggish West Indies team in Barbados in the first Test, then drew a rain-shortened match in Antigua when the situation on the fifth day was set up for Shane Warne to produce another demolition job. In Port-of-Spain, Trinidad, the toss and therefore the pitch favoured the West Indies. With one game to go, the series was 1-1 and Ambrose was looking closer to his usual form.

Despite not reaching 150 in either innings in Trinidad, the Australian batsmen never wavered from their plan to be positive. It said much for Taylor's cool, attacking attitude that his team never lost its nerve. On a good pitch in Kingston, Jamaica, the Australians bowled out West Indies for 265 before the Waugh twins posted a fourth-wicket stand of 231 which helped take the Australians to a dominant total of 531 and a lead of 266 runs. They won by an innings and 53 runs within four days.

The loss was the first for the West Indies in 30 series, since they went down in New Zealand in 1980. It was their first loss at

*At last: Allan Border celebrates Queensland's defeat of
South Australia in the 1994-95 Sheffield Shield final.*

*The impossible victory: Justin Langer (far left) looks into the eyes
of his new captain, Mark Taylor, as the Australians celebrate
their historic win over the West Indies in the Caribbean in 1995.*

home since Ian Chappell's Australians won in 1972-73 and their first loss against Australia since Greg Chappell led Australia to a 5-1 win in 1975-76.

With some justification, several commentators argued that one lost series did not mean the West Indies had forfeited their unofficial crown as world Test champions. But, as Taylor argued, surely the win meant that Australia had to be rated the best team in the world on current form. At least the series and the debate that ensued added some impetus to the idea of a world championship of Test cricket, an idea supported by no less an authority than the 1995 edition of *Wisden Cricketers' Almanack*.

Whatever the international pros and cons of that debate, it was clear that for Australian cricket, the highest mountain peak had been reached. The long climb back from the chaos of December 1984 had been completed.

A number of factors tipped the balance in Australia's favour in the Caribbean in 1995. The West Indies were certainly weaker than at any time in recent memory, especially with Ambrose out of sorts. They looked tired, worn out by the heavy demands of international cricket and the grind of the English county scene, where most earn a living when not required by their national teams. As well, the fierce pride which inspired the teams of Clive Lloyd and Viv Richards had faded.

However, the Australians did not just beat Richie Richardson's West Indians, they thrashed them. They were in the stronger position in the drawn Test and lost the third only because of a sub-standard pitch. Whether the Australians would have won under Border is debatable, although it seems harsh to say so given that his side came within two runs of beating a better West Indian team in 1992-93. As well, Warne's improvement in the years between those series was immense. Border was never able to use Warne at his best against the West Indies; Taylor enjoyed that advantage.

Still, a change *had* come over the Australian team since Taylor took over from Border. The players' on-field behaviour improved, thanks mainly to Taylor's prompt intervention whenever trouble was brewing. The dressing-room was happier and more relaxed because the new captain maintained a more even temper and kept his mind on the game at all times, and because the coach was no longer the tactically conservative, politically active and administratively powerful figure he had been under Border. On the field, Taylor was quicker in his tactical moves and more imaginative in his ideas than Border.

Most importantly, Taylor won the mind game, which, against the West Indies, was more important than against any other team. As Taylor said of the 1992-93 series: 'We weren't strong enough to hang on. This time we were strong. We lost in Trinidad, but we wanted it that badly. They came up against a very good cricket team.'

The 'recent trauma syndrome' Border had diagnosed in 1992-93 had been cured. After the 1995 series, Border noted that Taylor had brought 'a different focus' to the Australian team. Most critics agreed that Taylor's captaincy was the major difference.

That psychological leap was best illustrated by the attitude of the batsmen. With Taylor's approval, all but Steve Waugh played the hook. As Taylor explained mid-series: 'That's the way you have to play. You've got to challenge these guys. If a side bowls five half-volleys an over, you have to play the drive. If you nick a ball every now and then, you're going to be out. If a side bowls a lot of short balls, you have to hook and pull.'

In contrast, Border thought that the best way was to 'wait for them and score off the bad balls. The trap a lot of players fall into is trying to fight fire with fire'.

The one Australian batsman who did not hook was the most successful, Steve Waugh, but Waugh never hooked. Although his success may have been due partly to his refusal to play that risky shot, the point was not so much how many runs the Australians scored off the hook, but the fact that they showed they were prepared to take on the West Indians. It was as much mental as physical or tactical. It was the attitude that mattered, that carried the psychological weight.

Ian Chappell, who had long advocated a more aggressive attitude towards the West Indies, used his famous hook shot as a philosophical statement as well as a means to score runs. So it was with the 1995 Australians. With the ball, McGrath's brave decision to bounce the West Indian fast bowlers when they batted sent a similarly powerful message.

Steve Waugh was named Man of the Series in what was undoubtedly the finest achievement of his career. For the previous two years, he had taken over from David Boon as the best batsman in the team. In the Caribbean, Waugh battled a great deal of public animosity after the legality of his diving catch to dismiss Brian Lara in the first Test became a major controversy. Viv

Richards inflamed that debate when he publicly accused Waugh of maintaining an Australian tradition of claiming unfair catches.

When Border retired from Test cricket, Steve Waugh said: 'Just playing with him has brought something out in me that might have taken longer or might never have come out.' Whatever it was, it was 'out' in full measure in the Caribbean in 1995.

In many respects, Waugh's triumph in that series was a reminder of Allan Border's major contribution to the Australian team. Border, along with Simpson, built a team in his own image: physically tough, disciplined, patriotic, often touchy when things went against them. In 1995 in the West Indies, Steve Waugh's six innings produced 429 runs at an average of 107.25, with three fifties and one century. Mark Waugh averaged 40; the other four specialist batsmen, in the mid- to low twenties. Steve Waugh's was a virtuoso performance, easily the best batting by an Australian against the West Indies since Border's great feats in the Caribbean in 1984. And Waugh did it all in a no-frills, organised and determined way – very much like Border at his best.

Another notable event in this series was David Boon's hundredth Test appearance. Like Waugh, Boon was the personification of the Border era. Similar in many ways to his long-time captain – stockily built, mentally resilient, physically tough, a thorough professional – Boon became the second Australian after Border to play 100 Tests.

Boon's hundredth match happened to be played on that wet wicket in Trinidad. From the time he saw the pitch two days before the game began, he must have realised his chances of marking the milestone with a big score were slim – and so it proved.

Boon's first ball was a massive in-swinger from Courtney Walsh which began a long way outside off stump, sliced through his defence and ended up being taken by the wicket-keeper wide outside the line of leg stump. When the next ball beat the outside edge by moving a long way off the pitch in the opposite direction, Boon, no longer able to contain his vigorous sense of humour, looked down the damp and green pitch and laughed – at the wicket, at Walsh and, it seemed, at the world. Boon averaged only 25 in the series but his contribution, as batsman and short-leg fieldsman, to the Australian team throughout Border's time as captain was outstanding.

In the May/June issue of *Inside Edge*, Allan Border offered his assessment of Australia's win in the Caribbean:

> *Great teams will battle their way out of tight situations and that's exactly what Australia did at key times against the West Indies. The side has built up a tremendous resilience and spirit . . . This side was never daunted whereas Australian sides in my early Test career got drawn into the portrayal of West Indians as supermen breaking bones and bats. The West Indies really played on that aura and psychological stuff, and I know I was one who felt totally out of my depth when I first played them. The aura didn't exist for Taylor's squad. They took it right up to the opposition and won.*

Of his successor, Border said: 'A final credit to Mark Taylor for his handling of the Australian side. He hasn't been inhibited by anything. He's said, "this is the way I want it", with no "umming and arrhing" about the old regime. He's come in straight away and stamped his own authority on the captaincy and now he's holding one of the greatest prizes of all.'

The 'umming and arrhing' Border mentioned might well have been a reference to his own hesitant early approach to the captaincy compared to Taylor's decisive work. The 'old regime' obviously referred to the Border-Simpson partnership. Although it must have been difficult for Border to watch a team he had helped build go one step further and take the prize he had never won, his comments were gracious.

Not so gracious was Bob Simpson's assessment, published in the *Sydney Morning Herald* on Monday, 8 May, five days after the win in Kingston. The article, appropriately headlined 'They Did It My Way', was a long and immodest catalogue of the various improvements Simpson had brought to the Australian team during his nine years as coach. There was no acknowledgement of Taylor's captaincy nor Border's long struggle for collective excellence.

The article, riddled with the words 'I', 'me' and 'my' and reading more like a job application than a cricket column, prompted several letters to the paper, the first coming from Tim Bowden of Northbridge in Sydney. Published on 12 May, the letter began: 'The article by Bob Simpson (*Herald*, May 8) headed "They did it my way" is truly remarkable. While I (like most Australians) rejoiced in the fantastic victory over the West Indies, I cringed at Simpson's amazing smugness in claiming personal credit for every aspect of the win.' It ended: 'Simpson's embarrassing self-adulation went on for column after column. Was there no one else available – or willing – to write such a glowing testimonial to the long-serving Australian coach? Blowing one's own trumpet is not a normally accepted Australian virtue. Simpson has demeaned his role and himself by basking in such an orgy of self-congratulations.'

Although the win in the Caribbean produced tributes from all over Australia, and the premiers of New South Wales and Victoria offered civic celebrations, the welcome home did not match that for the 1989 Ashes team. This time, the Australian players did not return together. Some went for holidays to the United States and Europe, others to join county or league teams in England. Those who were not playing in England returned by late June to enjoy a ticker-tape parade through the centre of Sydney. The celebrations might not have matched the euphoria which followed the win in '89, but most people agreed that Taylor's was the greater achievement. The days of stagnation were over. The Taylor era had begun in impressive fashion.

BORDER:

THE PROFESSIONAL

I N the southern spring of 1994, former prime minister Bob Hawke was trooping around the country promoting a huge chunk of his post-retirement handiwork, *The Hawke Memoirs*. In its 23 August edition, the *Bulletin* ran a review of the book by former New Zealand prime minister David Lange. The cover picture for that edition was an unusual choice – a shot of two modern Australian heroes, two men of the people.

Allan Border and Bob Hawke are sitting on a dressing-room bench, caught at an awkward moment. Hawke, in a politician's grey suit, seems to be striving for intimacy – and for something to say. Border, also in his work clothes, looks ill at ease, both with the famous figure next to him and with his own fame, the fame which had attracted Hawke in the first place. As a study in contrasting leadership, Lorrie Graham's photograph of two of the most famous Australians of the 1980s is simple, understated and eloquent.

From the time his parents conveyed to him their feeling that he was destined for great things, Hawke believed he would be

Men of the people: Allan Border chats with Prime Minister Bob Hawke during their heyday in the 1980s.

prime minister. Throughout his public career, he craved the affection of the people, and at the end, could not believe that his parliamentary colleagues had dumped him.

Border was Hawke's opposite in every way. He never sought high office and never felt comfortable in it. He never craved fame and valued the praise only of those he knew and respected. Unlike Hawke, Border could see that his time had come and that a new man deserved a chance in the top job. Hawke loved to be seen in the company of sporting champions; Border had to be dragged to any official function, let alone to a do at Parliament House.

Both in their differing ways were successful and popular leaders – it takes all sorts.

When Border had the Australian captaincy thrust upon him in 1984, Australian cricket was in turmoil. The players were really only part-time professionals, despite the advances of the World Series Cricket revolution, and the Test team was being beaten by every other side in the world. When he retired, Australia was a few wins away from being the best team in the world. The country's leading players could manage nicely as full-time professional cricketers.

Allan Border had been the first Australian to call himself a professional cricketer. Even if he did so only because he couldn't think of anything better to do, he still set the trend, still showed the way. Border did not always know where he was going, but because of his qualities as a great batsman and his determination to pursue his chosen career to the best of those formidable abilities, he did come to symbolise modern Australian cricket. The two grew together, side by side, occasionally at odds with each other but mostly on the same path. Border did not create the modern era, but he did become the ultimate example of it. He was no great fan of one-day cricket, the modern era's major innovation, but during his time no one played more one-day games nor played them so well.

If the modern era produced a tough, pragmatic style of cricket which preferred percentage play to the daring of old, Border was the perfect specimen. He was no poet like David Gower, but he was far more reliable, a quality highly valued in any professional. Border was practical, hard-working and cautious. He rarely soared to great heights, but he was always highly competitive and always earned his pay packet. If Test cricket needs more flair than that as it heads towards the twenty-first century, then the game might

Worried man: Allan Border in familar pose, checking the scoreboard and worrying about the fate of another Test match. Adelaide, February 1989.

need someone other than a Border. Border was of his time, and that is no failing.

Border's greatest achievement as Australian captain was that he was able to maintain his batting at a consistently high standard and so set an example for teammates to follow. If Border's batting had fallen apart in the mid-1980s when he was the only experienced, world-class cricketer around capable of taking on the captaincy, Australian cricket would have been in chaos instead of a deep hole. All of Border's teammates learned something from him. He instilled in his team a genuine pride in playing cricket for Australia, a disciplined attitude to training, preparation and playing essential at a time when so much international cricket is played, and a durability that saw the national team through that difficult campaign in the Caribbean in 1995.

Captaining any cricket team can be difficult, lonely work. Captaining a losing Test team can break the spirit. It broke Kim Hughes. During Border's years, England went through captains every series or so then often recycled them a couple of years later. The laconic Richie Richardson took over the West Indies team from the undefeated Viv Richards in the early 1990s, but two years later, had to take a year off from all cricket involvement because of physical and emotional fatigue. When he returned as captain for the 1995 series against Australia, Richardson had lost weight and muscle bulk as well as the carefree attitude that had made him such a popular figure.

Border outlasted them all – he was that tough. Admittedly, one reason he lasted was that he delegated many responsibilities to his coach, the first ever full-time coach of an Australian team. Again, Border created the role of coach because he knew he needed help, not because he looked into the future and saw the way the game was developing. In some ways, Border's delegation of some of the captain's duties to Simpson reduced the primacy of the Australian captain. But it was not a permanent change, it just suited the pragmatic Border. Mark Taylor reverted to the more traditional role when he took over although it is likely the full responsibilities will limit Taylor's captaincy to fewer than Border's 93 Tests.

Simpson followed his self-congratulatory article in the *Sydney Morning Herald* with assertions in the media that he had no intention of standing aside. His latest contract was due to expire after the World Cup in early 1996 but he was already talking of another term. By then he would be 60 and, as one of his stronger supporters, Keith Stackpole, noted in the *Sunday Herald Sun*, coaching an international team was a younger man's job. As well, Simpson had been forced into hospital twice during the series in the Caribbean with a blood clot in his left leg. At 59 and with persistent back problems, Simpson was no longer the active practice general he had been under Border. Whether the ACB would be prepared to look to someone else after the World Cup remained to be seen. Certainly the Board's decision-makers would encounter more of Simpson's typically fierce lobbying before they ruled on his future.

In some ways the success in the Caribbean had been a confirmation of Simpson's contribution during the previous eight years. The team's discipline and, in particular, its brilliant fielding, reflected Simpson's work. Yet, as ever with such a controversial figure, there was another interpretation: that one of the reasons why Australia under Taylor took that next step and actually beat the West Indies was due in part to the reduced role Simpson played under Taylor. Essentially, Simpson belonged to the Border era. The first year of Taylor's reign proved that there could be life after Border; surely it also proved that there could be life after Simpson.

If Simpson did continue as team coach after the 1996 World Cup, it would again be in a more subdued role than the one he played under Border. The definition of the job had changed. When asked in April 1995 by Michael Horan of the *Herald Sun* if he would be interested in taking over from Simpson, Greg Chappell said: 'Australian cricket doesn't need a Bob Simpson or a Greg Chappell. The job had evolved into what is good for Simmo, not what's good for Australian cricket. What is needed is some sort of assistant to the captain. That's all.'

Simpson's successor, whenever he was appointed, was likely to be such an 'assistant', a far less powerful figure than Simpson had been from 1986 to 1994.

The English writer Quentin Crisp once said that 'to be a man of destiny is to arrive at a point in history when the only gift you have to offer has suddenly become relevant'. That applies to Allan Border's period as Australian captain: his greatest gift was his determination and, in 1984, that was the quality which the Australian captain and the Australian game needed more than any other. Just as in 1994, with talented players educated and inspired by Border, the Australian team needed a captain with flair and imagination to finally take them to the next level. As Allan Border was right for his time, Mark Taylor seems to be right for his.

Although Allan Border's retirement brought more freedom to the team system and allowed a more daring captain to beat the West Indies in a Test series, no one questioned the value of Border's role in preparing that 1995 Australian team. During a long and difficult period, Border laid a solid foundation upon which Mark Taylor was able to build quite an impressive structure.

Taylor certainly appreciated the work that had gone before him. On the rest day in Kingston, Jamaica, with Australia in a strong position to win the fourth Test and the series the next day,

Taylor made a point of inviting all the former Australian players present in Kingston to the dressing-room at the end of the match to share in the celebrations.

When Border made his way self-consciously into the noisy room after that great victory, Taylor came straight over and handed him the Frank Worrell Trophy. 'Here, mate, this is for you too,' Taylor said.

An hour earlier, Border had been high up in the television commentary area looking down to the other end of the field where Michael Slater and David Boon were lifting their new captain onto their shoulders for the start of the celebrations. Justin Langer had not played a Test on the tour but had been his usual enthusiastic, supportive self throughout. Proudly wearing his creams and his baggy green Australian cap, Langer ran onto the field to join his teammates.

In a photograph used on the cover of the souvenir edition of the *Australian* the next day, Langer is on the far left of the picture, his right hand on Boon's shoulder, his eyes fixed firmly on the laughing face of his captain, Mark Taylor. Things had certainly changed since that depressing day at the Adelaide Oval, 1 February 1993, when Langer saw Allan Border's disappointed face and vowed he would one day play in an Australian team which beat the West Indies in a Test series. In Jamaica in May 1995, Langer was still looking on from the edge, as was Border, but in their own very different ways they had been part of a great Australian victory.

BIBLIOGRAPHY

BOOKS

The ABC Cricket Almanac, ABC Books, Sydney, 1990-94 edns.

The Age: World Cup Cricket, Five Mile Press, Melbourne, 1992.

Richie Benaud (ed.), *Wide World of Sports Cricket Yearbook*, Hamlyn Australia, Melbourne, 1986-94 edns.

Scyld Berry, *Cricket Odyssey*, Pavilion Books, London, 1988.

Allan Border, *Allan Border: The Autobiography*, Methuen, Sydney, 1985.

——*Ashes Glory*, Swan Publishing, Sydney, 1989.

——*Beyond 10,000*, Swan Publishing, Sydney, 1993.

Ian Botham, *Botham: My Autobiography*, Collins Willow, London, 1994.

Ian Chappell, *Chappelli: The Cutting Edge*, Swan Publishing, Nedlands, WA, 1992.

Mike Coward, *Cricket Beyond the Bazaar*, Allen & Unwin, Sydney, 1990.

Mike Coward and Michael Rayner, *Caribbean Odyssey*, Simon & Schuster, Sydney, 1991.

——*Australia vs the New South Africa*, Simon & Schuster, Sydney, 1994.

Roland Fishman, *Calypso Cricket*, Margaret Gee Publishing, Sydney, 1991.

David Gower with Martin Johnson, *Gower: The Autobiography*, Collins Willow, London, 1993.

Gideon Haigh, *The Border Years*, Text Publishing, Melbourne, 1994.

Michael Holding with Tony Cozier, *Whispering Death*, André Deutsch, London, 1993.

David Hookes with Alan Shiell, *Hookesy*, ABC Books, Sydney, 1993.

Dean Jones, *Deano: My Call*, Swan Publishing, Perth, 1994.

Geoff Lawson with Mark Ray, *Diary of the Ashes*, Angus & Robertson, Sydney, 1990.

Geoff Lawson, *Henry: The Geoff Lawson Story*, Ironbark Press, Sydney, 1992.

Craig McDermott with Phil Derriman, *McDermott: Strike Bowler*, ABC Books, Sydney, 1992.

Alan McGilvray with Norman Tasker, *McGilvray: Captains of the Game*, ABC Books, Sydney, 1992.

Adrian McGregor, *Greg Chappell*, William Collins, Sydney, 1985.

Rob Steen, *Desmond Haynes: The Lion of Barbados*, Witherby, London, 1993.

Mark Thomas, *David Boon: In the Firing Line*, Sun Books, Melbourne, 1993.

Steve Waugh, *Steve Waugh's South African Diary*, Ironbark Press, Sydney, 1994.

Dirk Wellham with Howard Rich, *Solid Knocks and Second Thoughts*, Reed Books, Sydney, 1988.

Mike Whitney, *Quick Whit*, Ironbark Press, Sydney, 1994.

Wisden Cricketers' Almanack, John Wisden & Co. Ltd, 1984-1995 edns.

Tim Zoehrer, *Tim Zoehrer: The Gloves Are Off*, EMW Publishing, Perth, 1995.

NEWSPAPERS

The *Age*
The *Sunday Age*
The *Sydney Morning Herald*
The *Sun-Herald*
The *Sun*
The *Herald*
The *Herald Sun*
The *Independent* (UK)
The *Sunday Telegraph* (UK)
Today (UK)
The *Courier-Mail*

INDEX